MW00438876

"Like many of us, I have been infatuated with rocks and crystals since young, intuitively realizing they convey healing and manifesting properties. Travels around the world, and client work, have convinced me the most solid and sparkling of stones are brilliant gateways to transformation, as explained by Margaret Ann with wisdom and practical insight. As she points out, when energetically used with the understandings and tips provided in this A–Z essential guide, all good things are possible. Your "everything" go-to for crystals!"

—Cyndi Dale, best-selling author of *The Complete Book of Chakra Healing, Beyond Soul Mates,* and *The Subtle Body*

"I love stones and crystals! My pockets magically fill with treasures no matter where I am and my house is full of long-loved and new-found friends. Each August when we return to the U.S. from camping in the solitudes of Canada my husband jokes that the International Bridge is going to collapse under the weight of the rock friends that wanted to come home with us. It is from this deep love that I devoured every page of *The Essential Guide to Crystals, Minerals and Stones* so exquisitely written by Margaret Ann Lembo. It is clear in the reading of this gem of a book that Margaret is spirit guided, extensively trained, deeply connected to, and appreciative of the spirit energies and beauty of our mineral relatives, in addition to being a gifted writer. As a person living the shamanic way, I especially appreciate the extensive metaphysical wisdom, spiritual insights, and potent teachings on intention and focus that *The Essential Guide* imparts. These fundamental teachings eloquently woven into the multitudes of clearly explained ways and means for working with the sacred tools from the earth, and sometimes from the stars, makes this book a must have for, well, everyone!"

—Colleen Deatsman, author of *Energy for Life* and *Inner Power*

"Margaret Ann Lembo's *Essential Guide to Crystals, Minerals and Stones* proves to be a must-have guide for anyone who even enjoys picking up rocks. Her straight-from-the-hip approach is matched by her passion, love, and knowledge of each and every geode, multifaceted crystal, and everything in between. Her organized and detailed approach is why we all loved *Chakra Awakening,* and this equally gleams like a polished rock to be carried for good luck!"

—Joan Ranquet, author of *Communication with All Life*

"With *The Essential Guide to Crystals, Minerals and Stones*, Margaret Ann Lembo has created a dazzling array of information that leaves no stone unturned! Gorgeously illustrated and written in an easy to understand format, Margaret Ann brings over thirty years of experience into this cohesive and indispensable guide. It has earned a permanent place on my bookshelf!"

—Radleigh Valentine, co-author of
Angel Tarot Cards with Doreen Virtue

Praise for
Chakra Awakening:

"Brimming with great tips on how to give your body's complex energy centers an almighty cleanse and boost, *Chakra Awakening* is a must for everyone who's on a spiritual path. Expect your life to blossom after reading this guide."

—*Prediction* (UK)

"Get out your highlighter! Margaret Ann Lembo's wonderful book is filled with profound ancient wisdom, but at the same time it's overflowing with usable and transformational information. It's a great resource for anyone's library. This book can truly help you to balance all of your chakras (and your life) with ease and joy!"

—Denise Linn, best-selling author of *Sacred Space*

"*Chakra Awakening* brings the ancient knowledge and sacred use of crystals and gemstones into present-day focus. This wonderful book is a very useful reference for anyone interested in the healing power of gemstones."

—Caroline Sutherland, author of *The Body Knows*

"Filled with valuable information for personal growth, spiritual practices, and Margaret's unique insights and warm humor, her crystalline and loving intent shines through the many facets of guidance offered in what I hope to be the first of other books of hers to come in the future."

—Josie Ravenwing, author of *The Return of Spirit,*
A Season of Eagles, and *The Book of Miracles*

"A straightforward and far-reaching, complete guide that clearly takes you on the wondrous and magical path of personal evolution in this lifetime. Read this book and follow it! Be prepared to take off with this flight manual for your spiritual ascent."

—James Wanless, creator of *The Voyager Tarot*
and author of *Intuition @ Work*

The Essential Guide to

CRYSTALS,
MINERALS
and
STONES

About the Author

Margaret Ann Lembo (Boynton Beach, FL) is a spiritual practitioner and owner of The Crystal Garden, a spiritual center and gift shop. For more than twenty years, she has led workshops and classes around the country. Her audio CDs (guided meditations and more) are distributed nationally. She is also the president of the Coalition of Visionary Resources (COVR). Visit her online at www.margaretannlembo.com.

To Write to the Author

If you wish to contact the author or would like more information about this book, please write to the author in care of Llewellyn Worldwide, and we will forward your request. Both the author and publisher appreciate hearing from you and learning of your enjoyment of this book and how it has helped you. Llewellyn Worldwide cannot guarantee that every letter written to the author can be answered, but all will be forwarded. Please write to:

Margaret Ann Lembo
⁄ Llewellyn Worldwide
2143 Wooddale Drive
Woodbury, MN 55125-2989

Please enclose a self-addressed stamped envelope for reply,
or $1.00 to cover costs. If outside the USA, enclose
an international postal reply coupon.

Many of Llewellyn's authors have websites with additional
information and resources. For more information, please visit
our website at http://www.llewellyn.com.

The Essential Guide to
CRYSTALS, MINERALS
and
STONES

Author of *CHAKRA AWAKENING*

MARGARET ANN LEMBO

Llewellyn Worldwide
Woodbury, Minnesota

FIRST EDITION
Second Printing, 2013

Book design by Bob Gaul
Cover art: Rose quartz and crystal © iStockphoto.com/mykeyruna
      Scroll rule © iStockphoto.com/Claudelle Girard
Cover design by Adrienne Zimiga
Editing by Laura Graves
Interior art: Gemstone photos © Andy Frame except cube
      image on page 18 by Llewellyn art department
      Appendix illustrations © Llewellyn art department
      Scroll rule © iStockphoto.com/Claudelle Girard

Llewellyn is a registered trademark of Llewellyn Worldwide Ltd.

Library of Congress Cataloging-in-Publication Data (Pending)
978-0-7387-3252-7

Llewellyn Publications
A Division of Llewellyn Worldwide Ltd.
2143 Wooddale Drive
Woodbury, MN 55125-2989
www.llewellyn.com

Printed in the United States of America

This book is dedicated to the customers and the staff of The Crystal Garden. It is also dedicated to all the rock hounds, rock dealers, New Age metaphysical stores and retail owners, numerologists, astrologers, and spiritual teachers around the world. Thank you for all that you taught me over the years, enabling me to compile the information, wisdom, and knowledge in this book.

Contents

The A-to-Z Essential Guide ... 35

Name of stone; Key phrase; Color; Chakra(s); Planet(s);
Number(s); Element(s); Mohs scale; Astro sign(s);
Affirmation; Spiritual uses; Mental uses; Emotional uses;
Physical uses; Divine guidance; About the stone

Appendices ... 361

Acknowledgments

I would like to acknowledge the energy of the muses, spirit guides, angels, and Master Teachers who have helped me recall the information that has been poured into this book. There were many times when I felt and knew that a force much greater than myself was providing the deep insight into the energy of the crystals, stones, and minerals discussed within these pages. Perhaps this deeper insight came from the Gemstone Guardians or a higher level of myself. Whatever the case may be, it is not important what that force is called. What is important is my gratitude for my ability to be a channel for this information.

My gratitude goes to all my rock dealers, especially Bob Nelson at Raiders of the Lost Art, Quasar Gems, Joseph Neto and Delson Correa at Underground Crystals, Susan and Bobby Buchannan at Seeds of Light, and Pat Diamond (and dearly departed Michael Diamond) for their generosity in helping to find the stones for the photos in this book—as well as for their years of friendship and camaraderie.

Special thanks goes to Bill Krause at Llewellyn. It is because of his request that I've written this book. Thank you for recognizing that this book was in me! I am grateful to everyone at Llewellyn. I give special kudos to Elysia Gallo for her love of gems and geology. Thanks for your extensive input and advice to make this a complete guide.

Thank you Carol Rosenberg, my personal editor. She is an answer to my prayers. She has grace and finesse as she helps me polish my writing to make it the best it can be.

I am forever grateful to The Crystal Garden. I would like to acknowledge my customers, who have taught me so much. I especially bow to and salute my staff for holding the energy of love and well-being while providing excellent service. Their dedication allowed me the space to leave my store for many months at a time to sequester myself to write while on book tour. During the time this book was written, Pam Moore managed my store, which allowed me to be free to write. Thank you, Pam! I want to also acknowledge Dawn Seiler, Caitlin Ten Eyck, Darla Mini, Melissa Applegate, Judy Waters, and Chrissy Clark.

I would like to acknowledge certified gemologist Michael Zeff for his contribution to this book. The information in the About the Stone entries and the Gemology Basics section was provided by him to ensure accurate gemological information. Michael began his career in the jewelry business in 1974 as owner of Zeppo Merchandisers, Inc., and has been importing gemstones from Thailand, Mexico, and Brazil since 1975. He completed the GIA Graduate Gemology Program in 1985. I am honored to have had the opportunity to work with him.

Gratitude to Andy Frame Photography. Thanks to the good work of Andy and Julie Frame and their kids.

I send my thanks and blessings to all my readers and those who love crystals, minerals, and stones. It is you for whom this book came forth.

And I would like to give special honor to the many metaphysical, New Age, and earth-centered bookstores, gift stores, centers, studios, and rock shops around the planet that hold the energy of the magnificent gemstone kingdom. Thank you for hosting my events and sharing your customers with me throughout the years.

Most important, I have deep love and honor for my beloved, Vincent Velardez. His presence, love, and unwavering support allow me to be all that I can be. I am thankful to him for being my companion on all my book tours, waiting patiently for me during events, listening to my talks over and over again, and keeping me grounded and safe. Thank you, Vincent, for holding the space so I can write and share love.

Introduction

This book is about how to use crystals, minerals, rocks, gemstones, and metals in your everyday life. The uses described within are based on metaphysical principles. The word *metaphysical* pertains to that which transcends the physical. In other words, metaphysics encompasses what the physical and scientific world cannot define but we know clearly exists. The majority of the principles and information you will find here is based on higher wisdom and knowledge, which were channeled through me.

I know firsthand that these beautiful tools can help you in your spiritual, mental, emotional, and physical realignment and personal development. Crystals, minerals, rocks, metals, and gemstones are tools from the earth that can be used to assist you in staying focused on your intentions to create and maintain positive change in your life. In fact, intention is the foundation for the practice described in this book.

How did I get to where I am today? Like most children, rocks fascinated me as a young girl, and I collected them in little boxes over the years alongside my collection of seashells. As an adult, I was drawn to work with quartz crystals and various minerals, rocks, and gems as part of my spiritual development and intuitive practice. The use of gemstones is wide and varied. I see them as beautiful friends from the earth, sparkling with beauty and innate vibration.

In the 1980s I was invited to participate in a crystal-buying venture with two friends who were off to Arkansas. I made the investment as a silent partner, but before I knew it, I wasn't so silent and my love for crystals and rocks was reignited with my childhood enthusiasm. Not only was this a business venture, but it also became my passion and a main part of my life purpose.

Soon after I made this investment, the mortgage-banking industry catapulted me out of the corporate world of finance and into the creation of my own metaphysical store and center, The Crystal Garden. Memories of my lifetime in Atlantis flooded to the surface of my consciousness. The legendary island of Atlantis—a land mass which sunk beneath the Atlantic Ocean—was first mentioned by Plato, the Greek philosopher, in his writings. In metaphysical circles, Atlantis is known for the crystal chambers and spiritual techniques that used sound, color, and vibration to heal. Many of my memories from that lifetime are woven into these pages, and so this book comes from that place of innate knowledge and wisdom.

The more I interacted with rocks through buying and selling them for my store, the more I knew about the stones. Of course, I also read books by some of the forerunners in the crystal-healing field in the early days, which confirmed what I was finding to be true based on my personal experience. I also learned much from the customers who frequented my metaphysical bookstore and spiritual center. My customers would ask me for a stone for this purpose or that, and I would direct them to the gemstone display to pick what they were naturally attracted to. The decades of interacting with people regarding their gemstone choices were the best training ever! As my customers shared their challenges and issues, I would observe which stones they chose for their collection to help them heal, realign, attract relationships, or create prosperity in their lives. This fieldwork was invaluable, although at the time I didn't realize it would become part of my knowledge base for a book.

The metaphysical perspectives and uses of gemstones come naturally to me. Shortly after the creation of my store, I began offering my clients crystal alignments—a deeply healing and restorative meditation experience. I fondly recall how the shop was basically devoid of furniture and displays at the time, and I would place a blanket on the floor, kneel down beside my client, place gemstones and crystals on and around the body, and guide him or her through a meditation using imagery to restore balance and regenerate well-being.

Over the past three decades I've taught many classes and workshops around the country to hundreds of participants. I developed the Crystal Healer Certification course now also known as Chakra Awakening Workshop, named after my first book. Many massage therapists and complementary medicine practitioners incorporate these teachings into their daily work. Much of this work is intuitive and is also based on the understanding of the chakras and the belief systems stored within the chakras. You are a spiritual being in a human body. Your body is composed of seven main chakras or energy centers. These energy centers begin at the base of the spine with the root chakra and end at the head with the crown chakra.

I've been connected with the angelic realm throughout my life. I've shared many lectures, events, and workshops in a variety of settings to help people connect with their angels. Throughout this book, you will find references to angels and archangels. Just as gemstones have attributes, the same is true for angels and archangels. You can add the vibration or assistance of an angel to your intentions or request for realignment. The gemstone associated with the angel or archangel is based on the color ray and the attribute of the angel or archangel that is most closely associated with the spiritual energy of the gemstone.

In order to create the life you want, your focus must be on what you *do* want, not on what you *don't* want. Whatever you focus on becomes your reality. In other words, all of your conscious thoughts and feelings—as well as the subconscious and unconscious ones—create the life you are currently living. This basic principle is at the heart of most universal laws, including the law of attraction and the laws of physics.

It is important to have an intention and to focus on the positive so that life reflects your highest potential. Everything created is done so through intention. We create our lives with our thoughts, actions, words, and deeds. Our intentions vibrate out into the word and return to us in the form of our personal reality.

When a gemstone is paired with a daily affirmation, the stone amplifies that intention. It is a tool that helps you maintain your focus on what you *do* want. In my work with color and crystals over the course of three decades, I've found that to use a stone most effectively, it is best to associate an intention with it. And the more information you have about the qualities associated with certain stones, the more creative you can be with using these valuable tools to improve your life. That's why I have compiled the information in this book—to provide you with what you need to know to set about using these gifts from nature to make positive changes in your life. Some of the affirmations in this book are more detailed versions of the ones you'll find in my *Angel Gemstone Oracle Cards*. As you read about the stone, use the affirmation combined with your intention to transform your reality.

The 160 crystals, minerals, and stones listed in this book are those that you can commonly find in metaphysical bookstores and rock shops and are typically used by spiritual practitioners. This book is a comprehensive metaphysical directory to these stones, and it is intended to help you achieve or maintain a more balanced existence. This guide provides you with the opportunity to open your mind, body, and spirit to accepting assistance from the vast mineral kingdom. The following sections are helpful in how to select stones, clear them, and use them in your daily life; each gemstone entry in the guide contains the following information:

- **Name of stone**

- **Key phrase:** A phrase of a couple of words to capture the essential meaning of the stone.

- **Color:** The various colors in which the gemstone typically appears.

- **Chakra(s):** The energy center typically associated with the gemstone.

- **Planet(s):** The planetary body with which the stone is associated based on astrology.

- **Number(s):** The matching numerological vibration.

- **Element(s):** The associated element derived from either how the stone grows or the energetic components provided by the stone.

- **Mohs scale:** The degree of hardness based on the Mohs scale. (A diamond, one of the hardest substances on earth, is 10 on this scale. Talc is 1.)

- **Astro sign(s):** The sign of the zodiac with which the stone is associated.

- **Affirmation:** A positive statement of affirmation associated with the gemstone that helps to focus an intention.

- **Spiritual uses:** Ideas on how to use the stone to further develop your spiritual connection.

- **Mental uses:** Ideas on how to use the stone for mental focus or clarity and situations in which it can be helpful.

- **Emotional uses:** Ideas on how to use the stone as a tool for dealing with feelings to unblock underlying challenges.

- **Physical uses:** Ideas on how to use the stone as a complementary tool to heal your physical body or to help you on a mundane level such as with your career. It is important to realize that the stone is an *external* tool to be used to overcome physical challenges. Do not use the stone internally in any way. The use of gemstones or energetic healing is not a substitute for traditional medicine. It is a complementary practice to enhance a plan of action established by a professional healthcare practitioner.

- **Divine guidance:** Guidance for uncovering self-knowledge and self-realization for the purpose of personal development and spiritual awakening.

- **About the stone:** A short gemological summary of the type of stone.

While each entry under the gemstones provides valuable insight for personal growth, the key to getting the most out of this directory is focusing on the affirmations. Use the color, energy, and feel of the stone to complement the positive thoughts you have established regarding your goals and desires. Allow yourself to replace negative thoughts or fears connected with the goal with the positive statements that the affirmation provides. Repeat the affirmation again and again and soon you'll find that any negative thoughts and fears disintegrate. There is no room for anything but love and goodness where love and goodness reside.

Use the appendices in the back of this book. You will find information to direct you to stones to invite and invoke archangels in the Archangels list. Astrology lovers will enjoy the Astrological Signs and Planetary and Asteroid lists. Refer to the Careers and Professions appendix when dealing with challenges or situations in the business world.

New Age and Metaphysical Concepts for Beginners

Throughout this book, you will find references to numerology, astrology, intuition, channeling, past lives, various healing therapies, and much more. Information about crystal alignment, chakra balancing, and other energy-healing modalities are referred to throughout for the readers who are energy healers or who wish to learn about energy healing. If some of these concepts are new to you, look for them in the glossary and check out the suggested reading to learn more about them. As you become familiar with these concepts and techniques, integrate the ones that resonate with you with into your life as you deem appropriate.

Gemology Basics

While this book is primarily a metaphysical guide, I want to provide you with some basic gemological information on crystals, minerals, and stones that you may find helpful as you delve into this vast world of color and form. This *very* brief gemology lesson will give you some insight into the names or types of the stones and a few of the associated terms so that you can move forward with your practice with some relevant background.

Rocks are mineral aggregates containing one or more minerals.

Minerals are naturally occurring inorganic materials with generally consistent chemical, physical, and optical compositions.

Crystals refer to the smooth, angular forms assumed by minerals when they solidify. The inner atomic structure of the mineral forms the outward structure of the crystal. Each mineral crystallizes in a consistent crystal group, and the shape of the crystal can aid in identification. When conditions are not present that would allow a mineral to crystallize into its well-known faceted structure, it can occur in massive form, in veins or in nodules, within a matrix of another form of rock.

Gemstone is a broad term that encompasses both organic materials and synthetically created inorganic gemlike materials cut or polished by man.

Fossils are the preserved remains of animals, animal parts, plants, and other living organisms from the past. Generally, fossils are composed of rocks that contain limestone.

Quartz is silicon dioxide that crystallizes and is also found in masses. Quartz is found in several forms. The varieties that crystallize are known as amethyst, citrine, smoky quartz, rose quartz, and rock crystal quartz depending on color.

Chalcedonies, which comprise agates, onyx and sardonyx, and jaspers, are cryptocrystalline or microcrystalline quartz composed of microscopic quartz crystals. Agate, jasper, and chalcedony all have chemical and physical properties that are virtually indistinguishable.

A general distinction can be made that agates are banded while chalcedony is not banded; jasper is heavily colored with minerals and may contain iron and other impurities that impart the color and density of the stones.

Obsidian is a natural glass formed during the cooling of volcanic lava. As a glass, it is amorphous and has no crystalline structure.

The study of these naturally occurring materials can be fascinating, but this subject goes beyond the scope of this book. Although gemological references are made throughout, this guide transcends the physical; the information provided is meant to enhance your spiritual and energetic practices. There are many books about gemology, a deep and interesting subject all its own.

WORKING WITH GEMSTONES

The most important thing about working with crystals, minerals, and stones is to remember is that they are simply tools that provide you with a reminder of your intentions and goals. Just as you might light a candle to help you focus on your intention or tie a string around your finger to remember something, a gemstone can provide that same nudge. These sparkling treasures from deep within the earth can help distract you from any troubling thoughts that might be getting in the way of your progress. They remind you to focus on what you *do* want instead of what you *don't*. Here is a good way to get started:

1. Pick a stone, any stone.

2. Hold the stone in your hand, or if it's too large to hold, gaze at the stone.

3. Read the divination provided in this book for the stone and contemplate what that gemstone is trying to awaken in your awareness.

4. Use an affirmation (either the one provided for the stone in this book or one that you create) to help you maintain your focus on what you want, thus replacing thoughts of things you do not want.

5. Every time you touch the stone, look at it, or think of it, remember why you are working with it, and reaffirm your intention.

You can carry smaller stones around with you to stay focused on your intentions while you go about your day, or you can place them strategically around your house or workplace. In fact, there are many methods for incorporating crystals into your daily life, including:

- Carry smaller gemstones in your pocket. Every time you touch your chosen stone, bring your mind back to your intention.

- Put smaller crystals in your pillowcase. Set your intention as you fall asleep and let your subconscious mind work with the crystals to amplify your intention.

- Put the chosen stone on your desk, workstation, or even on the dashboard of your car so that every time you look at it, the rock will remind you to be mindful and conscious of your thoughts and the actions you are taking to actualize your reality.

**Crystals can become part of your everyday life
as beautiful reminders of your intentions and goals.**

- Create a grid of stones in your room, house, property, or office. Set your intention by charging the group of gemstones to be used. (To charge a crystal, focus all your attention on the stone and mentally transfer your intention into the stone with a confident, forceful breath.) Decide which geometric formation best suits you. Place gemstones in the corners of rooms, on furniture, and on windowsills while imagining that you are mentally drawing an energetic geometric line of light to establish a grid of love and well-being to uphold your intention. (There's more about creating a grid in the Crystal Grids and Alignments appendix.)

- Transform your reality using gemstones as they relate specifically to your chakras as discussed here and in my book *Chakra Awakening*.

- Use gemstone hydrotherapy: Place a collection of small charged stones into a net or organza bag, and drop it in your bathtub to infuse your bathwater with your intention. As you relax in the tub, allow the positive energy to seep into your skin.

Regardless of the method used to incorporate healing gemstones into your life, be sure to form clear intentions you can associate with particular stones every time you see them when choosing crystals. For example, if you are looking for more love in your life, you may choose a rose quartz after reviewing the various gemstones in this directory. When you see or touch the rose quartz, any other thoughts you have will melt away, and you will be filled with the love you wish to attract into your life. Need more self-confidence? You might choose a citrine from among the stones that boost self-confidence. Every time you touch the citrine, look at it, or even think of it, you will have the opportunity to reaffirm your intention that you are filled with confidence. The A-to-Z Essential Guide will help you choose your stones for this purpose, or you can choose a stone, look it up in the guide, and see what mysteries it reveals to you.

How to Choose Crystals

You can use this book as a guide for choosing stones to assist you with your life, but quite often, the stones you are drawn to are the stones that have important lessons or messages in store for you. Browse through your local metaphysical store, and allow yourself to be attracted to the stone that is right for you at this moment in your life.

You don't have to spend a lot of money to work with stones. The most affordable are small tumbled stones you'll find in most metaphysical stores and rock shops. Larger stones usually carry a higher price tag. However, with a little money, you'll always find a stone for you at the right price. I recommend starting a collection of tumbled stones, since you can easily accumulate a reasonably priced variety of choices to use with this book.

The majority of the stones listed in this book is naturally occurring and come straight from the earth. In a few cases, you'll find that I have included synthetic, dyed, or slightly altered stones. I've purposely included some of these sparkling options because they are commonly found in metaphysical shops, and you may be drawn to one. Based on my own experience, I still like to use them and want to share how they can also be useful.

As you are looking through the tumbled stones (and the larger stones, if you wish), think about what you want to attract or change in your life—in other words, what do you hope to accomplish by working with the crystal you will choose? Contemplate what you will think about every time you touch or look at the stone. Continue looking at the various stones. Allow your higher self to be naturally attracted to one of them. Choose the stone by color and how attractive it is to you. If you think a stone is pretty or if it piques your interest in some other way, pick it up and see if you like the way it feels in your hand. Ask yourself, "How does this stone make me feel?" Begin your work by using your intuition and feelings about the chosen stone without searching out its description. Then look it up in the pages that follow to find out why you were attracted to it and the many ways you can use the stone to awaken your awareness. Learn how it can assist you or affect you on all levels—spiritually, mentally, emotionally, and physically.

Which stones do you find appealing?
Perhaps there's a message hidden in your preferences!

You can also use this book as a guide for choosing the right stones for you. As you flip through the pages, see if your eyes are drawn to a particular photo, then read about that stone. If you relate to what you read, put that stone on your shopping list. Or maybe it isn't the photograph that draws you in but a particular affirmation or any of the other material under a gemstone entry. With your shopping list in hand, you can seek out those stones when you visit the rock shop. Even when you are seeking out specific stones, be open to others that might be "calling" to you as well.

To choose stones that specifically relate to the chakras you wish to align as described in this book and more in depth in my book *Chakra Awakening*, turn to the Chakra appendix.

Pick stones that seem appropriate for your purposes from the chart and then read the associated affirmations. When you find one that feels right, put that on your shopping list as well. While it's best to use your intuition when choosing stones, you can also choose stones by color and shape to amplify your intentions.

The Shapes and Sizes of Crystals

Crystals come in various shapes and sizes, either directly from the earth in their natural state or polished and cut into various geometric configurations. Gemstones are especially delightful in jewelry, amulets, and pendulums. In fact, your home, office, and jewelry box probably contain some of these sparkling treasures already. After reading this book, you will look at your gemstone paperweights, book ends, and rings from a new perspective. The various shapes of the stones provide you with further insights when setting your intentions.

Arrowheads

Arrowheads are often carved out of black obsidian, but you can find other types of stones carved into arrowheads as well. I use arrowheads as a reminder that there are always signs pointing me in the right direction. (Some people have assigned the negative connotation of being "stabbed in the back" to the arrowhead, but I choose to see the positive in everything!)

Use this shape of stone to help remind you that there is always direction available to help you know what to do, where to go, and what to do next. I encounter many clients who just don't have any direction and are waiting for someone to tell them what do to with their lives. I remind them that each of us is solely responsible for deciding what to do with our own life. You can use an arrowhead to help you focus your intention on identifying what you enjoy doing. When you do what you love, prosperity, peace, and love will be more abundant.

Geodes

Geodes are rounded rock formations that, once broken open, expose a beautiful crystalline interior. You never know what you'll find inside a geode until it has been broken open. Geodes are typically sold only after the center has been revealed. The interiors are agate, quartz, amethyst, or chalcedony. Geodes are often dyed various colors for an added effect. (I believe that color-infused crystals are equally as delightful and as effective for the purposes described in this book.) Children love geodes. The miniature cavern is reminiscent of the land of little fairies and gnomes. The word "geode" comes from the Greek word *geodes,* meaning earthlike. You can use geodes to help focus your attention on being more grounded while contemplating your innermost thoughts.

Hearts

Many stones are cut and polished into the shape of a heart. Heart-shaped stones are dedicated to approaching whatever you are working on from the center of yourself—your heart chakra. Heart-shaped stones remind you that love is always the answer. Allow love. Love yourself. Nurture yourself. If you are attracted to heart-shaped stones, you may want to improve your relationships—the relationship you have with others as well as the relationship you have with yourself. Use a heart-shaped stone to help focus your attention on attracting romance or more love into your life.

Pyramids

Pyramids are a popular shape in crystal shops. The base of a pyramid is a polygon (a straight-sided flat shape); the sides are triangles that meet at the top, or the apex. Pyramids can be square, triangular, pentagonal, and so on. The common feature is that they are three-dimensional figures with a flat base and straight edges (polyhedrons). Use pyramids to amplify your focus and the preservation of knowledge, wisdom, love, and protection. The foundation of the pyramid is the grounding force. The triangle represents focus, and the point aligns you with your intentions.

Spheres

A sphere (also called a crystal ball or orb) is a three-dimensional object shaped like a ball. Every point on the surface is the same distance from the center. Virtually every type of stone has been polished into a sphere, so the choice of color and size is plentiful. This shape is helpful during times when you are connecting with the oneness of all life. Spheres are pleasant to gaze at during meditative practice. Use a sphere to help focus your attention on receiving intuitive information to help yourself or another person. Use it as a companion tool during readings or in a work setting on your desk as a decorative item to help you read—and hear—between the lines.

Cubes

A cube is a relatively common shape for some crystals. The cube itself represents the energy of the triple-digit vibrations of numbers. In basic geometry, to cube a number is to multiply the same number three times. For example, 3x3x3=27. Take that number, 333, without multiplying it, and it represents the realm of the Ascended Masters (see "Ascended Master" in the glossary). To take this further, the number 27 becomes a 9 in numerology (2+7=9), which represents the completion of a cycle.

Use a cube-shaped gemstone to help you experience completion of a life cycle with awareness and good intentions. The gemstone cube you choose for this purpose will amplify and strengthen your intentions. You can also choose cubes when you need to affirm that everything will turn out for the best.

Octahedrons

An octahedron is three-dimensional form consisting of eight equilateral triangle facets. Four of the eight faces form a pyramid pointing in one direction and the exact replica forms in the other direction—with the bases of the pyramid back to back. It has twelve edges and six vertices or corner points, and four edges meet at each vertex. Fluorite octahedrons or clusters with octahedral formations are naturally occurring.

There are many numerological meanings behind all of these faces and edges. The eight faces lend the ability to be strong enough to execute your abilities in a leadership-type role. Eight adds great financial success and the vibrations for good business judgment. The three edges of each face offer access to the subconscious mind, producing growth through imagination. The twelve edges represent the connection with super-consciousness and all that is. It provides inner strength and tolerance. The six corner points offer justice, comfort, beauty, and love. An octahedron has the vibration of embracing community responsibility and the interplay that has with each person's domestic life. Use an octahedron to help focus your attention on any of these concepts or qualities.

Clusters

Every gemstone cluster is entirely unique. Clear quartz and all types of gemstone clusters grow within the veins of mountains throughout the world. Clusters are a family of points that share a common matrix. The cluster, therefore, represents happy community connections, starting first with a happy family life and learning how to share common ground while each individual point/person is unique within itself. Use a gemstone cluster to help focus your attention on community and global connection. The cluster is a reminder of the interconnectedness of all life on this planet and beyond. Use clusters when setting intentions that will have wide-reaching effects.

Wands

A wand shape occurs naturally in many types of gemstones. Wands are also often fashioned from larger chunks or pieces of stone into points or massage tools. Wands can be used in a variety of ways. They direct energy, help focus attention, and ground the force of thoughts into a steady, single force.

Wands are often used by body workers, reflexologists, acupressure workers, and massage therapists as a tool in their healing modality. They are useful in crystal grids to connect the matrix of the grids by adding a link to amplify the grid's intention. Wands are employed for ritual and magical purposes.

Use a crystal wand for memory recall, to maintain focus, to amplify vital life force, and to strengthen concentration. Wands help gather energy and direct energy through the transference of thought and intention.

Gemstone-Adorned Everyday Items

Gemstone-adorned rings, earrings, bracelets, and necklaces are not only attractive but can also be worn with intention as a reminder to keep your focus on your positive affirmations and desires. Dress with consciousness: when you establish your goals for the day, charge the gemstone jewelry you will use as an accent to your outfit with your intentions. You can also adorn your keychain, bags, and cell phone with crystals specifically intended for this purpose. As you see the gemstones dangling or adorning these everyday items, you will be frequently reminded to keep your awareness on your goals and desires throughout the day.

Other items you may consider of the everyday variety, such as pendulums and amulets, also benefit from crystal energy. A simple piece of string and a button make a simple divining pendulum, but a faceted crystal point at the end of a chain adds a rich dimension to your dowsing practices. Similarly, while an amulet, which is meant to bring good luck and protection, can be made of practically any type of material, a crystal brings the added benefit of positive associations and intentions attached to it.

Clearing and Charging Crystals

Intention is the simplest, most effective, and least costly way to clear and charge a crystal. To begin, roll the crystal in a clockwise direction with your dominant hand, pressing firmly on each of the crystal's facets. This creates a piezoelectric charge. (Piezoelectricity is simply the ability of some materials, including certain types of crystals, to have electrical properties under stress.) Next, press the forefinger of your dominant hand onto the tip of the crystal, and place the forefinger and thumb on your other hand on the sides of the crystal to create a crosscurrent. Next, focus all of your attention on the stone and mentally transfer your intention to clear the stone into the stone itself. Think something to yourself along these lines: *My intention is to clear this crystal, releasing whatever is not for my highest good and for the highest good of all concerned.* Then complete the process with a confident, forceful breath through your nose (a pulsed breath). The force of the exhaled breath is similar to the force of a breath you would use to extinguish a candle.

Repeat this process for each pair of facets on the crystal. For example, a quartz is a six-sided gemstone, so you need to repeat this process three times because you're holding on to two sides at a time. In the case of tumbled stones, larger crystals, or a large assortment of crystals, it isn't necessary to hold the crystal or the group of crystals in your hand to clear them. Simply look at each stone you want to clear and make the strong intention that it will be cleared. Follow this with a pulsed breath.

Breath, intention, mental focus, transference of thoughts, and visualization performed remotely are effective as well. You can clear your house, office, or car in the same manner. The plan is to hold the intention and visualize and *know* it is effective.

Other ways to clear your crystals include smudging with herbs and resins, salt baths, running them under tap water, holding them tightly in the ocean as the water cleanses them, and placing them for a time in the sunlight or moonlight. If you choose to use salt baths to clear your crystals, quickly pass them through the saltwater, then rinse and dry. Many polished stones will lose their shine after sitting in saltwater. This goes for the ocean as well. Be sure to hold on to your stones at the beach very tightly. Many a stone has returned to Mother Earth this way!

Gemstones for the Chakras

Gemstones come in a vast array of colors. The use of color is a powerful tool for bringing balance into our lives. It is a vital part of our body, mind, and spirit. According to some Eastern philosophies, chakras are the energy centers that comprise our energy field. These energy centers are responsible for regulating the functions of many levels of our being. There are seven main chakras, each of which has a color associated with it; in turn, each color corresponds to a stone of the same color, as described here and in each entry in the A-to-Z guide.

First Chakra

The first chakra is the root chakra. Its basic color is red. This energy center is located at the base of the spine and is responsible for our basic needs. This is where we store our vital energy for providing food, shelter, and water for ourselves. It is the base of Maslow's pyramid. These are our very basic needs, and money is strongly associated with this center. A gemstone for the root is garnet.

Second Chakra

The second chakra is the navel or sacral chakra. Its main color is orange. It is obviously located at the navel. This is the center for reproduction and creativity. We often store emotional memories in this center. It is a center that allows us to create and take action in our lives. A gemstone for the navel is carnelian.

Third Chakra

The third chakra is the solar plexus chakra, and it is located at the solar plexus (the area of the body between the belly button and the center of the chest). The main color associated with the chakra is yellow. This is the place of joy, personal power, self-confidence, mental clarity, and the ability to shine our light. We often store verbal abuses here that may have reduced our self-esteem, and likewise store kudos and praises that we have received that raised our self-confidence.
A gemstone for the solar plexus is citrine.

Fourth Chakra

The fourth chakra is the heart center. This chakra is green and/or pink. It is located in the center of the chest. This center is the bridge between the lower three chakras of the physical, mundane world and the upper chakras of the spiritual world. This is the part of us where our true self resides; the "Love That We Are." It is where and how we integrate that we are spiritual beings having a physical experience. Some gemstones for the heart are green aventurine and rose quartz.

Fifth Chakra

The fifth chakra is the throat center. This chakra is blue (like the color of the sky) or turquoise. This center is located at the throat and provides us with our ability to communicate and express ourselves. This is not exclusively our verbal expression, but also the way we express ourselves in the world, including writing, speaking, singing, cooking, or however else we may express who and what we are. A stone for the throat center is aquamarine.

Sixth Chakra

The sixth chakra is the third eye center. This chakra is indigo blue. It is located in the center of the forehead. This is the location of our ability to see the unseen, know the unknown, and hear what is not being said. It is the place of intuition, knowing, and dreaming. A stone for the third eye is lapis lazuli.

Seventh Chakra

The seventh chakra is the crown chakra. The color associated with the crown ranges from golden white light to a violet flame. This is the place of higher intuition, channeling, and connection with divine consciousness. This is the place where our connection to miracles resides. Some gemstones for the crown chakra are selenite, amethyst, and clear quartz.

Making conscious connection with the chakras with the intention of balancing and aligning them with each other provides an avenue for balancing various aspects of your life. It is beneficial to meditate on each of the chakras using visualization to spin off what you no longer need and replace that with goodness, love, and well-being. Using guided meditation CDs and placing gemstones on each of these chakras will bring peace and balance to your life. You can use my CD, *Color Meditation: Align Your Chakras,* as a tool to assist you in balancing your life. *Chakra Awakening* goes into great detail of all of the chakras, and you can read it for an in-depth understanding of the chakras and color usage.

Crystal Alignment: Chakra Balancing

A crystal alignment is also referred to as the laying on of stones. It is the process of placing gemstones and crystals on and around the body with the intention to restore balance. It's a meditative experience that elicits extreme relaxation.

Although a crystal alignment is usually performed by someone else rather than for oneself, there is no reason you can't give it a try. You can perform a crystal alignment with little or no experience simply by placing the crystals, stones, and minerals you are attracted to on or around you for meditation, prayer, or contemplation. If you are lying down for this experience, first line up the suggested crystals next to you and then place them on each chakra, beginning with the root and work your way up to the crown.

To provide this alignment for someone else, establish intention with the recipient of a crystal alignment. Engage in conversation prior to the actual meditation experience. During the preparation for the alignment, determine the ultimate goal and develop a strategy together to restore balance. The section below gives you some guidance for offering this type of session for another person. The same applies when you are doing this for yourself; just ask yourself the questions.

Choosing Gemstones for the Alignment

There are a number of ways to approach the process of deciding what crystals to use for the actual laying on of stones. With the participation of the person receiving the alignment, determine the reason for the session. Why does he or she want a crystal alignment? What feels out of balance? Once you are proficient at pinpointing colors and chakras either through extensive reading or attending workshops related to becoming a crystal healer, you will automatically know which crystals will be most beneficial. However, not everyone has the time or money for that kind of training. Each entry in this book lists the chakras associated with the individual gemstones, but you can use the following for a quick reference:

- **Crown chakra:** Selenite—Divine connection, miracle worker, and channel

- **Third eye chakra:** Lapis lazuli—intuition, spiritual sight, and meditation

- **Throat chakra:** Angelite—communication, divine timing, angelic communication, and spirit-guide awareness

- **Heart chakra:** Green tourmaline—love, compassion, kindness, and tolerance

- **Solar plexus chakra:** Golden calcite—self-confidence, courage, joy, and enthusiasm

- **Navel chakra:** Carnelian—creativity, fertility, and realization of goals and intentions

- **Root chakra:** Garnet—prosperity, vitality, passion, sensuality, and action

A reliable alternative to choosing stones for a crystal alignment listed here or elsewhere is to use a technique I call the Gemstone Oracle. To use the Gemstone Oracle technique, place your collection of gemstones and crystals in front of the person for whom you are performing the crystal alignment, and ask him or her to choose seven gemstones. Advise the person to choose the stone he or she is attracted to in that moment. This is extremely revealing, as everyone innately knows what they need and where they need help or guidance. The choice of gemstones also often reveals a pattern of colors that the person needs or wants to rebalance.

Once the stones have been chosen, use your intuition along with the knowledge that you have gained about the chakras, the associated colors, and complementary colors. Refer to the gemstone meaning found in this book, and use the matching affirmation.

Laying On of Stones

After choosing the stones for the alignment, place them on and around the person as he or she reclines on a massage table or another flat surface. You may want to drape a blanket or a sheet over the person for a feeling of security. Be sure to clear your area ahead of time with one of the methods you have available to you, such as Florida Water or Smudge in Spray.

Encourage the person to let you know if anything feels uncomfortable at any time. Sometimes the stones can feel too hot or too cold. Some of my clients have expressed to me that stones felt too heavy. Let the person know that there should never be any physical pain associated with this type of healing. Keep in mind that some people are too self-conscious to tell you if something is bothering them. Reassure and check in with the person from time to time to ask if everything feels okay as you place stones on his or her body.

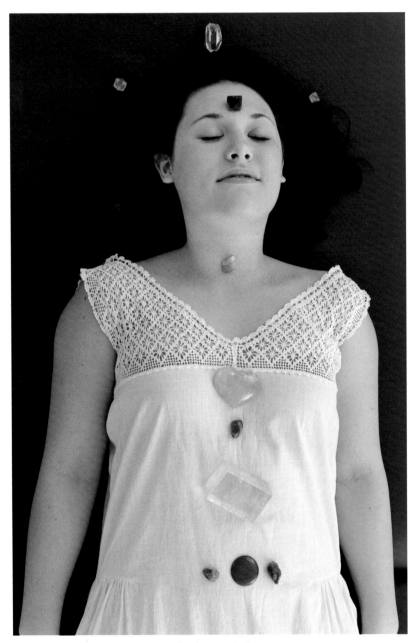

An example of a crystal alignment.

In a crystal alignment, the stones are placed
on the body's chakras for rebalancing.

Stones will often fall off or roll to some other part of the body during this experience. This can be caused by the body breathing, or even because the crystal healing session has taken on a life of its own. Occasionally, when a stone moves, I will replace it in its original location, yet I assess my intuition to determine if perhaps that is where the stone wants to be. At times, even when I replace the stone, it rolls right back to where it wants to be, so I let it be.

Crystal Grids for
Home, Office, and the Planet

A crystal grid is the use of gemstones in geometric configurations placed on or around a person, place, or thing to achieve a desired intention. Crystal grids can be combined with crystal alignments with larger groups of people at sacred sites. The use of sacred geometry to realize a goal is often employed by metaphysicians, spiritual teachers, and many spiritual practitioners.

Crystal grids are simply a much bigger, larger-than-life version of a crystal alignment used with the intention of realigning the body of Mother Earth through the activation of the Grids of Light. The Grids of Light can be likened to the grid of electricity you live within, or the (worldwide) web created via the Internet. The Grids of Light are around and within the body of Mother Earth. To create crystal grids, use people and crystals to create geometric configurations in conjunction with intention, meditation, guided imagery, and prayer.

I've been to sacred sites to activate the grids of light and love that surround our planet. My travels have included Chichen Itza, Mexico; Uxmal, Mexico; Dzibilchaltún, Mexico; Teotihuacan, Mexico; Machu Picchu, Peru; Mesa Verde, Colorado; Stonehenge, England; and other sacred places. We've performed meditative crystal grids using telepathy which connects crystals held by participants, activating love and well-being at the location.

Sacred geometry is geometry used in designing temples, pyramids, cathedrals, churches, and other places of worship and spiritual connection. Sacred architecture sets a foundational vibration and vortex or channel for an easier connection with spiritual wisdom.

This type of geometry is also found within sacred art. Sacred art is designed with the intention to uplift your consciousness to the spiritual. Geometry and mathematical ratios, harmonics, and proportion are found in music, light, and the philosophical study of the universe.

You don't have to be an architect nor must you understand sacred geometry to make a grid. It's easy to make one by placing stones intuitively with intention. The key phrase here is *intuitively with intention.* Although I provide formulas for successful grids in the Crystal Grids and Alignments appendix, I encourage you to think with your heart and follow your intuition. Brush up on the energy represented by the colors of the stones; familiarize yourself with the color meanings.

If you know the color and know what you want to achieve, all you need to do is place stones strategically around the space you are gridding. Stay focused on the intention of infusing love and well-being in and around that space. Imagine that these gemstones are energetically connecting with each other and are creating a network of well-being above, below, and around the room or space. This process can be used both indoors and outdoors.

1. Write down a clear intention that defines the purpose of the grid.

2. Pick the crystals and gemstones that will positively effect change.

3. Stand in the center of the room or space, and state your intention aloud while gazing at the stones. If the stones are small enough, hold them in your hands while you speak. Otherwise, place them on a surface, hold your hands over or around the stones, and gaze at the stones as you infuse the gemstones with the intended energy.

4. Intuitively place the stones around the room or space. As you do this, continue to stay focused on love and well-being, and visualize the positive outcome. Use your imagination to see, sense, feel, and know the intention completed.

5. Now, really stretch your imagination, and visualize beams of light or particles of energy that connect each and every stone to create an energetic web of love, light, and well-being. See or know that this web extends far and wide around the space.

**Placing crystals, minerals, and stones around your home
has many benefits both for the house and all its inhabitants.**

In summary, place crystals, minerals, and stones around the space you wish to realign or bless. Instill your intention and visualize the stones creating a matrix of love and well-being. I have included sample diagrams and suggested stones for various places and purposes in the Crystal Grids and Alignments appendix.

The appendices in the back of this book are intended to assist you when choosing stones for all parts of your life. You have the Careers and Professions appendix to refer to when you are picking a stone for your workspace or the office of a friend. Use the Archangels appendix for spiritual assistance to align you with the Divine. The Astrological Signs and Planetary and Asteroid appendices are geared to help connect you with a deeper understanding of the cycles of our stars, planets, and your own personal astrological chart and transits.

THE A-TO-Z
ESSENTIAL GUIDE

In the pages that follow, you will find a directory of stones listed in alphabetical order. Each entry includes the following categories:

- **Name of stone**

- **Key Phrase:** A phrase of a couple of words to provide a quick insight into the information regarding the specific stone.

- **Color(s):** The various colors in which the stone typically appears. The most common color is listed first. The meaning of a stone is often revealed by the color of the stone. The color directly relates to one or more of the seven chakras.

- **Chakra(s):** Indicates the chakra for which this stone would be most beneficial. An in-depth understanding of the chakras provides you with a strong foundation for using stones. Knowing the chakras is like knowing your alphabet prior to forming words and sentences.

- **Planet(s):** The planetary body with which the stone is associated. Sometimes the choice of planet corresponds with the astrological sign assigned, and sometimes it doesn't. Some stones have an asteroid listed under this entry as well, such as Chiron, Ceres, Pallas, Vesta, and Juno. This is based on my chart-reading experience, which includes the asteroids. Including the asteroids provides a deeper understanding of geometric formations revealed in astrology charts.

- **Number(s):** The matching numerological vibration. This number is based on my knowledge of numerology, and in some cases, the number was provided by divine inspiration. In some instances, double digits followed by a single digit separated by a slash are listed to give the stone a more complete numerological portrayal.

- **Element(s):** The choice of the element—air, fire, water, metal, or earth—is determined by a number of means. Sometimes the element is based on how the mineral grows or formed on the earth. Other times, it's based on the human interaction—how it affects the four subtle bodies. And, of course, there are moments when the element was revealed to me through Divine inspiration and has nothing to do with the chemical elements of the mineral, stone, or metal.

- **Mohs scale:** The degree of hardness based on the Mohs scale. This scale rates the scratch and abrasion resistance of various minerals and stones (but not durability or toughness) when affected by rougher materials. It was created by the German geologist and mineralogist Frederich Mohs in 1812, and applies to stones, materials, minerals, and rocks. (A diamond, the hardest known substance on earth at the time the Mohs scale was created, is 10 on this scale. Talc is 1.)

- **Astro sign(s):** Short for "astrological signs." The sign of the zodiac with which the stone is associated. There are many opinions from many gemologists, authors, astrologers, metaphysicians, and others providing their take on the assignment of the zodiac sign for each gemstone. The astrological signs listed here are based on more than three decades of study with many different teachers.

- **Affirmation:** A positive statement of affirmation associated with the stone that helps to focus an intention. The most powerful use of stones is through the use of setting an intention, focus, or goal for the stone in question. The affirmation provided at the beginning of each entry gives you various phrases to state, repeat, or think about every time you look at, touch, or use the stone. It is my recommendation to set an intention when working with a stone; the affirmation is provided to help you form the intention.

- **Spiritual uses:** Ideas on how to use the stone to further develop your spiritual connection. The spiritual use of the stone is the manner in which it can help you develop your spiritual nature or your spiritual practice. Common suggestions are offered regarding connection with the Divine, regression therapy for a better understanding of spiritual lessons, meditation practice, and connection with guides, angels, and other master teachers in a variety of ways.

- **Mental uses:** The use of the gem for mental focus or clarity and situations in which it can be helpful. The use of the stone for the mind and the various ways we think and use our mind is provided in this section. The mental subtle body contains all the thought forms in your consciousness. It is these thought forms that create your reality. To manage and balance your thought forms is paramount in creating a happy, healthy, and productive life. Use the stone with intention to keep your mind focused on the positive: what you *do* want, not what you *don't* want.

- **Emotional uses:** A tool for dealing with feelings to unblock underlying challenges; the emotional body is just as real as the physical body. You don't have to be convinced that you have feelings—or do you? This section is dedicated to how the stone can help you get in touch with, embrace, or transform and transmute your feelings. Balance is always the goal, and it starts by understanding and recognizing how you feel.

- **Physical uses:** The most obvious part of our existence—the physical realm. This section provides uses for gemstones for the mundane world, including the physical body and financial security. Important note: never use stones internally in any way. Do not put gemstones in water you plan on drinking. See the section "Working with Gemstones" for methods of applying crystals for uses described in this book.

- **Divine guidance:** Guidance for uncovering self-knowledge, and self-realization for the purpose of personal development and spiritual awakening. Here the Gemstone Oracle speaks and gives you a message to tell you what it could mean if you are attracted to this stone. The word *oracle* refers to a person, place, or thing through which advice or prophecy is given. In this setting, the stone you pick is a clue to part of your unconscious (or subconscious) thoughts and beliefs, helping you uncover hidden or buried truths, a bit like uncovering computer programs that run in the background. Use the divine guidance to awaken your awareness. Personally, using gemstones as an oracle became natural across many years as a crystal shop owner.

- **About the stone.** A basic geological description of the stone.

AGATE, BLUE-DYED
Love, Wealth, and Abundance

COLOR(S)	blue
CHAKRA(S)	throat, third eye
PLANET(S)	Uranus, Earth
NUMBER(S)	77/5
ELEMENT(S)	air
MOHS SCALE	6.5–7
ASTRO SIGN(S)	Aquarius, Virgo

Affirmation I am at peace. All is well in my life. I am grateful for my ability to stay focused on what is truly important. I am a blessing to myself and others. I have many blessings. Love, wealth, and abundance come naturally to me.

Spiritual uses With its peaceful blue energy, blue-dyed agate emits calming vibrations. This stone infuses peacefulness into the surrounding area. Use this stone to integrate grounded meditation experiences into your practices. This agate, which is often attractive to children, helps provide calm, grounded experiences for children's spiritual activities in the metaphysical realm.

Mental uses Blue-dyed agate is useful for gaining insight and clarity. In cases where confusion or distractions exist, this stone can assist in gently guiding your attention back to the matter at hand. Use this stone with children for relieving stress regarding school work or any type of study. It's helpful for children as well as adults with ADD and ADHD.

Emotional uses With blue-dyed agate in hand, set your intentions on balancing your emotions and bringing yourself into a place of calmness. If you have a tendency to be up and down in your emotions, this is one of the stones that can help you maintain that focus. All agates are very grounding, and the blue energy in this stone will calm any inflamed emotions you may be experiencing.

Physical uses Blue-dyed agate is a good stone to work with if you frequently strain parts of your body. Using this stone can help keep your attention on what you are doing. If you tend to become angry easily, this stone can remind you that everything is okay at the deepest level. Breathe deeply and allow the blue energy to dissipate the angry red energy from your consciousness. It is also a stone of good fortune and many blessings. Use this stone to discover your life's work and fulfill your divine purpose.

Divine guidance Are looking for grounding and focus? Are you also experiencing some frustrations or agitation? Perhaps you are feeling aggravated or angry with someone or some situation. This is a reminder to focus your attention on a peaceful place within you and in all your interactions. Don't sweat the small stuff.

About the stone:
Silicon dioxide formed into microcrystalline quartz with synthetic blue color enhancement.

AGATE, BLUE LACE
Opportunities Abound!

Color(s)	translucent pastel blue with white swirls
Chakra(s)	throat
Planet(s)	Venus, Uranus, Neptune
Number(s)	7, 11, 12
Element(s)	air, water
Mohs scale	6.5–7
Astro sign(s)	Virgo, Libra, Pisces

Affirmation Favorable opportunities present themselves to me in many ways, and I follow through on their promise. I am always in the right place at the right time. I have divine timing. It is easy for me to express myself. I am understood. I truly hear what others are communicating.

Spiritual uses The pastel blue vibration of blue lace agate aligns you with the ability to hear divine guidance from angels, spirit guides, power animals, fairies, and the Other Side. With this alignment, the ability to follow your intuition is increased. This stone helps you to develop trust of the spiritual realm. This stone is associated with Archangels Haniel and Thuriel.

Mental uses Blue lace agate improves your ability to communicate with others and speak your truth. Use it when you want to be heard and truly understood. It also helps you listen more closely when others speak and really hear and understand what they are trying to express. It aids your ability to read between the lines.

Emotional uses Blue lace agate increases your ability to stay calm and peaceful in times of stress and turmoil. It is an aid for appropriately communicating your emotions and feelings. This stone's pastel blue color is ideal to use to calm children who have a tendency to be hyperactive and extremely loud. On the other hand, it assists children who have a hard time expressing themselves. In other words, this agate balances out either extreme.

Physical uses The pastel blue of this lacy agate promotes health for the throat, neck, ears, mouth, gums, teeth, and nose. Blue lace agate encourages peace and calm and is beneficial for healing all types of physical ailments. This stone helps you to reduce stress and calm inflammation. Use it for laryngitis, sore throats, and canker sores and to calm outbreaks of herpes anywhere on the body.

Divine guidance Do you feel like you keep missing promising opportunities? Do you simply wish to recognize opportunities when they knock? Have faith: divine timing is at play in your life. Allow yourself to recognize this powerful force and believe that you are always in the right place at the right time with the right people.

About the stone:
Blue lace agate is silicon dioxide forming into microcrystalline quartz with blue and white banding in lace-like patterns. The stones are translucent.

AGATE, BOTSWANA
Abstract Thinking

Color(s)	a combination of translucent to opaque banded swirls of pink, peach, gray, black, white, beige, brown, and/or orange
Chakra(s)	heart, root, solar, navel
Planet(s)	Mercury
Number(s)	13
Element(s)	air
Mohs scale	6.5–7
Astro sign(s)	Virgo, Gemini

Affirmation I think abstractly. I am extremely creative. Creative thoughts are constantly coming to me. Patterns and different perspectives give me insight and understanding. I am imaginative, and I easily arrive at solutions to challenges as they present themselves. My creative endeavors come to fruition. I am enthusiastic and confident.

Spiritual uses The banded patterns within this stone form a vortex of energy that opens your spiritual ears and eyes, enabling you to receive channeled messages. Being an agate, this stone keeps you grounded while you "download" spiritual wisdom and knowledge. It is helpful to integrate complex and abstract spiritual beliefs and concepts. It's a great aid in studying spiritual texts.

Mental uses The swirling colors of Botswana agate amplify the creative vibe for connecting with artistic ideas. With its banded patterns, this stone also assists you in recognizing the patterns in your life and within yourself. It is beneficial to be conscious of repetitive patterns and clarifies what shifts you might choose to make. When you are in the process of changing your reality, one of the first assignments is to use the tool of self-observation. This tool gives you the ability to observe if you are stuck in a rut or limiting belief systems.

Emotional uses Botswana agate can help you step into your swirling emotions by using abstract thinking. Because it aids with the ability to look at things outside the box, it provides objectivity. It promotes observing your emotions from many different angles, thereby removing the strong attachment to those emotions. Use this stone to tap into the expression of emotions through art.

Physical uses Botswana agate is a good stone for improving skin tone, texture, and collagen production. Regardless of the stone's color, the underlying energy of all agates is grounding and stabilizing. When you combine the lofty energy of creativity that lies within this stone with the energy of groundedness, you receive additional assistance in manifesting conscious action to make your intentions a reality. This is a stone for artists and inventors.

Divine guidance Do you find that you are able to see things from a different angle than most people? Are you able to see solutions to challenges? You are extremely intuitive and creative. Use your innate gifts to make your life and the lives of others a bit easier. You are capable of maintaining your focus and accomplishing great things.

About the stone:
Botswana agate is silicon dioxide forming microcrystalline quartz exhibiting white and gray banding. The stones are translucent to opaque and are found in Botswana, Africa.

AGATE, BROWN
Open Up!

Color(s)	translucent to opaque brown
Chakra(s)	root
Planet(s)	Saturn, Ceres
Number(s)	4
Element(s)	earth
Mohs scale	6.5–7
Astro sign(s)	Capricorn

Affirmation It's easy to open myself up to allow the light in. I unlock the secrets of my soul. I am aware of my thoughts and belief systems. I am a caretaker of the earth. I spend time in nature. My connection with fairies is strong. I am a talented gardener!

Spiritual uses Brown agate is a perfect stone for connecting with the elemental spirits, devic forces, and the fairy kingdom. The plant and other earth spirits are aligned with this stone. With it, you can tap into the wisdom of the earth stewards. This stone opens up the "trap doors" on the soles of your feet, grounding you so that you can communicate with the nature spirits.

Mental uses The color of the earth, brown agate is a useful tool for grounding your awareness by connecting to the soil. It is easy to get distracted, go off on tangents, and never get anything done, but this stone can gently keep you on task while still allowing the energy of fun, play, and creativity.

Emotional uses Brown agate reminds you that laughter and play are keys to a balanced emotional state. This stone wants you to make mud pies and reactivate your childlike nature. The carefree energy of this stone, which is strongly aligned with the nature spirits, helps you heal your inner child and issues from the past. This stone also helps you to sort out your emotions so that you can recognize that all that exists is this present moment.

Physical uses Brown agate is a good tool for balancing the absorption and elimination processes of the physical body. This stone helps you remove toxins from your physical body through your reconnection with nature. It reminds you to spend time with the trees, grass, and flowers, which aid in physical health and well-being. This is a good stone for gardeners, landscape architects, herbalists, aromatherapists, and ecologists.

Divine guidance Have you been spending time in nature? How does your garden grow? Whether you live in a small city apartment or on an expansive farm, you can always find a way to establish your roots in the earth and nature. Use the negative ions of the mountains, sea, or air for your overall good.

> **About the stone:**
> Brown agate is silicon dioxide forming microcrystalline quartz with a brownish hue. Stones can be translucent to opaque.

AGATE, GREEN-DYED
Be Green!

COLOR(S)	green
CHAKRA(S)	heart
PLANET(S)	Neptune
NUMBER(S)	9
ELEMENT(S)	water
MOHS SCALE	6.5–7
ASTRO SIGN(S)	Pisces

Affirmation It's easy to "be green." I make conscious, informed purchases. I recycle used materials. I reuse as much as possible. It is my aim to leave this world a better place than it was when I arrived. I am dedicated to leaving a minimal footprint on the planet.

Spiritual uses Green-dyed agate opens your mind to understanding the spiritual dimensions of plants and plant-life forms. Plants have a consciousness in similar alignment to the consciousness of animals. This stone allows you to hear messages from the plant kingdom and to benefit from its vast knowledge.

Mental uses With green-dyed agate in hand, contemplate the limiting belief systems and outdated thoughtforms (mental energy) that need to be removed from your consciousness. Set the intention to release this clutter from your mind and energy field, and foster positivity in its place.

Emotional uses Green-dyed agate helps you to remember to cleanse and purify your body as well as your environment. As you release toxins or unnecessary clutter in your life, you will make a healthier and clearer space in which to live. With this stone close by, take advantage of the healing properties of a swim in a pool, lake, or ocean, or simply relax in a bath.

Physical uses Green-dyed agate reminds you that there is great power in "being green." Recycling keeps your physical space in order and this stone keeps you aware of how the materials you leave behind might affect the next seven generations. This stone can be used by vegetarians and/or vegans for making peace with the plant kingdom and thanking it for the sustenance it provides.

Divine guidance Are you in the process of reinventing yourself? This is a time for self-renewal and realignment. Take time to reflect on where you've been and where you are going. Connect with the power of the future generations and decide how you will make this world a better place.

About the stone:
Silicon dioxide formed into microcrystalline quartz with synthetic green color enhancement.

Agate, Green Moss
Mountain Air

Color(s)	translucent to opaque green fern-like sprays within clear or milky quartz
Chakra(s)	heart, root
Planet(s)	Earth, Venus, Ceres
Number(s)	2
Element(s)	earth
Mohs scale	6.5–7
Astro sign(s)	Taurus

Affirmation I spend time in nature. I have an intimate connection with Mother Earth and tools for natural healing. Essential oils and herbs bring balance to my life. I am aware of the sacred ground beneath my feet. The green energy of plants and trees restore my body, mind, and spirit.

Spiritual uses Green moss agate holds within it the spiritual wisdom of the keepers, or devic forces, of the plant kingdom. Working with this stone provides a portal through which you can access the world of fairies, gnomes, and elves. This stone helps inspire you when working with herbs and aromatherapy for body, mind, and spirit. Green moss agate is good for aligning your energy with Archangels Raphael and Thuriel.

Mental uses With its mosslike pattern, this stone helps you remember to ground yourself. Use green moss agate when you are experiencing mental fatigue. This stone helps you replenish your mental focus. When you aren't able to make it outdoors, gaze into the stone's inner structure and imagine that you've stepped into a forest or glen for a quick break. It's helpful for people who spend a good deal of time inside buildings with limited time in nature.

Emotional uses With its earthy appearance, green moss agate helps you to reclaim your balance through nature. Infuse this stone with an intention to take time to walk in the grass, visit the water's edge, or embrace a tree. Give your emotional challenges to the earth through the use of imagery. For example, imagine that a flow of emotional toxins is draining from the soles of your feet, and envision Mother Earth transforming the toxins into rich compost or fertilizer.

Physical uses Grounding and healing, green moss agate aids you in understanding aromatherapy and herbal essences. This stone aligns you with nature and gardening. Hold the stone to the light and look through it to see the mineral inclusions that resemble fern or moss inside the stone. This stone reminds you that you are a steward of the earth. Learn how to compost, recycle, and take the extra step to take care of the planet. This is a good stone for gardeners, aromatherapists, and herbalists.

Divine guidance When was the last time you gardened or just enjoyed the healing, nurturing power of nature? You may tend to love gardening, nature spirits, and working with the green vibration of Mother Earth. Mother Earth wants to spend more time with you, to feel your hands and feet upon her body, and to fill up your senses with her loving gifts. Investigate the use of nature's pharmacy, such as herbs and essential oils, for holistic health.

About the stone:
Green moss agate is silicon dioxide forming into microcrystalline quartz forming colorless to white gemstones with dendritic (branchlike) inclusions. Gemstones are transparent to translucent.

AGATE, MAGENTA-DYED
The Feminine Christ

Color(s)	hot pink or fuchsia
Chakra(s)	heart
Planet(s)	Venus
Number(s)	33
Element(s)	air
Mohs scale	6.5–7
Astro sign(s)	Aquarius, Pisces

Affirmation I am love. I align my consciousness with gentleness, compassion, and goodwill toward all. I am compassionate and kind. I am aligned with the healing powers of inner peace and kindness. I am able to help others by vibrating love through my presence, words, and actions.

Spiritual uses Magenta-dyed agate reminds you to be receptive to your intuition and accept the part of you that is able to hold a vision and imagine a better way of life for all beings. Archetypes for this energy are Mother Mary, Kuan Yin, Isis, and Mary Magdalene (the Feminine Christ). The associated archangels are Tzaphkiel and Uriel. Use this agate to awaken your awareness of your spiritual purpose. Visualize brilliant magenta at your higher heart chakra, between the heart center and the throat center. Use this stone to activate the zeal point at the notch at the base of your skull, the occiput. (The zeal point regulates multidimensional telepathic communication. Currently, this point is just in the beginning stages of awakening.)

Mental uses The thoughtforms, or mental energy, associated with magenta align the consciousness with the Feminine Christ. This archetypal energy embodies compassion, nurturing, and great wisdom. Through meditation on the thymus area (above the heart and below the throat), you can begin to grasp the difference between information, knowledge, and wisdom with magenta-dyed agate. Strive for wisdom, and the information and knowledge will always be available.

Emotional uses Magenta-dyed agate can help you to balance your emotions, thereby increasing your emotional maturity. The color magenta is a reminder of the Divine Mother within, who hears and knows truth and accepts you unconditionally. This stone amplifies retribution, both positive and negative. Make use of the energy to amplify your intention through your heart and thymus to project love into all your thoughts, goals, and actions.

Physical uses With its deep pink vibration, magenta-dyed agate activates the opening of your heart center to allow love to enter. There are many sensual feelings that naturally arise when the heart center opens. With this stone in hand, use the breath and discipline to harness the sensual energy for the higher good of all.

Divine guidance Are you seeking unconditional love? You have natural abilities to love and be loved. You really want others to demonstrate the love they have for you. You are well loved by many people. Allow love. Become a receptacle for all this is love.

About the stone:
Silicon dioxide formed into microcrystalline quartz with synthetic magenta or fuchsia color enhancement.

AGATE, PURPLE-DYED
Grounded Spirituality

Color(s)	purple
Chakra(s)	crown, solar plexus
Planet(s)	Jupiter
Number(s)	5, 9
Element(s)	fire
Mohs scale	6.5–7
Astro sign(s)	Sagittarius

Affirmation I adjust my attitude to create a happier life. I am discerning about the people I allow into my circle. I am mindful of being in peaceful places to support my loving vibration. I take good care of myself. I sleep well every night.

Spiritual uses Purple-dyed agate helps to keep you grounded during your spiritual quest while allowing your consciousness to open up to unlimited possibilities. This stone aids in opening channels in the crown chakra and the third eye to all wisdom, enabling information to flow through you with ease. It is protective and grounding, which is beneficial when opening the upper chakras.

Mental uses Purple-dyed agate helps you to transform negative thoughts or beliefs by awakening your awareness to the incessant chatter. This is a stone of unlimited possibilities. Use it to think outside the box and find different ways to approach a problem or any mind-bending challenge.

Emotional uses Purple-dyed agate carries the transformative power to remove people, places, or things from your life that upset you emotionally. With this stone, you can lovingly release people from your life who keep hurting your feelings. This agate is useful to let go of feelings of insecurity, depression, and lack of confidence.

Physical uses Purple-dyed agate can help you beneficially readjust how you take care of your physical body. Use the grounded vibration of its transformative energy to transmute aches, pains, weight issues, and a whole plethora of potential health challenges.

Divine guidance Are you ready to change your life? Do you need to shift whom you spend your time with? Make the necessary changes to adjust your life to be healthy, happy, and fully supported by loving family and friends.

> *About the stone:*
> Silicon dioxide formed into microcrystalline quartz with synthetic purple color enhancement.

AGATE, TREE
Standing Ones

COLOR(S)	translucent to white with green inclusions
CHAKRA(S)	crown, heart, root
PLANET(S)	Venus, Ceres
NUMBER(S)	2
ELEMENT(S)	earth
MOHS SCALE	6.5–7
ASTRO SIGN(S)	Taurus

Affirmation The earth is my mother. I am one with all that is. I am connected with the sacred energy of the trees, plants, shrubs, vines, and smaller vegetation. I embrace the sunshine as well as the rain. I am in balance with all life.

Spiritual uses Tree agate is useful for taking on the earthy characteristic of trees. With this stone, you can visualize that you have branches extending from your body, rising up to connect with the cosmic consciousness while firmly established in the present moment. Your feet connect you with Mother Earth through deeply embedded roots. Use this stone for earth-centered spiritual pursuit, earth-based rituals, and shamanic journeywork.

Mental uses Tree agate amplifies your ability to gather knowledge and wisdom from the universal consciousness. It also helps you to more readily access the vast information stored within your own mind. Imagine that the crown of your head is like branches of a tree reaching out for and absorbing information while you stay rooted in the earth. When your to-do list is lengthy, this stone will help you stay grounded and focused.

Emotional uses Tree agate reminds you to sway with the winds of change as they occur so that you can readily and easily adapt to new things and situations. This stone encourages you to take yourself into nature to rebalance raw emotions, feelings, and out-of-control responses. Use the negative ions of nature to reestablish your emotional balance.

Physical uses Tree agate is the perfect stone for arborists, gardeners, florists, farmers, aromatherapists, herbalists, and anyone aligned with plants and nature. It's beneficial for the feet, ankles, and legs as well as the mind and the brain. Use tree agate when you are detoxifying and cleansing your physical body, as it will lend support for your process.

Divine guidance Are you a self-proclaimed "tree hugger" or environmental rights activist? Take the time to sit beneath a tree and connect with the qualities of its firmly planted roots, its ability to flex and bend in a storm, and its amazing power of growth. Remember your roots, but always remember how much you can grow to reach great heights.

About the stone:
Tree agate is silicon dioxide forming into microcrystalline quartz forming white gemstones with dendritic (branchlike) inclusions. Gemstones are translucent to opaque.

AMAZONITE
The Truth, the Whole Truth, Nothing but the Truth

COLOR(S)	blue-green (aqua) with white flecks
CHAKRA(S)	throat, navel
PLANET(S)	Mercury
NUMBER(S)	3
ELEMENT(S)	air
MOHS SCALE	6–6.5
ASTRO SIGN(S)	Gemini, Virgo

Affirmation I live my truth. I easily and honestly communicate what is on my mind. I speak eloquently. I am heard. My courage helps me communicate with ease. I stand up for myself. I say what I need to say. I surround myself with people who easily speak their truth.

Spiritual uses Amazonite's energy offers a direct connection to the heavenly realm and makes you receptive to its assistance. Angels must be invited to help you, so ask your angels for help in any area of your life. Use amazonite to invite Archangel Haniel to assist you in connecting with your truth. Nothing is too insignificant or mundane. Spiritual help is always available. This stone also keeps you aware of divine timing and divine orchestration in your life. Wouldn't you like God and the angels to orchestrate your life with you? Decide what you want, make a plan, take action, and be mindful of the signs and symbols the angels have placed along your path.

Mental uses This aqua stone helps you focus on the truth. Use amazonite when you want to know the truth or when you need to speak the truth. Let it be your reminder to act with integrity or to attract people of integrity into your life. Hold the thought or intention of honesty while you work with this stone.

Emotional uses Amazonite helps you graciously speak up for yourself and reminds you to listen to what others have to say. This helps both parties avoid making inaccurate assumptions that might lead to hurt feelings. With this stone in hand, you are better able to discern the truth and set the boundaries with those around you who are not coming from a place of genuineness and integrity.

Physical uses If you have laryngitis, tonsillitis, a sore throat, or any physical challenges located in the neck or throat area, amazonite can speed your recovery. This stone also aids in clearing physical challenges of the ears and nose. It helps improve your ability to speak, sing, or make any type of vocalization in general. This is a good stone for judges, lawyers, mediators, public speakers, teachers, bankers, brokers, journalists, and writers.

Divine guidance Are you holding back something that needs to be said? Perhaps the truth about a certain matter needs to be spoken. Honesty is very important at this time, so have the courage to speak up with grace. When your words come from a loving and compassionate place, they have the power to heal or improve a situation.

About the stone:
Amazonite is a microclinic feldspar composed of potassium aluminum silicate. Forms in opaque, well-defined (sometimes quite large) triclinic crystals. It is often found in Colorado alongside smoky quartz crystals.

Amber
Boundaries

Color(s)	various shades of yellow, gold, brown, and sometimes green
Chakra(s)	solar plexus, navel
Planet(s)	Mercury, Jupiter, Sun
Number(s)	3, 5, 12
Element(s)	fire, water
Mohs scale	2–2.5
Astro sign(s)	Gemini, Leo, Aquarius

Affirmation I have the courage to set boundaries with love and grace. I am protected. Experiences from the past empower me. I am connected with powerful ancient wisdom. I know how to make positive changes. It is safe to be powerful in loving ways.

Spiritual uses Amber is a tool for recalling past lives with the intent to uncover how those memories can help you in your life now. All regression therapy, whether it is a regression in this life or a past life, should have the intention to assist you in understanding and breaking unwanted repetitive patterns. Amber can help focus your attention on that purpose. Use this resin to align with Archangels Jophiel and Seraphiel.

Mental uses Amber enhances your conscious understanding of the messages within past memories to favorably assist you in your decision-making processes. When you are more conscious of your innate strengths and weaknesses through your work with this ancient stone, you can create circumstances with more dedication and force.

Emotional uses With conscious intention, amber gives you the courage to establish healthy boundaries in your relationships in all areas of your life. This fossilized resin helps you to clear out the unwanted energies from energy-sucking acquaintances, friends, colleagues, and family members. Carry this stone or wear it in jewelry with the inward knowing that you are deflecting energy that doesn't belong to you. According to its connection to tears in Norse, Greek, and Lithuanian mythology, amber is a good stone to use during the grieving process.

Physical uses Amber is the sap, or blood, of the pine tree—the resin from within that has petrified. Use this stone to help remove toxic substances from your physical body when performing a cleanse, since it amplifies your intention to remove harmful matter from your body.

Divine guidance Are you allowing someone or something to drain your energy? Establish clear boundaries by surrounding yourself in a protective shield that will deflect any negative energy that comes your way. Ancient wisdom resides within you, and when you subconsciously tap into it, it has the ability to keep you protected and transform your life.

About the stone:
Amber is an organic tree resin which has hardened over a 30-million-year period. It is composed of several resins, succinic acid, and a volatile oil, as well as hydrogen sulphide.

AMETHYST
Transformation

COLOR(S)	purple
CHAKRA(S)	third eye, crown
PLANET(S)	Uranus
NUMBER(S)	11, 22, 33
ELEMENT(S)	air
MOHS SCALE	7
ASTRO SIGN(S)	Aquarius

Affirmation I create my reality. I can change my reality. It's easy for me to transform and transmute challenging situations. I use my intuition and follow my hunches. I am aligned with higher wisdom. I pay attention to my dreams and easily interpret them.

Spiritual uses Amethyst stimulates the third eye and all six "clairs" (or sensory gifts): clairvoyance, clairaudience, claircognizance, clairsentience, clairolfaction, and clairgustation. These are terms for the ability to spiritually see, hear, know, sense, smell, and taste the truth. Use this purple-toned quartz to ward off nightmares and encourage sweet dreams and restful sleep. It is also good to help you remember your dreams. Amethyst helps protect you from psychic attacks and clear out the negative thoughts of the day. This stone is perfect to invite the angelic vibes of Archangels Gabriel, Metatron, Raziel, Tzaphkiel, and Zadkiel.

Mental uses The purple vibration in amethyst has powerful transformative qualities. To use this vibration in changing unwanted situations, imagine yourself surrounded by a vibrating, glowing bubble of violet light emanating from the stone. As you imagine this, know that all that you are upset about or challenged by is currently being transformed and transmuted into something powerful. Imagine the situation changing to what you *do* want versus how it currently is. The vibration of your imagination of how you want your life to be combined with the violet light will effectuate change.

Emotional uses When you realize your emotions need to be transformed or significantly shifted, amethyst's purple energy gives you the strength and wherewithal to make the change. Imagine yourself surrounded by the purple energy of this gemstone as you focus on how you would like to feel.

Physical uses Since amethyst derives its name from the Greek word *amethystos* meaning "not drunk" or "not intoxicated," carry or wear this stone to remind you to avoid harmful distractions and to change old habits through conscious intent. The association to drinking stems from a Roman myth involving Bacchus, the Roman god of wine and intoxication. Every time you touch the stone or see it, imagine your new reality as if that old habit is a distant memory. What would your life be like without that habit? Take the time to imagine it and daydream your new reality into being.

Divine guidance Are you in touch with your spiritual side? Have you been having prophetic dreams? Are you ready to transform your life? Through your spiritual connection with the Divine, you can receive intuitive insights to help you in your daily life. Dreams bring realizations through symbols and metaphors. You have the ability to transform your reality using the spiritual guidance you receive.

About the stone:
Amethyst is the variety of quartz (crystalline silicon dioxide) with a natural violet color due to the presence of iron, other trace elements, and irradiation. Amethyst crystallizes in the trigonal system and is found in open cavities.

AMETHYST, CHEVRON
Personal Excellence

Color(s)	purple and white
Chakra(s)	crown, third eye
Planet(s)	Uranus, Neptune, Mercury
Number(s)	3, 11
Element(s)	air
Mohs scale	7
Astro sign(s)	Aquarius, Pisces, Gemini

Affirmation I use the experiences from the lessons I have learned to improve myself. I've earned my stripes. I strive to earn more badges of honor and knowledge as I continue this journey. I see with higher perspective because of the benefits of hindsight.

Spiritual uses A stone of integrity and honor, chevron amethyst reminds you to commit to excel on all levels. With its ability to help develop intuition and prophetic dreaming, this stone can guide you through the dream world, enabling you to use your dreams to help you on your spiritual path. Encourage thoughts of Ascended Masters and spiritual teachers to help you in the dream state and remember your dreams so you can apply their messages in your daily life.

Mental uses The pointed bands of chevron amethyst direct your energy toward whatever you need to focus on. Use this stone when you feel mentally challenged. With this stone in hand, allow your mind to open to new pathways and think unconventionally.

Emotional uses With its bands and swirls, chevron amethyst can help you unravel the source of unresolved feelings and emotions. Gaze into the white bands, follow the lines of energy, and allow them to guide you toward remembering why certain emotional patterns and blocks keep recurring in your life. Once you can see the pattern, uncover the source, and embrace it, then you can heal it.

Physical uses Like its sister stone ametrine, chevron amethyst alleviates headaches and digestive challenges. Use this banded variety of amethyst with the intention to put an end to unhealthy patterns and habits such as smoking, excessive drinking and eating, and drug usage.

Divine guidance Are you being the best you can be? Have you been living your life with integrity? Are you honest with yourself and in your interactions with others? Strive for personal excellence. Be the best you can be, and be impeccable with your word.

About the stone:
Chevron amethyst is banded amethyst with purple and white lines forming angular patterns of approximately 60 degrees.

Amethyst Druzy
All That Is

Color(s)	purple
Chakra(s)	crown, third eye
Planet(s)	Earth
Number(s)	7
Element(s)	air
Mohs scale	7
Astro sign(s):	Aquarius, Gemini

Affirmation I am one with all that is. I am tuned into the forces of the universe. I easily access wisdom and knowledge. I have excellent concentration skills. I am aware of the results of my actions. I am mindful of my feelings and others'.

Spiritual uses Amethyst druzy is ideal for activating the energy field that connects you to the spirit realm. The points reaching upward are like antennae tuning into the cosmic forces of the universe, providing you with a direct link to wisdom and knowledge. Draw on the energy of spirit quartz in meditation practice as well as to align yourself with the Ascended Masters and other teachers of the higher realm.

Mental uses Amethyst druzy awakens awareness, providing you with more focus and concentration. This stone expands thinking from ego-centered thinking to "we-centered" thinking. It is the stone for humanity coming together in global consciousness.

Emotional uses Amethyst druzy helps you get in touch with your feelings and to become more sensitive to the feelings of others. This stone is a reminder that everything is interconnected, including our feelings.

Physical uses Shaped by the formation of a second generation of smaller points sometimes known as druzy quartz, amethyst druzy is beneficial for those who are becoming ecologically aware of how each action we take affects the next seven generations. This stone helps raise the consciousness of the collective toward green thinking and living. This is a good stone for environmentalists, waste management specialists, green celebrities, and conservationists.

Divine guidance Are you reaching out in prayer asking for help? Are you in touch with your connection with all life—the seen and unseen? Tap into your innate ability to intuit whatever you need whenever you need it. Acknowledge your intuition, and trust your awareness of your own feelings as well as the feelings of others.

About the stone:
Druzy (or drusy) amethyst, also known as spirit quartz or cactus quartz, is the term for amethyst occurring in formations of very small crystals. The crystals form a lining on the surrounding rock mass by the deposit of mineral-rich waters in druzy cavities.

AMETRINE
Empowered Transmutation

Color(s)	purple and yellow
Chakra(s)	crown, third eye, solar plexus
Planet(s)	Uranus, Mercury
Number(s)	3, 11
Element(s)	air
Mohs scale	7
Astro sign(s)	Aquarius, Gemini

Affirmation Power and strength are mine. It is safe for me to be powerful in loving ways. The transformation of challenges, negative patterns, and unhealthy habits occurs daily in my life. I release what is no longer for my highest good. I am confident.

Spiritual uses Ametrine is a powerful spiritual tool; it has the power of amethyst to transform and transmute negativity and the power of the citrine to boost self-confidence to achieve your heart's desires. This stone contains complementary colors—purple and yellow—which promote balance by connecting the crown chakra and the solar plexus. Focus on the Divine will, not the small lower ego for things to manifest in your life. The amethyst and citrine facilitate high connections with Ascended Masters and spiritual teachers.

Mental uses Ametrine helps clear your mind, allowing you to realize the power of your intention and your thoughts. You can do anything, but first, you have to have the mindset to believe it. This stone helps retrain your brain, mind, thoughts, and consciousness to stay on course with your decisions. Whether your decision is to become a nonsmoker or start a new business, this stone helps to clear the cobwebs and obstacles in your mind to achieve great heights.

Emotional uses The complementary colors of purple and yellow magnify ametrine's benefits. The vibration of the purple helps to transform and transmute negative emotions and releases the hooks that others have in your emotional body. The yellow encourages the ability to discern the right people, places, and situations you allow into your life. It helps you during times when you need to have the courage to set boundaries with others.

Physical uses Use this combination stone for headaches and digestive challenges. Ametrine is also beneficial for the kidneys, liver, spleen, pancreas, and gall bladder. Use it as an aid for uncovering the root cause of any imbalance or disease. Form the intention to have the source of your ailments revealed to you either through proper medical diagnosis or through more extraordinary means such as through medical intuitive readings and your own inner guidance. Use this stone to release unhealthy habits and patterns such as smoking, drinking, drugs, and overeating.

Divine guidance Are you trying to release a bad habit, addiction, or a relationship that is no longer for your highest good? Do you want to make changes in your life but your inner critic is telling you that you can't do it? It's time to take action and be determined and confident enough to make the necessary changes to transform your life!

> **About the stone:**
> Bi-color quartz (silicon dioxide) made up of amethyst and citrine. The Anahi Mine in Bolivia produces natural ametrine; much of the ametrine on the market before 1989 was heat-treated.

ANDALUSITE
All Four Directions

COLOR(S)	brown with a cross or X running through it
CHAKRA(S)	root, navel
PLANET(S)	Earth, Saturn
NUMBER(S)	4
ELEMENT(S)	earth
MOHS SCALE	7.5
ASTRO SIGN(S)	Capricorn

Affirmation I am aligned with the four elements and the four directions. I am grounded. Protective energies keep me safe always. I receive spiritual insight to easily resolve problems. I know I am never truly alone.

Spiritual uses With the cross or X in its center, andalusite helps you align with earth-centered spirituality, including the beliefs and practices of the indigenous people around the world as well as Paganism. This stone is ideal for aligning yourself with fairies, elves, gnomes, and the invisible realm of the earth plane.

Mental uses The grounding elements of andalusite aid in maintaining focus. It is especially useful if staying targeted on the task at hand is very challenging. It is a stone for those who jump from one great idea to another yet are seemingly unable to complete anything. Gaze at the cross running through the stone to find focus.

Emotional uses Andalusite enhances the healing power of the negative ions of the great outdoors to balance your emotions. If you are feeling out of sorts in your emotions, this stone helps motivate you to take the time to be in your garden. Its energy encourages you to go to the park, beach, lake, or somewhere where you can be renewed in nature. Take the journey to the center of yourself and find balance from the time outdoors.

Physical uses Andalusite is beneficial for the bones, spinal column, teeth, hair, and nails. Use it when you might have a tendency to stumble, trip, or fall, or when you are generally feeling clumsy. This stone is related to helping you keep your balance and equilibrium—to keep stable footing. On a worldly or root chakra level, you can use this stone to keep you on track. Financial security takes diligence, focus, and repetitive practice in your craft. Use this stone to remind yourself that X marks the spot and stay focused on your goal.

Divine guidance Are you in search of a deeper spiritual connection? It is time to find that connection in nature. Go outdoors and commune with the birds and the bees. Listen to the fairies and the messages being communicated to you by the trees, plants, and animals. You may need some time in a garden or the woods. Put your attention on your alignment with Mother Earth.

About the stone:
Andulasite is aluminum silicate with strong pleocroism of yellow, green, and red. It crystallizes in the orthorhombic system with squarish crystals, but well-formed crystals are rare. An opaque variety of andalusite with carbonaceous inclusions that form a black cross is known as chiastolite.

ANGELITE
Messages from the Angels

COLOR(S)	pastel blue
CHAKRA(S)	throat
PLANET(S)	Uranus, Neptune, Jupiter
NUMBER(S)	11, 12
ELEMENT(S)	air, water
MOHS SCALE	3.5
ASTRO SIGN(S)	Aquarius, Pisces

Affirmation I communicate with ease and grace. Guidance and inspiration from my angels and spirit guides come to me constantly. I easily interpret and use signs and messages from angels. I feel the entourage of angels orchestrating cosmic coincidence in my life. I feel calm and at peace.

Spiritual uses Heavenly blue angelite is a good stone for attracting divine intervention through communication with the angels. You have the ability to talk with and listen to angels—so much so that it is as real as being able to chat with your friends. Use this stone to open yourself up to communication with the angelic realm and the realm of invisible helpers. Messages from the other realms come in a variety of ways—for example, as signs in nature, on billboards, or through intuition. Pay attention. Archangels Haniel and Seraphiel are associated with this stone, and will assist with divine communication and the exploration of your angelic self.

Mental uses Angelite is a stone of communication, a two-way process of sending and receiving. Employ this stone when you need to be a better listener. Use it to sort out your thoughts and organize all aspects of your life. This is a good stone for writers, musicians, and artists, as it has a strong connection to the Muses of Greek mythology.

Emotional uses With angelite on hand, call on the angels to help with your emotional upsets. If you feel the need to cry or if you are experiencing internal emotional angst, touch this stone and gaze at the calming blue color while you form the thought or prayers asking your angels to help you. Ask for understanding and to be consciously aware when the messages are provided. Ask the angels to help you interpret the messages so you can apply them to your daily life.

Physical uses Angelite is a good stone for your throat and neck area, and for any ailments associated with it, such as tonsillitis, a sore throat, laryngitis, or muscular strain in that area. You can use this stone—the stone of divine timing—to manifest divine timing in your life. Just imagine that you are always in the right place, at the right time, with the right people, and it will be so! This is the perfect stone for spiritual counselors, intuitive readers, motivational speakers, and meditation facilitators.

Divine guidance Are you receiving intuitive messages? Do you wish to be more open to them? Quiet your mind and give yourself permission to communicate with angels and other spirit guides. Remember, true communication includes listening as well as speaking. Pay attention to the messages from nature and your other surroundings, and heed them.

About the stone:
Angelite is a blue variety of anhydrous calcium sulfate crystallizing in the orthorhombic system. It is usually found in nodules or masses.

APATITE
Taking It All In!

COLOR(S)	deep teal, blue, green, or yellow
CHAKRA(S)	throat, solar plexus
PLANET(S)	Mercury
NUMBER(S)	31/4
ELEMENT(S)	earth
MOHS SCALE	5
ASTRO SIGN(S)	Virgo

Affirmation I am healthy, whole, and complete. My body is perfect. I am the perfect weight for my height, build, and genetic background. I exercise regularly, drink plenty of water, sleep well, and eat nutritious foods. My digestive processes are healthy. I easily absorb and process all that goes on around me.

Spiritual uses Neon-blue apatite is a portal through which you can communicate with spirit guides. Communication with Ascended Masters and other inter- and intradimensional beings requires a good connection both above and below. This stone aids the information's assimilation process in a grounded way so it can be used and integrated into daily life.

Mental uses With its qualities of assimilation and absorption, apatite is a perfect stone to help clear your thoughts by sorting out which are valid and which only add confusion to your life. Use this stone to integrate your life with the events happening in your environment. With its ability to eliminate confusion, this stone is useful in helping you understand thoughts and concepts, especially when you are feeling overwhelmed.

Emotional uses Apatite is a good tool for becoming conscious of emotional eating. As you pinpoint the emotions that trigger the eating, you have a better chance of dealing with those emotions so you can break the cycle.

Physical uses Apatite supports the balance of electrolytes in the body. This electric-blue stone also helps to balance the absorption of food throughout the digestive process. Use this stone to help you focus on a healthy digestive system. This stone is also useful for improving the strength of tooth enamel and bone minerals. Additionally, it is an ally to gardeners, especially when fertilizing your garden, as it helps you tune into the environment to determine the nutrients required for healthy plants. This is a good stone for dieticians, nutritionists, gastroenterologists, and any type of weight management counselor.

Divine guidance Are you feeling agitated? Is there something you find hard to swallow? Perhaps you are having digestive difficulties. Pay attention to the food going into your body as well as what you are thinking or talking about while you eat. Wholesome food, thoughts, and conversation can make things easier to process and accept.

> **About the stone:**
> Apatite is a calcium phosphate that crystallizes in the hexagonal system with stocky prismatic to tabular crystals. The mineral can be transparent to opaque.

APOPHYLLITE
Universal Wisdom

COLOR(S)	white or mint green
CHAKRA(S)	third eye, crown
PLANET(S)	Venus, the Moon
NUMBER(S)	7
ELEMENT(S)	air
MOHS SCALE	4.5–5
ASTRO SIGN(S)	Libra

Affirmation I have a focused mind. I have mental clarity. I know and trust my inner truth. I accept myself without judgment. I meditate regularly. I am insightful. My connection with universal wisdom guides me daily. It's easy for me to quiet my mind and emotions. I am a miracle worker.

Spiritual uses Apophyllite helps you access the Akashic Records (the history of the cosmos) and assists in past-life recall, the ability to see and read the aura, and spiritual healings. It is a stone to use to connect with Archangels Metatron, Sandalphon, and Seraphiel. Use it during Reiki sessions to help you stay focus on allowing the universal life force to flow through you. This stone tunes you in so that you are a good channel who is aligned with the higher will rather than the egoic self. This sparkling gem brings higher levels of clarity to meditation experiences.

Mental uses With its natural pyramidal structure and excellent ability to refract light and sparkle so intensely, apophyllite is the perfect stone to clear your mind of incessant chatter. The result is clarity of consciousness. Use a clear apophyllite point on your third eye center to improve your meditation practice. This stone can help you quickly center yourself and quiet your thoughts.

Emotional uses With its profound ability to bring about mental clarity, using apophyllite automatically bestows a deeper understanding of yourself. This enables you to shift into accepting your feelings and relax. Once this is achieved, you can more easily let go of the cord that keeps you connected to the original source of emotional imbalance.

Physical uses Apophyllite is useful as a guide when choosing doctors, health practitioners, nutritional plans, or other means for healing any physical, mental, spiritual, and emotional challenges. This stone helps you be open to holistic methods of healing such as Reiki, CranioSacral Therapy, Emotional Freedom Technique (EFT), Integrated Energy Therapy (IET), and other whole-body healing therapies.

Divine guidance Do you wish to gain clearer insight or a better understanding of a situation? Make an appointment with yourself to meditate or sit in silence. Do this often. Open your consciousness and listen for your soul's truth, and embrace it without judgment. Mental clarity and self-acceptance are the gifts of a regular meditation practice.

About the stone:
Apopyllite is hydrated potassium calcium silicate which crystallizes in the tetragonal system. Generally colorless, it can also occur in pink, green, or yellow. It is commonly found in India.

AQUAMARINE
Call of the Mermaids

Color(s)	bluish-green
Chakra(s)	throat
Planet(s)	Uranus, Neptune
Number(s)	5, 11
Element(s):	air, water
Mohs scale:	7.5–8
Astro sign(s):	Aquarius, Pisces

Affirmation I am able to identify my feelings and resolve unsettling emotions. Negativity flows away effortlessly and lovingly. My emotional body is awash with positive, cleansing energy. I enjoy a wonderful sense of emotional balance. Inspiration flows effortlessly. I travel safely by land or sea.

Spiritual uses Aquamarine is a perfect stone for a lover of sea creatures, including dolphins and whales, as well as mermaids and undines (water nymphs). From the Latin *aqua marina,* this stone's name means "seawater," and is associated with Poseidon and Neptune. Connecting with sea creatures through this stone is a joyful way to awaken spiritually and an excellent tool for self-development. The practice of opening communication with fish and mammals of the sea helps the development of telepathic skills and the understanding of other types of spiritual communication, including channeling and mediumship. Aquamarine is the stone of Archangel Muriel.

Mental uses When your mind has hit a brick wall or has become stuck in some way, turn to aquamarine. Place it in your bathtub or hold it while you swim for best results. This gemstone helps with receiving inspiration in all areas of life. If you have a problem, hold aquamarine with the intention that the resolution will be communicated to you. Writer's block? Gaze at the stone and visualize yourself writing for inspiration.

Emotional uses Water, as represented by this stone, assists in regaining emotional balance. This seafoam-colored gem clears the consciousness, releasing emotionally charged thoughts. It also helps relieve negative energy from conversations and your own internal dialogue. With aquamarine in hand, learn how to allow tears to flow to wash away sadness and other emotional hurts. Tears are beneficial for cleansing your emotional, physical, and mental bodies. This is a stone of truth. Make it your intention to have the truth revealed and the compassion and tolerance to accept the truth with ease and grace.

Physical uses Aquamarine soothes the tonsils, larynx, throat, vocal cords, and neck. It is helpful for swimmers, hydrotherapists, water-birth coaches, pool-service personnel, scuba divers, high board divers, boaters, fishermen, and anyone who works or plays on, in, or near bodies of water. This stone is also good for people who have careers in writing, speaking, teaching, and other professions and hobbies that require good communication skills.

Divine guidance Are your emotions in turmoil? Are you feeling uneasy? When was the last time you went to the seaside or to another large body of water? Spend time at the water's edge to regain emotional balance. This will help clear away any negative energy you may have accumulated from unsettling conversations or negative internal dialogue.

> **About the stone:**
> Aquamarine is the blue variety of the mineral beryl. Beryl is a silicate mineral containing aluminum and beryllium, and it often occurs in a bluish-green color. Crystallizing in the hexagonal system, crystals are often light in color. Other beryls are distinguished by color, including emerald (green), morganite (pink), and heliodor (yellow).

ARAGONITE

Creative Chaos

Color(s)	brown
Chakra(s)	navel
Planet(s)	Neptune
Number(s)	2
Element(s)	water
Mohs scale	3.5–4
Astro sign(s)	Pisces

Affirmation I have a gift for creativity. I can see things others seem to miss. I stay focused on the task at hand, even when confusion is around me. I solve problems with ease. It is easy for me to stay calm, even when I have many responsibilities.

Spiritual uses Crystalline aragonite carries within it the vibrations of caves and the oceans. It is a storehouse of ancient knowledge. With this stone in hand you can channel spiritual wisdom, and allow yourself to follow the guidance of the still, small voice from deep within. Listen with spiritual ears, employing your innate sense of clairaudience.

Mental uses This gemstone gently guides you to go quietly within yourself to locate your center. In this way, aragonite directs you toward clarity, organization, and creative solutions. Use this stone with the intention to find answers within your own mind.

Emotional uses Aragonite shows you the way into your center; it helps you feel and know the depth of your emotions. This stone is a reminder that it is important to recognize and become aware of your emotions and define them, but it is also equally important to learn to detach from your feelings to become an objective observer, just as an artist observes art in nature.

Physical uses With its significant calcium content, aragonite lends itself to assist with disease or health challenges related to a calcium deficiency. Form the intention that aragonite's vibration will help you use nutrition and exercise to improve the health of your bones, muscles, and teeth. This stone is helpful for those with careers as a chiropractor, orthopedic doctor or surgeon, dentist, podiatrist, athlete, gymnast, and manicurist.

Divine guidance Are you an artist or someone who is in need of creative inspiration? Do you want to think unconventionally and find original ideas? Are you comfortable with organized chaos? Be willing to channel divine inspiration, and organize your thoughts and intuitive flashes into attainable reality.

About the stone:
Aragonite is a mineral composed of calcium carbonate that crystallizes in the orthorhombic system. Often twinned, the crystals are found in white, yellow, green, brown, and blue.

Aventurine, Green
As Luck Would Have It...

Color(s)	green
Chakra(s)	heart
Planet(s)	Earth, Neptune
Number(s)	10, 12
Element(s)	earth, water
Mohs scale	6.5–7
Astro sign(s)	Capricorn, Pisces

Affirmation I am so incredibly lucky! I have many blessings. Abundance and prosperity are constantly flowing in my life. I am grateful. I am safe. I am blessed with easy travel experiences. I am adventurous. My heart is open to love.

Spiritual uses Green aventurine opens the heart to divine love, good connections with all life, and a balanced and healthy view of the world. This green stone helps you make the connection between the earth and your heart, allowing your awareness of the elemental world to assist you in your daily life.

Mental uses With green aventurine in hand, focus on and believe in good fortune and well-being to create a more positive and stable reality for yourself. This stone of good fortune can amplify your intentions to create more abundance in your life.

Emotional uses Green aventurine grounds your emotional body and rebalances your heart's desires. The love you experience in romance, friendships, and other relationships can affect your emotional well-being, so be sure to keep a green aventurine near your heart while you sleep to "recalibrate" your emotions each night.

Physical uses Green aventurine helps you stay focused on eating healthy and exercising regularly to maintain a healthy heart. On another level, this is a prosperity stone. Keep one in your wallet, pocket, or cash drawer to continue to attract the physical rewards that comes with financial success. This is a good stone for bankers, realtors, professional poker players, brokers, hedge-fund managers, cardiologists, nutritionists, and farmers.

Divine guidance Do you wish for more luck? Be assured that you have all the luck you need at your disposal. It's almost as if you have a four-leaf clover in your pocket! Simply recognize your good fortune. Focus on the vast abundance in your life, and you will attract more. Believe that all your travels flow with ease.

About the stone:
Green aventurine is a form of metamorphic quartzite containing green fuchsite mica. The quartz crystals comprising aventurine are highly disorganized and may contain chromium and other impurities. The shiny mica within makes this stone easily identifiable.

AXINITE
Order Out of Chaos

Color(s)	reddish-brown, clove brown, brownish-black
Chakra(s)	root
Planet(s)	Uranus, Pluto
Number(s)	4
Element(s)	earth
Mohs scale	6–7.5
Astro sign(s)	Aquarius, Pisces

Affirmation I am grateful for all of my life's experiences. I have plenty of energy and stamina to get things done in a timely manner. I have a strong and healthy body supported by strong and sturdy bones. My mind is clear, and I stay focused on my priorities.

Spiritual uses Axinite helps you remember the teachings of your core spiritual essence. While you may not subscribe to the religious affiliation under which you were raised, you can use this stone to help you examine your core spiritual foundations from this lifetime (and perhaps other lifetimes, if you have that recall) to enable you to renew your faith or add to your eclectic spiritual "basket."

Mental uses Axinite grounds you and provides focus, helping you relax into the work or task at hand so you can accomplish what needs doing with self-assuredness. Use this earth-colored stone when you feel challenged by scattered forces, both from within and outside yourself. Let order ensue by allowing this stone to help you deflect what might appear to be chaos.

Emotional uses Axinite helps you strengthen your connection with the core of your being and assists you in embracing any issues you may find there. This stone helps you recognize that less-than-positive life experiences often provide you with the emotionally mature backbone required for dealing with other situations. It helps you to learn from those experiences and put the teachings into your emotional toolbox, providing you wisdom for another day.

Physical uses Axinite promotes strong bones, an aligned spinal column, and healthy teeth, hair, and nails. This stone helps you visualize iron-rich blood circulating throughout your body, providing you with the core strength and endurance you need for a healthy and prosperous life. This stone is also good for those who wish to have more energy in general.

Divine guidance Has chaos or confusion taken over your life? Are you going in too many directions at once and feeling energetically depleted? It's time to rest, regroup, and rejuvenate. Be sure to feed your body dark-green leafy vegetables or other iron-rich foods. Create a to-do list to get focused on what you need to accomplish. As you bring order to chaos, embrace the changes that come.

About the stone:
Axinite's chemical composition as a calcium aluminum borosilicate varies due to the replacement of calcium with iron, magnesium, and manganese. Crystallizing in the triclinic system, its name is derived from its crystals, shaped like ax heads or wedges.

AZURITE
Moving with Mindfulness

Color(s)	dark blue to navy blue
Chakra(s)	third eye, crown
Planet(s)	Jupiter, Mercury
Number(s)	6
Element(s)	air, fire
Mohs scale	3.5–4
Astro sign(s)	Sagittarius

Affirmation I am calm. I am at peace. My physical and energetic body flow with the currents and the rhythms of nature. I am extremely intuitive. My spirit guides and angels send me messages all the time. I am grateful for divine guidance.

Spiritual uses Azurite energy serves as a conduit for receiving information from spirit guides, angels, and your higher self—the part of you that is connected to the all knowing and all seeing. This stone is the color of the third eye chakra and can be used to exercise the six "clairs" (or sensory gifts)—clairvoyance, clairaudience, clairsentience, claircognizance, clairolfaction, and clairgustation.

Mental uses The vibration of azurite promotes mental clarity and the proper flow of the knowledge that is available in your consciousness. It helps you retrieve information as if you were pulling it out of a filing cabinet. This stone also calms the incessant chatter of your mind so you can sort out details and make sense of things.

Emotional uses The cobalt-blue vibration of azurite calms you and brings peace and harmony to otherwise discordant emotions. Use it specifically to ameliorate anger, hysteria, frustration, and overreaction to life circumstances. This gemstone is a perfect antidote for agitation and aggravation.

Physical uses Azurite supports the proper flow of blood through your circulatory system. This is a good stone for acupuncturists, reflexologists, or any healthcare practitioner who manipulates the energy of the body along its meridians. A good tool for dowsers, this stone is also helpful when you are dowsing to locate the energy meridians (ley lines) of the earth.

Divine guidance Do you crave peaceful environments? Are you attracted to moving meditation? Join a tai chi class or take a peaceful stroll to gently circulate the energy throughout your body, all the while moving with mindfulness.

About the stone:

Azurite is a copper carbonate with strong azure-blue color. It is opaque, found with botryoidal growth or as a mass in veins, and often occurs with malachite.

AZURITE-MALACHITE
Heavenly Connections

COLOR(S)	navy blue and dark green
CHAKRA(S)	third eye, throat, heart, navel
PLANET(S)	Jupiter, Mercury
NUMBER(S)	44
ELEMENT(S)	fire
MOHS SCALE	3.5–4
ASTRO SIGN(S)	Sagittarius

Affirmation I embrace the peace within. My innate healing powers are used to help others and myself. I am intuitive. Guidance from my higher self lights my path. I trust my intuition and my internal guidance system. I release ego, arrogance, and vanity. I am calm and flexible.

Spiritual uses Azurite-malachite represents the physical blending of two copper-carbonate minerals, which is symbolic of the symbiotic relationship between earthly existence and the entire cosmos. Use this stone as a conduit to channel the higher wisdom and knowledge of the universe while maintaining a grounded connection with the physical world.

Mental uses The azurite-malachite combination links the love of the heart chakra with the thought process of the third eye and crown chakras to achieve great mental clarity with divine wisdom.

Emotional uses Azurite-malachite helps you recognize heartfelt love, and furthermore, it helps you integrate the understanding of love into your consciousness so you can better heal emotional challenges. The gentle blending of the healing green energy of malachite combined with the cooling energy of azurite calms reactions brought on by hormonal imbalance. Azurite-malachite helps you connect with Archangel Camael to release anger, aggression, or out-of-balance emotions.

Physical uses Azurite-malachite is a combination stone that helps all your body's systems to work together. This stone also helps you to be aware of the words you speak and how these words affect your health. This combination is also good for supporting healing in cases of problems with the teeth, gums, jaws, throat, and neck. With its anti-inflammatory vibrations, this stone is useful for PMS, menopause, sprains, burns, arthritis, cellulitis, varicose veins, and phlebitis. This is a perfect stone for gynecologists, doulas, obstetricians, and vascular professionals.

Divine guidance Are you trying to comprehend all that is going on around you? Are you in the process of recovering from a time of upset or emotional challenge? Seek out calming experiences such as meditation. Take notice of the signs and symbols around you and contemplate their meaning.

About the stone:
Azurite-malachite is formed when both azurite and malachite occur together. They are both copper carbonates and are found in banded veins.

BISMUTH
Organized Creativity

COLOR(S)	yellow to blue metallic with iridescent tarnish
CHAKRA(S)	crown, third eye, throat
PLANET(S)	Venus, Mercury, Saturn
NUMBER(S)	44
ELEMENT(S)	earth
MOHS SCALE	2–2.5
ASTRO SIGN(S)	Taurus

Affirmation I realize my fullest potential—spiritually, mentally, emotionally, and physically. I think outside the norm and find creative ways to approach life. The rainbow of light and positive energy expands my consciousness.

Spiritual uses Bismuth helps you gain access to the part of your consciousness that connects with the Akashic Records (the history of the cosmos). Using this stone, tap into higher awareness and access the information and knowledge provided by angels, departed loved ones on the Other Side, and other spirit guides.

Mental uses The vibrations associated with bismuth's geometrical patterns help create pathways for the development of creative ideas in the mental body. With this stone in hand, think of untraditional approaches to any problem that needs a solution. When looking at things with a new perspective, other possibilities or ways of approaching life are revealed.

Emotional uses Bismuth is useful during meditation or open-eyed contemplation for sorting out emotional challenges. Gazing at its metallic structure helps to reorganize your thoughts and feelings.

Physical uses Bismuth is a good stone for businesspeople who work hard and must maintain focus and determined effort to succeed. This stone is also good for programmers, information-technology teams, and anyone who is learning how to use a computer or is learning a new computer program.

Divine guidance Are you interested in computers? Do you work in a very detailed job? Are you feeling challenged by the tasks ahead of you? Take one step at a time and know that the answers you need will be revealed as you work through things in a systematic, methodical manner.

About the stone:
Bismuth is an element that crystallizes in spectacular stairstep formations when grown in a laboratory. It is a metal with a naturally iridescent oxide tarnish.

BLOODSTONE
Birthing into Reality

Color(s)	dark green with red flecks
Chakra(s)	navel, root
Planet(s)	Moon, Ceres
Number(s)	2
Element(s)	water
Mohs scale	6.5–7
Astro sign(s)	Cancer

Affirmation My energy flows perfectly. My blood is full of life-giving oxygen, and it circulates through my system just as it should for good health. My life runs smoothly. My relationships with friends and colleagues and other areas of my life are aligned and in balance. Prosperity and blessings surround me.

Spiritual uses Associated with birth and the birthing process, blood-stone helps align you with the birth of your consciousness. Use this stone to bring forth your true spiritual nature. Allow it to help you bring your spirituality into everyday life in a grounded and real way.

Mental uses Bloodstone provides a mental boost when motivation is lacking. A stone of birthing, it is useful when you are developing an idea, such as an invention, a writing project, or any other creative endeavor that you have only just thought about previously. With this stone in hand, you are motivated to take action on your dreams and goals, cultivating it from the idea stage to actualization.

Emotional uses Bloodstone helps you truly recognize that your feelings and emotions are the juice behind what you manifest in your life, that your heartfelt emotions create your reality. Use this stone to clear your emotional birth canal so you have a clear channel for the emotions that help determine your life's purpose.

Physical uses Bloodstone is a good stone for women to keep on hand during their childbearing years. This stone helps ease the birthing process and lends supporting vibrations so the baby easily travels through the birth canal. This stone is also useful for hormonal balance, PMS, menopause, and any physical issue involving hormone imbalance or blood disorders. It is also good for the liver, heart, lungs, and spleen.

Divine guidance Are you a creative person? Do you have aspirations to give birth to something? A child? A book? A piece of art? Give it a go! You won't know until you try, so put your hand and your head to work and creatively play toward your true passion. Let creativity be born from you as easily as blood flows through your veins.

> **About the stone:**
> Bloodstone is a variety of chalcedony (microcrystalline quartz) displaying a dark green color with red spots of jasper.

BRUCITE
Flowing with Peace

Color(s)	white, light green, gray, or blue
Chakra(s)	third eye, navel
Planet(s)	Neptune
Number(s)	8
Element(s)	water
Mohs scale	2.5–3
Astro sign(s)	Pisces

Affirmation I receive new ideas all the time. Peacefulness, calmness, and serenity are mine, now and always. I am content. I go with the ever-changing flow of life, willingly and joyfully. I breathe deeply and oxygen replenishes my body. I feel protected.

Spiritual uses Brucite (especially the pastel blue variety) is extraordinarily helpful for communicating with the devic forces of oceans, lakes, and rivers. Communing with nature enables you to realize the oneness of all life, thereby expanding your spiritual awareness. When held, the energetic cleansing effect of this stone clears your auric field.

Mental uses Brucite expands your mental pathways so you can more easily generate new ideas. It helps you venture outside the norm of your regular way of thinking, allowing you to use your mind in different ways to achieve new results in your life.

Emotional uses Brucite assists in bringing forth tears that have been held back or the acknowledgement of upset feelings in a peaceful manner. If you are trying to achieve peace amid a tumultuous array of feelings, this stone can help the energy flow with ease while gaining a better perspective on the issues at hand. Use it for inner child work to heal the past.

Physical uses Brucite is a good tool when it is especially necessary to remain hydrated, as it is a good reminder to drink plenty of water. Use brucite to improve the integration of oxygen in your body. This stone also eases elimination and therefore assists in healing intestinal challenges.

Divine guidance Do you need to gain perspective on your feelings? Are you allowing the tears to flow when the emotion arises? It is always good to look at things from different perspectives. Go with the flow and find a unique way to perceive your reality. It's a good idea to increase your intake of water or take a walk by a lake, ocean, or river. Connect with nature and flow with the current.

About the stone:
Brucite is magnesium hydroxide. It crystallizes in the hexagonal system producing mostly flat tabular crystals that are not well defined. The material is mostly found in veins or in massive form.

CALCITE
Oh, Now I See!

COLOR(S)	translucent, yellow or pink
CHAKRA(S)	crown, third eye, heart, solar plexus
PLANET(S)	Moon
NUMBER(S)	0
ELEMENT(S)	water
MOHS SCALE	3
ASTRO SIGN(S)	Aries, Cancer

Affirmation I see life clearly now. All obstacles have fallen away. I have all the information I need at my fingertips. I see the good in all things. Through understanding, I gain awareness. I am at peace.

Spiritual uses Optical calcite increases the necessary energy to see information clearly and easily. Use it as a tool to develop your clairvoyance as well as the other five "clairs" (or sensory gifts)—clairaudience, clairsentience, claircognizance, clairgustation, and clairolfaction. Use this stone at the third eye and the crown chakra to amplify your connection with the Divine.

Mental uses The clarity of optical calcite allows you to see right through it. If placed on written material, the words can be read as you gaze through the stone. Because of this quality, this unique stone is beneficial to help you to "read the writing on the wall" or to "see through" situations. The golden variety amplifies the necessary self-confidence to trust what you see.

Emotional uses Optical calcite helps you to get a clear understanding of the source of feelings that disturb or upset you. It is a good stone for gaining clarity on the source of your "buttons." Through the awareness this stone brings you, you can clear away energetic hooks. Pink optical calcite helps remove hooks from your heart, while yellow optical calcite helps remove hooks from your solar plexus, where your self-confidence resides.

Physical uses Optical calcite is good for the eyes and all associated nerves and muscles of the eye. Use this stone in conjunction with intention to improve physical sight and to stay positive when in the healing process of eye disease. This is a good stone for optometrists, ophthalmologists, and neurologists.

Divine guidance Are you trying to gain some clarity in some part of your life? Do you notice the larger-than-life signs and messages all around you? Or perhaps it's time to believe what you see or perceive. Honor your intuition and your ability to see the truth.

About the stone:

Optical calcite (also known as Iceland spar) is the optically clear form of calcite, calcium carbonate crystallizing in the rhombohedral system. Optical calcite is colorless and occurs in crystal form. Well known for its property of double refraction, when a clear calcite crystal is placed over words on paper, letters appear twice.

CALCITE, BLUE
Words Speak Loudly

COLOR(S)	pastel blue
CHAKRA(S)	throat
PLANET(S)	Neptune, Uranus, Chiron
NUMBER(S)	11
ELEMENT(S)	water
MOHS SCALE	3
ASTRO SIGN(S)	Aquarius, Pisces

Affirmation I am impeccable with my words. I speak with love and kindness. I communicate softly regardless of what I need to express. I powerfully express loving kindness. Love vibrates through the sounds that come through me.

Spiritual uses Calcite's sky-blue energy aligns you with the celestial, spirit, and angelic realms. It helps you to focus on astrological or metaphysical pursuits as well as other visionary pursuits. This stone helps you expand your consciousness to receive inspiration. This is an excellent stone for writers, musicians, artists, and metaphysicians. This stone is associated with Archangel Haniel.

Mental uses Calcite makes you more aware of how you say things and what you say so that you can employ "word patrol" as necessary. As you move away from negative words to more positive expression, you will find that things in your life change to match your more positive approach.

Emotional uses With its calming pastel-blue energy, blue calcite chills out your angst when raw emotions are running rampant and shifts your perspective to that of peaceful acceptance. Blue calcite helps you to voice your feelings through conversation, song, or writing. It helps you change the manner in which you communicate your feelings.

Physical uses Blue calcite is helpful if you are making a career change that involves metaphysics, New Age, or other spiritual pursuits. This stone grounds you so that you can get your work done, which is especially helpful for those involved in visionary businesses. Employ blue calcite as a member of your staff to keep you on task.

Divine guidance Do you have an affinity for metaphysics, spirituality, astrology, and other associated arts? You are a natural. You have inherent abilities to hear, see, and know messages from the spirit world. It's time to use these natural gifts in your daily life.

> **About the stone:**
> Blue calcite is calcium carbonate that crystallizes in the rhombohedral system. It gains its blue color from impurities within the chemical composition.

CALCITE, COBALTOAN
Oh Joy Divine!

COLOR(S)	pink, fuchsia, magenta, and red
CHAKRA(S)	heart
PLANET(S)	Moon, Ceres
NUMBER(S)	10
ELEMENT(S)	water
MOHS SCALE	4
ASTRO SIGN(S)	Pisces, Cancer

Affirmation I am aligned with the vibration of the Feminine Christ. I embrace the wisdom of the Divine Mother. My emotions are balanced. I am clear and joyful. Events from my past have a positive effect on my present and future.

Spiritual uses Cobaltoan calcite activates divine love, which includes compassion, wisdom, tolerance, and kindness. This rich fuchsia stone aligns you with the ultimate recognition of unconditional love, mercy, and understanding. Use this stone when you are getting to know the energies of the Divine Mother in her various forms—Isis, Kuan Yin, Mother Mary, Mary Magdalene, Demeter, and so on. The archangels aligned with this stone are Auriel, Jophiel, and Uriel.

Mental uses A vibrant and joyful stone, cobaltoan calcite encourages positive thinking and a good mental outlook on all aspects of life. This stone relaxes your mind enough to stop the incessant chatter so you can just "be." It is best used when you need to arrive at a solution to a problem. Simply gaze at the crystalline structure to generate ideas.

Emotional uses Cobaltoan calcite is a stone of love that opens the heart center at the core of your consciousness. This stone is a conduit for allowing heaven and earth to meet at your center. Use it to see and feel the world through the vibration of love, and allow love in all facets of your life.

Physical uses Cobaltoan calcite carries vibrant energy for renewing your vital life force. It also helps you to get motivated to exercise and move your body. The rich color of this stone also carries the vibrations of wealth and abundance, encouraging the ability to manifest wealth. Overall, this stone provides a vibe of health and well-being.

Divine guidance Are you in love? Have you been a mother or nurturer? It is time to acknowledge the essence of the Divine Feminine in you. Take the time to nurture yourself. If you are dealing with a love challenge right now, imagine yourself in the arms of the Divine Mother.

> **About the stone:**
> Cobaltoan calcite is calcium carbonate that crystallizes in the rhombohedral system. As the name indicates, this calcite gets its striking color from the presence of cobalt.

CALCITE, DOGTOOTH
Grounded Determination

COLOR(S)	golden-yellow and green
CHAKRA(S)	crown, solar plexus
PLANET(S)	Pluto, Sun, Mercury
NUMBER(S)	0
ELEMENT(S)	fire
MOHS SCALE	3
ASTRO SIGN(S)	Gemini, Leo, Scorpio

Affirmation I am determined to achieve my goals and dreams. My clarity and focus are unparalleled. Confidence and courage are mine. It is time to shine my light and share my gifts with the world. I emanate love, light, and well-being.

Spiritual uses Dogtooth calcite activates the crown chakra as well as the etheric chakras above the crown to connect your consciousness with super-consciousness, raising your awareness beyond normal levels. What's "beyond normal" is determined by you and your spiritual beliefs. Use dogtooth calcite to improve your faith and confidence in spiritual pursuits. It aids in believing in the power of prayer.

Mental uses Dogtooth calcite holds the energy of dogged determination with mental clarity and focus. With this calcite in hand, focused intent can help you gain clarity on what you are doing, where you are going, and how to get there. Use it to actualize your goals with confidence and a strong sense of self.

Emotional uses Dogtooth calcite is a stone of self-confidence, which is best used to raise your self-esteem. It helps you realize that you deserve to be noticed, to be acknowledged, and to shine your light. It helps you realize you have a light to shine! Also called stellar beam calcite, this stone helps you to remember your stellar qualities. It amplifies all that is positive in your life and all that is positive about you. Use the dogtooth energy to help you set boundaries so you receive the respect you deserve.

Physical uses The dogtooth vibration of this calcite is helpful when you are dealing with health issues concerning the teeth and gums. Use this stone to align you with the perseverance needed to heal from both ordinary and life-threatening diseases. The golden variety of dogtooth calcite is beneficial for your digestion and absorption of calcium. This is a good stone for periodontists, dentists, and veterinarians.

Divine guidance Do you have a project or goal that you've been working on and you need a little boost in your self-confidence to achieve your goals? Reach inside to find the innate courage within you to be all that you can be. Change your mind, your consciousness, and any false beliefs about yourself—and become empowered!

About the stone:
Calcite (calcium carbonate) in a classic double pyramid form resembling a canine's tooth.

Calcite, Golden
Shine the Light on Me!

Color:	translucent yellow
Chakra(s):	solar plexus
Planet(s):	Mercury, Sun
Number(s):	12/3
Element(s):	air
Mohs scale:	3
Astro sign(s):	Gemini

Affirmation It is safe for me to shine my light brightly. I am self-confident. I recognize my self-worth. It is easy for me to set boundaries. I stay focused on the good in all things. My internal brilliance shines. I have the courage to be all I can be!

Spiritual uses Golden calcite is a great tool for shamanic journey-work, helping you access new and different realities. This stone serves as portal through which unusual spiritual truths are revealed, resulting in new realizations and perspectives. With this stone in hand, taking a different path often leads to deeper meditative experiences as well as more "aha" realizations. Use golden calcite to connect with Archangels Camael, Jophiel, and Metatron.

Mental uses Golden calcite is a good stone to use when you want to be more optimistic. Associated with the solar plexus chakra—the place where we hold our self-esteem and positive attitude—this stone can connect you with the center of your personal power. With a strong sense of yourself, you can achieve anything you put your mind to.

Emotional uses Golden calcite aids you in transitioning from one way of being to another. With its sparkling golden light, it illuminates your path to help you to sort out feelings and to release fear of change. Use it to remember your magnificence. This light will shine so brightly that you won't miss it.

Physical uses Golden calcite brings your awareness to the food that you eat, reminding you to choose your foods wisely. It is beneficial for the entire digestive tract. This is a good stone for visionary business owners like New Age retailers, feng shui practitioners, metaphysical gift wholesalers, metaphysical book publishers, organic food suppliers, dieticians, and nutritionists.

Divine guidance Have you been pondering if you've become the person you thought you would become? Do you feel like you are fulfilling your soul purpose? Do you know what your strengths are? It's time to become the person you are meant to be. Align yourself with a strong sense of self and actualize your full potential. Live up to your dreams, desires, and contracts, and radiate your excellence.

About the stone:
Golden calcite is calcium carbonate crystallizing in the rhombohedral system. Its golden hue stems from impurities that exist within its chemical composition. Golden calcite usually is found in massive form.

CALCITE, GREEN
Smooth Transitions

Color(s)	various shades of green
Chakra(s)	heart, solar plexus
Planet(s)	Venus, Neptune
Number(s)	5
Element(s)	fire, water
Mohs scale	3
Astro sign(s)	Taurus, Pisces

Affirmation I remain grounded and focused even when the world around me changes. I tap into the innate healing abilities within to realign my emotional, spiritual, and physical body. Nature brings me balance. I enjoy and absorb the positive green vibrations of plants, herbs, and essential oils.

Spiritual uses The soft green vibration of green calcite opens your sacred heart to receive love from the spiritual realm. This stone encourages tolerance, compassion, and understanding. Use it as a tool for communicating with those on the Other Side and for heart-to-heart communication with others on the physical plane. Use green calcite to call on Archangels Chamuel, Raphael, and Zadkiel.

Mental uses Calcite is the stone of transformation, and this green-colored variety helps your mind process any major changes you might be going through, including a complete overhaul of your life as well as traumatic, seemingly unwanted changes. Use this green stone to help you think good thoughts to heal yourself on many levels of consciousness.

Emotional uses Green calcite can be used to focus on balancing your emotions when dealing with a change of heart. It helps you stayed focused on the love that you are and the loving relationships(s) that you deserve. Use this stone to help you resolve anger toward yourself and others. It helps you release judgment and move on. It also helps heal a broken heart.

Physical uses Green calcite is useful for rebalancing your digestion when faced with challenges. It promotes healthy function of the gall bladder, liver, pancreas, spleen, and small intestine. It also helps you to realize what you can do to absorb and process life with more ease. This stone opens the channels of your heart to optimize the function of the physical heart on all levels.

Divine guidance Are you having a change of heart? Do you find you are having a hard time changing the way you look at love and friendships? The only constant in life is change. Take the time to adjust and nurture yourself as change takes place. Honor and accept the change.

About the stone:
Green calcite is calcium carbonate that crystallizes in the rhombohedral system. Its green color is due to impurities that exist within the chemical composition. Green calcite usually is found in massive form.

CALCITE, HONEY
One with Nature

COLOR(S)	brown
CHAKRA(S)	root
PLANET(S)	Pluto
NUMBER(S)	4
ELEMENT(S)	earth
MOHS SCALE	3
ASTRO SIGN(S)	Scorpio

Affirmation I am grounded. My ability to focus and stay on target is very good. I enjoy playing outdoors and spending time in nature. I take in the sweetness of life and take pleasure in fairies, elves, and all of nature. I walk gently on the earth.

Spiritual uses The brown energy of this calcite helps you realize your spiritual connection with Mother Earth. This stone grounds you in your spiritual practice and is ideal when delving into earth-based religions or philosophies. Use this stone to connect with gnomes, fairies, and the devic forces of nature.

Mental uses Honey calcite helps you stay focused on whatever you are doing in the moment. Gaze at this amber-colored stone or hold it in your hand when you are feeling scattered to regain your focus. This stone is also beneficial when you are working through mental processes that center on the environment, ecological concerns, and/or being a good steward of the earth. It is the perfect planning aid for architects and builders who want to work in harmony with nature.

Emotional uses Honey calcite reminds you of your emotional connection to all that is. With this stone in hand, go to a natural environment such as a desert, stream, mountain, ocean, or lake to calm your emotions, regain your composure, and find your inner peace. Honey calcite is a good stone to use to embrace the power of gardening as emotional therapy. This stone provides a sense of safety and security.

Physical uses Honey calcite aligns your energies with gardening or when doing any work that is close to the earth. With its ability to morph and harden into marble with heat and pressure, this stone carries the vibration of regeneration and rejuvenation of bone tissue and other structural parts of the human body. It is a good stone for aligning the spine and is a useful tool for chiropractic physicians.

Divine guidance Are you feeling disconnected or scattered? When was the last time you had your hands in the earth? Make some time to connect with nature. Go outside and ground yourself. Find solace and inner security through a deeper spiritual connection with Mother Earth. Relax in the great outdoors, and know all is well.

About the stone:
Honey calcite, also known as brown calcite, is calcium carbonate and crystallizes in the rhombohedral system. Calcite occurs in many colors due to impurities that exist within the chemical composition, and this brownish variation is usually found in massive form.

CALCITE, ORANGE
Creative Strength

Color(s)	orange
Chakra(s)	navel, solar plexus
Planet(s)	Ceres, Moon
Number(s)	6
Element(s)	water
Mohs scale	3
Astro sign(s)	Cancer

Affirmation I embrace change. I create my own reality. My energy is balanced. My physical structure is strong. My imagination is active. I have creative ideas that I easily bring into reality. I trust in the relaxed flow of the day.

Spiritual uses Orange calcite is a good stone to use when doing shamanic journeywork. It's a gentle guide to the inner workings of the emotional body through spiritual means. Keep this stone nearby to improve the quality of rebirthing, Reiki, Emotional Freedom Technique (EFT), Integrated Energy Therapy (IET), and other spiritually aligned healing practices.

Mental uses Orange calcite entices you to use your creativity, encouraging action and play, and fostering a fertile life. When you are fertile with ideas, the orange vibration will catapult you into taking the action required to bring your ideas to fruition.

Emotional uses Orange calcite helps you process feelings that have been stored in your consciousness for a long time. The gentle orange vibration of calcite helps you release stuck emotions with a gentle push. This is the perfect stone to install positive thoughtforms or mental energy in the emotional body immediately after an emotional release. Use this stone to increase your self-esteem. It is especially helpful when you are learning to set boundaries with others. This stone is good for self-nurturing.

Physical uses Orange calcite supports the positive effects of spinal-cord alignments and is the perfect stone for chiropractors and body workers. Within that speciality, it helps self-care and knowing how best to serve a client. This stone also helps to ease the aches and pains of arthritis and muscular tension. It is also a fertility stone and is beneficial for positive thinking while preparing for conscious conception. Use it support your reproductive system, large intestine, kidneys, bladder, and mammary glands.

Divine guidance Are you experiencing major changes in your life that challenge your emotional state? Trust in the process of change and acknowledge and honor your feelings. Take the time to balance your physical, mental, emotional, and spiritual energy. Pay particular attention to the health of your nerves, bones, and muscles.

About the stone:
Orange calcite is calcium carbonate that crystallizes in the rhombohedral system. The orange color comes from impurities that exist within the chemical composition.

CALCITE, PINK
Love, Sweet Love

COLOR	pink
CHAKRA(S)	heart
PLANET(S)	Venus
NUMBER(S)	4
ELEMENT(S)	water
MOHS SCALE	3
ASTRO SIGN(S)	Taurus

Affirmation I am blessed with nurturing vibrations wherever I go! I am gentle with myself. I recognize that kind-heartedness brings about better life situations. I am kind and compassionate with myself and others. I enjoy loving relationships.

Spiritual uses The soothing cotton-candy shade of pink calcite helps you align with the Divine Mother, the highest form of motherly love. The Divine Feminine is within everyone regardless of gender. Use this stone to connect with Kuan Yin, Mother Mary, Isis, or any other highly regarded spiritual icon of feminine wisdom and truth. Pink calcite is the gemstone for Archangels Auriel and Chamuel.

Mental uses Pink calcite activates loving thoughts. It transforms less ideal mental musings into thoughts of self-love, thereby increasing your ability to love and receive love from others. Hold this stone when you are concentrating on thinking positive, uplifting thoughts about yourself and others.

Emotional uses Pink calcite activates the opening of your heart chakra so that you can release prior feelings of hurt or fear. Feelings of anger and frustration can be assuaged by keeping this stone on hand. It is also a good stone for children who cry or whine often. Give one to a grumpy friend and watch his or her energy transform.

Physical uses Pink calcite helps you put your attention on your heart, strengthening it and supporting its proper functioning. This stone can be used with the intention to make your blood flow easily throughout your circulatory system. It is helpful for healing from various diseases such as cancer, skin problems, lung disorders, diaphragm weakness, or any disease that might be associated with a lack of feeling loved or being loving. The soft pink vibration helps relieve insomnia.

Divine guidance Do you need more sweetness in your life? Are you gentle with yourself in your words and thoughts? Treat yourself with kindness. When you treat yourself well, you can cultivate loving friends, family, and environment. Be your own best friend, and be the best friend you can be to others. Love and accept your emotional nature.

> **About the stone:**
> Pink calcite is calcium carbonate crystallizing in the rhombohedral system; specimens are transparent to opaque. If not colored by cobalt (*see* Calcite, Cobaltoan), it is often colored by manganese; these varieties can be called manganocalcite or manganoan calcite, especially when banded. When more than 50 percent of the calcium in such calcite is replaced by manganese, it becomes rhodochrosite.

CALCITE, RED
Magnified Passion

Color(s)	red
Chakra(s)	root, navel
Planet(s)	Mars
Number(s)	4
Element(s)	earth
Mohs scale	3
Astro sign(s)	Aries, Capricorn

Affirmation I am energized and enthusiastic. My endurance levels are strong. I've got "get up and go"! I move forward with focus and determination. I am grateful for the abundance and prosperity in my life.

Spiritual uses Red calcite can be used to amplify the understanding of the teachings of Native American spirituality or the way of the Good Red Road (walking the road of balance). Its energy lends itself to a stronger connection with Mother Earth and earth-centered spirituality. It is good for use in medicine wheel ceremonies, sacred circles, and altars related to Native American ceremonies.

Mental uses Red calcite helps you integrate new core beliefs into your mindset surrounding money, wealth, and prosperity. Use this stone to activate your "millionaire mind." It can also be used as a grounding stone to help you stay focused on the goal at hand.

Emotional uses Red calcite helps you to uncover core issues stored in your root chakra and navel chakra. Use it to dredge up what needs to be addressed and dealt with. It helps you get to the moment in time when the emotional issue started so that you can awaken your awareness of it and heal it once and for all.

Physical uses Red calcite is the perfect stone to use when an activity requires physical endurance. Employ this stone when you are starting a new business or a new facet of an existing business. This is also a good stone for physical trainers of all types as it adds vigor and power to any workout. It also supports a healthy flow of lymph and blood through the genitals, feet, ankles, and knees. Keep it nearby to aid with the healing of your large intestine and add life to your sensuality, sexuality, and libido.

Divine guidance Do you need to improve your vim and vigor? Do you need a bit of motivation to get things done? It's time to get things moving. Use your creative energy to manifest your heart's desire. Take the time to connect with Mother Earth. Perform a simple ceremony stating your intention and watch how you move forward to complete your goals.

About the stone:
Red calcite is calcium carbonate and crystallizes in the rhombohedral system. Its red color is due to impurities that exist within its chemical composition. Red calcite is found in massive form or as rhombohedral crystals.

CARNELIAN
Creativity

COLOR(S)	deep orange or brownish-red
CHAKRA(S)	navel
PLANET(S)	Mars, Sun
NUMBER(S)	5
ELEMENT(S)	fire
MOHS SCALE	6–7
ASTRO SIGN(S)	Aries, Leo, Virgo

Affirmation I am fertile in body, mind, and spirit. Creativity flows through me in myriad ways. I am courageous and bravely bring my ideas into actuality. My imagination is the key to my success. I envision my future and joyfully participate as it unfolds.

Spiritual uses Carnelian can be used to reveal past-life experiences to help you on your spiritual path in this life. This stone activates the desire to uncover mundane patterns that prevent you from attaining self-realization. Use this stone with the intention of knowing yourself to the core and embracing all that you are on all levels. You can attain greater heights in meditation practice through self-acceptance and self-knowledge, developing your spiritual nature. Use carnelian to align with Archangels Ariel and Camael.

Mental uses Carnelian carries the vibration of creativity to help you give birth to new projects. This stone acts as a catalyst to put things in motion so that they can come to fruition. Use this stone to mentally integrate the true meaning of active courage. Carnelian is an ideal stone for improving visualization skills.

Emotional uses Carnelian is a good tool to help you dive into your emotions either through art, music, writing, or any creative outlet. It reminds you to give yourself the time to create and the courage to take the action to make it so. This stone also helps you embrace the emotions and feelings of past challenges, accept them, and move on. A stone for action and moving forward in life, it is useful when you are up against an emotional block.

Physical uses Carnelian is helpful for relieving the pain of arthritis as well as for supporting respiratory function, which makes it easier to breathe. A stone of fertility, it is helpful for manifesting ideas or for getting pregnant. Its orange vibration activates the part of you that needs a push or the motivation to move forward to take action on your projects, ideas, or business pursuits. This is a good stone for fertility specialists, artists, and writers.

Divine guidance Are you involved in a creative project or thinking about starting one? You are "fertile" with good ideas and/or with the ability to conceive something magnificent. Have the courage to take action to make your dreams and ideas into a reality, and allow yourself the time to create.

> **About the stone:**
> Carnelian is the light to dark red variety of chalcedony. The red color is caused by the presence of iron.

CELESTITE
Legions of Angels

COLOR(S)	translucent pastel blue
CHAKRA(S)	throat, third eye, crown
PLANET(S)	Neptune
NUMBER(S)	7
ELEMENT(S)	water
MOHS SCALE	3–3.5
ASTRO SIGN(S)	Pisces

Affirmation I know that angels exist. I remember to ask them for help or divine intervention when I am in need of it. I hear, see, notice, and understand the messages from the angels. I receive messages every day in every way. I interpret the signs from above with great accuracy.

Spiritual uses Celestite is the stone of angelic or heavenly communication. Use this stone to quickly reach the angels when you need things in your life to be a little easier. This lovely stone helps you recognize the heavenly messages in everything, from billboards, TV shows, and news headlines to innocent eavesdropping, number sequences, songs, dreams, and the voice within. Celestite is a stone of communication with loved ones on the other side as well. Sit in silence with this gem, bring to mind the face or essence of your departed loved one, and contemplate or imagine what it would be like to sit with them in conversation about the subject on your mind. Be open to receive their guidance. Celestite is associated with Archangels Gabriel, Haniel, and Seraphiel.

Mental uses Celestite can be engaged with the intention of calming the incessant chatter of the mind. Providing a sense of serenity, this stone is beneficial for times when too many things are happening at once and you need to regain your mental focus. An attractive stone, it is great to keep on your work desk to avoid becoming overwhelmed by paperwork and the like.

Emotional uses Celestite brings composure to turbulent emotions. The pastel blue vibration instills a sense of peace and comfort during tumultuous emotional times. This stone can help console you when you are sad from grief and reminds you to connect with the Divine Mother, who rocks you in her arms while you release the emotions, feelings, and perhaps the tears to relieve your grief.

Physical uses Celestite helps you to be truly present in your body while still being connected to the spiritual world. Use this stone to help you synchronize with the highest realm. If you are in a visionary business like a New Age store, a metaphysical practitioner, visionary artist, or any other spiritual related business, keep this stone close by. It's also helpful if you are running a conscious business engaged in integrating spirituality and ethics into business practices. It helps you to still be prosperous while providing conscious or spiritual services.

Divine guidance Do you feel a strong connection with your angels? Are you hearing messages from your angels? Have you noticed your life flows easily as if divine timing is working in your life? You have a team of angels on your side orchestrating your life. They respond to your thoughts, wishes, and dreams according to the divine plan.

About the stone:
Celestite is a sulphate of strontium. It crystallizes in the orthorhombic system with crystals being tabular in nature.

CHALCEDONY, BLUE
Peaceful Resolution

COLOR(S)	blue
CHAKRA(S)	throat, third eye, crown
PLANET(S)	Venus
NUMBER(S)	7
ELEMENT(S)	water
MOHS SCALE	6–7
ASTRO SIGN(S)	Libra, Aquarius

Affirmation I am calm and at peace within myself. I embrace the oneness of all life, and my peaceful attitude promotes goodwill for all. I am generous with my time, attention, and resources, and in this way, I spread love and joy.

Spiritual uses Chalcedony is named for the ancient seaport, Chalcedon. Cylinder seals made of this stone date back to 2500 BCE. Chalcedony was used in the Jewish high priest's breastplate with inscribed gems representing the twelve tribes of Israel, worn by Moses' brother Aaron. The historical lineage associated with this stone provides spiritual power and innate wisdom. Blue chalcedony specifically can be used to tap into your connection with the ancestors and the wisdom and knowledge of those who have walked on this planet before you. Historically, chalcedony was sacred to the goddess Diana.

Mental uses The pastel blue of this chalcedony elicits the soothing energy of a peaceful lake. Use this stone to help turn off the incessant chatter going on in your mind. Breathe deeply and relax. The calming vibration of this stone slows inner talk, aiding you in sorting out the many mental images and conversations going on inside.

Emotional uses Blue chalcedony relieves hostility and irritability. It promotes feelings of kindness and compassion. Just as the gentle lapping of the calm blue ocean on the shore promotes balance and healing, this stone brings your emotions to a balanced state when used with conscious direction. With this stone in hand, set your intention to realign your emotions and sort out all those unsettling feelings.

Physical uses Blue chalcedony is useful for healing problems associated with the throat, neck, or head. Use this stone for a headache, a sore throat, or an earache. This stone is beneficial for calming inflammations and sinus conditions.

Divine guidance Are you feeling angry and frustrated? Are you having trouble finding the right words? Are you looking for inspiration? Now is the time to quiet your mind and tap into the higher frequencies of the angelic realm. You'll release the anger and frustration by doing this because you'll have accessed inner knowing and find peace.

About the stone:
Blue chalcedony refers to the blue variety of chalcedony, which is cryptocrystalline or microcrystalline quartz.

CHALCOPYRITE
Boundless Abundance

COLOR(S)	golden yellow or iridescent bluish-purple
CHAKRA(S)	crown, solar plexus, third eye, root
PLANET(S)	Saturn, Sun
NUMBER(S)	10, 5
ELEMENT(S)	fire, air
MOHS SCALE	3.5–4
ASTRO SIGN(S)	Capricorn, Leo

Affirmation I shine my light brightly. There are plenty of people with plenty of money who need the goods or services that I offer. There are many opportunities for employment. I am open to moving forward with work, no matter how great or small the job may seem.

Spiritual uses The brassy gold of chalcopyrite represents the golden flecks of light sparkling in your auric field, specifically in the halo around your head. Use this stone to amplify your connection with the Divine, and keep it close as a reminder that you are a miracle worker.

Mental uses Chalcopyrite's color lightens up your consciousness, bringing mental clarity. This stone helps you think clearly, stay focused on the task at hand, and remember what you are doing. Writers can keep it handy when working on their manuscript so they remain focused and clear on what they are trying to convey.

Emotional uses Chalcopyrite helps you to locate the courage and strength that resides deep within you. This stone is beneficial for helping you overcome and discard any negativity impressed upon you during your developmental years.

Physical uses Chalcopyrite supports you when you are engaging in strength training to build your muscles, especially when it involves outdoor activities. This stone reminds you to get sufficient sunlight to maintain a healthy body. Use it as a tool to encourage you to move your body, thereby helping to prevent arthritis and other diseases of the joints, bones, and muscles. This stone also increases your physical vitality and endurance when used with conscious direction. This vitality often translates into prosperity and abundance because you're motivated to complete tasks and goals.

Divine guidance Does your self-esteem need a little boost? Have you been experiencing mental cloudiness? Are you ready to accept prosperity into your life? Recognize your inner strength—mentally, physically, emotionally, and spiritually. Step into your courage. Follow your dreams. Believe in yourself.

About the stone:
Chalcopyrite is a sulphide of copper and is sometimes known as copper pyrite. It crystallizes in the tetragonal system, although it is usually found in massive form.

CHAROITE
Metamorphosis

COLOR(S)	swirls of light and dark purple
CHAKRA(S)	crown, third eye, solar plexus
PLANET(S)	Uranus, Neptune, Pluto
NUMBER(S)	13/4
ELEMENT(S)	water
MOHS SCALE	5–6
ASTRO SIGN(S)	Aquarius, Virgo

Affirmation I have a deep understanding of myself and the circles of life around me. I am aligned with the Divine. I am profoundly clairvoyant and extremely intuitive. I clearly comprehend the details of everything set before me. I am empowered. I am at peace.

Spiritual uses Charoite activates the swirling energy of the crown chakra, jumpstarting the movement of the vortex in alignment with the cosmos. This stone is an excellent choice for channeling, trance medium-ship, psychic development, and spiritual awareness. Its vibration is connected with Ascended Masters Merlin and St. Germain. Charoite is also associated with Archangels Uriel and Zadkiel. The swirling energy of this stone assists in the process of spiritual transformation.

Mental uses A mineral for sorting out the details, charoite untangles chaotic thoughts and sheds light on confusing circumstances and complex situations. Initially, the intensity of the chaos expands in order to draw attention to the key elements that require attention.

Emotional uses A stone of metamorphosis, charoite is the perfect tool to keep in your pocket when you need courage in the face of change and challenges. The transformational properties of this stone will expand your ability to set boundaries and amplify your personal power.

Physical uses Charoite supports your skeletal structure. It is also a very powerful tool to use when trying to determine the source of disease so proper treatment can result. It helps to attract the right nutrition, doctors, and other healthcare practitioners to heal all types of disease.

Divine guidance Are you finding that life is out of control? Do you need to sort out exactly what's going on to get to the reason for the chaos? Take the time to go within and call on the Ascended Masters, spirit guides, and angels to provide you with the inspiration you need to transform your life.

About the stone:
Charoite is a unique silicate containing a plethora of elements, including potassium, sodium, calcium, barium, strontium, oxygen, silicon, and fluorine. It is commonly believed to be named for the only area in the world it has been found, near the Chara River in Russia, but others say its name comes from the Russian word *chary*, meaning wizardry or magic, for its enchanting effect.

CHRYSANTHEMUM STONE
Ancient Wisdom

Color(s)	black with white flowerlike pattern
Chakra(s)	root, crown
Planet(s)	Moon
Number(s)	7, 34
Element(s)	water
Mohs scale	4.5
Astro sign(s)	Cancer

Affirmation I easily tap into universal wisdom. I am one with the knowledge of my ancestors. I am aligned with the movement of the moon, sun, and stars. I am grounded and focused. The divine spark resides within me. I get great ideas all the time and act on them.

Spiritual uses The flowerlike sprays of celestite and calcite crystals in this rock represent the divine spark within each of us. Use this stone as a reminder that the Divine is within you, now and always. Tap into the universal wisdom available within the recesses of your consciousness to remember that you are one with All That Is. Use this stone to stay grounded when you communicate with the angels. This stone is also beneficial to strengthen your connection with the moon and the movement of the celestial realm to help align you with the cycles of life.

Mental uses Chrysanthemum stone, with its white crystalline sprays, can be used as a symbol of the light within the darkness. It is like the proverbial light bulb going off above your head when you suddenly become inspired. The ideas for anything and everything are available to everyone; this stone simply helps you tap into those ideas, offering you inspiration regarding any part of your life that you focus on. Use this stone to awaken the light within your mental body.

Emotional uses Most often collected from riverbeds, the watery nature of chrysanthemum stone helps you to find the beauty within the vast array of your emotions. Employ this stone to assist you in uncovering your true feelings. With this stone in hand, embrace the light within, accept your feelings and emotions just as they are in the moment, examine the source of the feelings, and use this information as a tool for growth and self-development.

Physical uses Carrying the vibration of both black and white energy, chrysanthemum stone can be used to balance the yin and yang energy flowing through your physical body. It opens the meridians for the smooth flow of energy. Use this stone in meditation and contemplative exercises to find answers from within regarding your health or the cause of imbalance or disease within your body. Regain balance through tai chi, chi gung, or acupuncture.

Divine guidance Are you at a point in life where it's important to see the light within the darkness? This ancient stone reminds you to tap into the wisdom of the ancestors and the celestial realm. Find the light within by aligning with the stars, planets, and movement in the sky above your head. If you are attracted to this stone, it would signal a time in your life to find balance through tai chi, chi gung, acupuncture, or other avenues to balance the body, mind, and emotions.

About the stone:
Originally found in Japan, most of the material is now coming from British Columbia, Canada. Usually found in boulders, this black basaltic rock contains white inclusions which mimic the chrysanthemum flower. Classically, the inclusions are celestite, but depending on their origin, the "flowers" can also be composed of calcite, chalcedony, dolomite, aragonite, or even xenotime and zircon.

CHRYSOCOLLA
Balance

Color(s)	blue-green with brownish-red inclusions
Chakra(s)	all
Planet(s)	Earth
Number(s)	33
Element(s)	earth
Mohs scale	2.5–3.5
Astro sign(s)	Libra

Affirmation My body is healthy. All of my systems are in balance. The cells in my body naturally regenerate and rejuvenate. I exercise often. I enjoy my meditation practice on a regular basis. I am relaxed. I am calm.

Spiritual uses Chrysocolla aligns your consciousness with the Divine. Use it at the third eye and crown chakras during meditation. Allow it to be your ally when doing shamanic journeywork or engaging in deep meditative practices. This stone evolves from a combination of other minerals over time, symbolizing the evolution of your spirit as it travels through time and experience. Use chrysocolla to call on Archangel Camuel.

Mental uses If you find yourself disturbed by negative repetitive thoughts, work with chrysocolla to absorb and transform your angst. With this stone in hand, imagine putting those negative thoughts into a compost pile and watch them being transformed into fertile earth to support the positive seeds planted in their place.

Emotional uses Chrysocolla helps you achieve balance in the face of emotional challenges. It is beneficial for those who have experienced abuse—physically, mentally, spiritually, or emotionally. Allow the healing vibes of its blue-green energy to envelop those old wounds like healing salve. This copper-based mineral is good for calming anger in cooperation with the foundational azurite-malachite composition of chrysocolla.

Physical uses Chrysocolla reduces inflammation in the body. Before surgery or dental work, keep this stone close at hand. Afterwards, hold it with the intention of reducing bleeding, swelling, and inflammation while promoting healing. This stone can be used as a tool of support when healing from cancer. It can also be a girl's best friend from puberty to menopause, as it provides a calming vibration to ease PMS and menopause symptoms.

Divine guidance Are you dealing with an inflamed or unbalanced situation—physically, mentally, spiritually, or emotionally? Have you been challenged by imbalances in your body? Take steps to balance your emotions through journaling, exercise, and healthy communication. Nurture yourself through rest and by taking good care of your body, mind, and spirit. Yoga and meditation are beneficial.

> **About the stone:**
> Chrysocolla is a hydrous copper silicate with the color caused by a variety of impurities. Chrysocolla may be found mixed with malachite, azurite, cuprite, and other copper minerals, as well as rock crystal quartz.

CHRYSOPRASE
Nurturing

COLOR(S)	sea-foam green, apple-green, or yellow
CHAKRA(S)	heart, solar plexus
PLANET(S)	Neptune
NUMBER(S)	11, 22
ELEMENT(S)	water
MOHS SCALE	6–7
ASTRO SIGN(S)	Pisces

Affirmation I am cared for, loved, and appreciated. My heart is open. I allow love to fill me up—body, mind, and soul. I nurture myself. Today I take good care of myself. I honor my body and my sacred space. I love myself. I love my body.

Spiritual uses With its sea-green appearance, chrysoprase brings to mind the Atlantean age, a time of great abundance. This stone can be used to help you learn about the use of color, sound, and vibration as a spiritual tool to open your consciousness to unlimited potential. It's a heart chakra stone, opening you to love, compassion, and kindness. Using this stone allows you to accept yourself and increases your tolerance for others, allowing you to accept people as they are. Chrysoprase is associated with Archangels Camael and Sabriel.

Mental uses Chrysoprase heightens your compassion for yourself when you realize that your repetitive thoughts are attracting unwanted situations. With this stone in hand, you can consciously decide to have the courage and confidence to allow love into your life. Yellow chrysoprase helps with mental clarity and is beneficial when trying to integrate a large amount of information or activity into your life.

Emotional uses Chrysoprase is a heart chakra stone. With this stone in hand, open your heart to give love and, even more important, to let yourself receive love. The yellow variety of this stone helps you increase your self-esteem, self-confidence, and courage. It is also useful for helping raise you out of depression. Use this stone when you are mentally overwhelmed to help rebalance and clear out the feelings associated with information overload.

Physical uses In our multitasking society, we often work excessively without taking a sufficient break to restore the body. Chrysoprase reminds us to take a break and relax so we can recharge yourselves, not only physically but mentally, spiritually, and emotionally, as well. Yellow chrysoprase, specifically, is useful for overcoming digestive challenges.

Divine guidance Are you overworked? Take the time to nurture yourself, and know you are loved by the Divine. Open your heart chakra by showing yourself and others more compassion. Engage in nurturing practices such as taking long baths and drinking enough water to nourish yourself.

> *About the stone:*
> Chrysoprase is a microcrystalline quartz (silicon dioxide) denoted by its green color, which is caused by the presence of nickel.

CITRINE
Brilliance

Color(s)	yellowish-orange or orangish-brown
Chakra(s)	solar plexus, crown
Planet(s)	Sun
Number(s)	3
Element(s)	fire
Mohs scale	7
Astro sign(s)	Leo

Affirmation I am confident and courageous. I shine my light brightly. I honor and respect myself. I allow others to see my magnificence. Prosperity abounds in my life. Goodness multiplies. Whatever I desire, imagine, and passionately act upon becomes a reality. It is safe for me to be powerful!

Spiritual uses Citrine activates the golden flecks of light vibrating in your halo which shimmers and connects you with your divine nature. The more aware you are of this aspect of your spiritual body, the more you will actualize the benefits of the connection with higher consciousness. Use this joy-filled stone as a reminder of your divine essence. Use citrine to connect with Archangels Ariel and Jophiel.

Mental uses Good for mental clarity, citrine reminds you that whatever you ardently believe, desire, and work passionately toward will manifest. Use this stone to awaken your awareness and become conscious of the repetitive patterns of self-limiting thoughts that are holding you back. Then develop and focus on positive thoughts to replace those negative beliefs.

Emotional uses Citrine activates self-confidence and joy. Use this stone to help you out of depression and relieve any feelings of inferiority or unworthiness. The radiant vibration that citrine emits helps remind your emotions that you are one with joy, peace, and love. Let the golden rays of this stone dissipate whatever challenge or negative emotion is blocking your way to happiness.

Physical uses Citrine helps improve digestive difficulties, bladder and kidney problems, allergies, and eating disorders. It has been known as the "merchant's stone" throughout the ages and also has the ability to increase your courage to accept abundance in your life. Keep this stone along with a green aventurine in your wallet, pocket, piggybank, cash drawer, or wherever you keep your money to remember your intention to accept prosperity, abundance, wealth, and good fortune into your life.

Divine guidance Are you lacking confidence in your abilities? What about yourself do you find difficult to accept? Acknowledge your magnificence as well as your shortcomings, and then focus on what you do well to increase your self-esteem. Trust that it is safe to be powerful in a loving way. Shine your light to reach your full potential!

> *About the stone:*
> Citrine is the yellow variety of quartz (crystalline silicon dioxide). Citrine crystallizes in the trigonal system and the yellow color is thought to be caused by traces of iron. Natural citrine is rare, and most citrine is produced by heating amethyst, which turns its color to yellow.

Copper
Bandwidth

Color(s)	metallic orange-gold
Chakra(s)	navel, solar plexus, heart, third eye
Planet(s)	Venus
Number(s)	29
Element(s)	air
Mohs scale	3
Astro sign(s)	Gemini, Scorpio

Affirmation I am a conduit for goodness, prosperity, and love. I am open to receive inspiration, wealth, and good health! My power is immeasurable. I easily transform anger and frustration through conscious release and awareness. My body naturally removes toxic substances from my system.

Spiritual uses Copper has been used by humans for a variety of purposes for nearly ten thousand years. Though orange-gold, it also carries the vibration of blue and green. The historic nature of this metal combined with its colorful variations when exposed to the elements and its thermal and electrical conductive qualities increases your ability to tap into the cosmos to garner wisdom, knowledge, and surprising information that can be applied to your spiritual practice of meditation, prayer, and contemplation.

Mental uses Copper provides a clear conduit for messages and inspiration. This metal is beneficial when working on an invention, formula, or any project that requires a download of insight to complete the task at hand. It is beneficial for writers, musicians, and inventors who feel stumped or stuck.

Because of its historical use as money, use it to encourage prosperous thinking and allow it to activate your ability to attract wealth and abundance.

Emotional uses Copper opens your heart despite aggravating or demeaning situations that took place in the past, enabling you to gaze into the sacred mirror to find the lustrous beauty within yourself and to connect with the Divine Feminine energy available to everyone regardless of gender.

Physical uses Copper has a history of assisting people with arthritis and associated diseases and imbalances. Wear or use copper with the intention that your body easily releases any toxins that have accumulated in the joints. This stone benefits the health of the tissues, muscles, bones, and liver. Use in it conjunction with chrysocolla to ease inflammation associated with arthritis.

Divine guidance What kind of bandwidth do you have? Are you receiving a clear signal and comprehensible messages from others and the universe? It's time to clear your channel and allow wisdom to flow through you. Believe in yourself. Have confidence in your ability to tap into universal knowledge and wisdom.

About the stone:
Copper is a metallic element usually found in rounded masses without crystal form. When found in its mostly pure metallic form it is a reddish color. It is responsible for the blue and green coloring of copper sulfides such as chalcopyrite and peacock copper, copper carbonates such as malachite and azurite, and other copper-containing minerals like dioptase, chrysocolla, and turquoise.

Covellite
Holding the Vision

Color(s)	metallic indigo blue
Chakra(s)	third eye, root
Planet(s)	Mars, Pluto
Number(s)	9
Element(s)	fire, water
Mohs scale	1.5–2
Astro sign(s)	Scorpio

Affirmation I am blessed with good health, peace, and calm. I consciously create circumstances to fulfill my dreams and destiny. I believe in the power of my imagination and have strong visualization skills. I visualize my dreams as if they have been realized. I create miracles in my life.

Spiritual uses Covellite—a conductive copper sulfide mineral—provides a conduit for messages, wisdom, and information from the universe and higher realms of consciousness. This mineral enhances your ability to recall past lives as well as tap into potential future realities for the purpose of self-actualization. It supports your innate intuition, allowing you to trust your sixth sense.

Mental uses A calming stone, covellite promotes a positive outlook on life. It can help you ground and focus your attention so you can stay aligned with your goals and intentions. It is good to keep nearby when you are in the process of achieving your dreams.

Emotional uses The calming, grounding effect of covellite can keep emotions balanced when used with conscious intent. It is very helpful when you are dealing with anger and frustration. This stone helps you gradually accept emotions you are feeling, embrace them, and then allow them to help polish your spirit and personality. It is through the eruptions life offers that we develop our strength, character, and wisdom.

Physical uses Covellite can be used as a reminder to purify your body in releasing excessive stomach and uric acids. It helps alleviate inflamed joints and tendons and is therefore beneficial for those challenged with the symptoms and causes of arthritis.

Divine guidance Are you in the process of creating a new reality? Do you realize that you are on the precipice of a wonderful shift in your life? Get ready—your dreams are about to become a reality. Don't stop now…keep moving forward, and trust in the process.

> **About the stone:**
> Covellite is a copper sulfide crystallizing in the hexagonal system. It is associated with other copper minerals and is usually found in massive form or as platy crystals.

DANBURITE
Harmony and Happiness

COLOR(S)	translucent white or pinkish
CHAKRA(S)	heart, solar plexus
PLANET(S)	Venus
NUMBER(S)	6
ELEMENT(S)	air
MOHS SCALE	7–7.5
ASTRO SIGN(S)	Libra

Affirmation Success is mine! I sparkle and shine. I emanate harmony and love. I am grateful for my fantastic significant other, presently known or unknown. I allow love. I have the best friends! Angels guide me wherever I go. Angels surround me, protect me, and inspire me every day.

Spiritual uses Danburite is an excellent tool for connecting with the angelic forces. This stone naturally resonates at a crystal-clear tone, attracting the angels of love and well-being. Archangels Chamuel, Gabriel, Metatron, and Seraphiel are associated with this stone. These archangels assist in spiritualizing your relationships. Danburite empowers you to connect with your highest vibration, aligning you with your divine purpose and your sacred heart.

Mental uses Danburite helps you overcome negative thoughts about yourself that were imposed upon you by others—either recently or at a young age. Step into your personal power, and have the courage to set boundaries with others with this stone in hand. Likewise, this stone of cooperation helps you learn the importance of collaborating with others, and it helps you take notice when others are establishing boundaries with you. This stone's harmonious vibrations calms the mind and reduces stress.

Emotional uses Danburite is a stone of harmony, marriage, and beneficial relationships. This stone helps you maintain a cooperative attitude to create an atmosphere of happiness. This energy will help forge valuable friendships, love relationships, and even a solid marriage.

Physical uses Danburite is beneficial for a successful career in the creative arts or design. The sparkling diamond-like energy of this stone amplifies prosperity and abundance. Use it for maintaining balance of the kidneys, adrenals, and heart. This stone is also beneficial for relieving stress and lowering blood pressure when used with conscious intent.

Divine guidance Do you know how to activate your inner sparkle? Are you focused on romance right now? Decide to create happiness and harmony. You'll start to see an increase in loyal and caring friends in your life as soon as you decide you're willing to accept love. Allow the development of a new romantic relationship or the rekindling of an existing one.

About the stone:
Danburite is a calcium borosilicate mineral that crystallizes in the orthorhombic system. Crystals are usually prismatic and striated.

DIOPTASE
Heart-Centered Communication

COLOR(S)	deep emerald green to bluish-green
CHAKRA(S)	heart, throat, third eye, crown
PLANET(S)	Venus, Saturn, Mercury
NUMBER(S)	4
ELEMENT(S)	metal
MOHS SCALE	5
ASTRO SIGN(S)	Capricorn, Virgo, Taurus

Affirmation All thoughts, words, and actions that come through me first flow through my heart center. I process and integrate information into my being with great ease. I am a good listener. I communicate my own thoughts with loving kindness and confidence.

Spiritual uses Gaze at dioptase to connect with your sacred heart by imagining that it is glowing at the center of your chest. Use this brilliant green stone as a tool to radiate to others your true spiritual nature—love.

Mental uses Often found alongside copper deposits or in mines, dioptase is good for sending and receiving communication via your heart's voice. With its ability to dissolve illusions, the brilliant green stone helps you see through falsehoods in a situation to get to the truth.

Emotional uses Dioptase can help calm emotionally charged conversations so each party can truly be present for the other. This stone is a reminder that when you are really listening and hearing what another is saying, reaching a resolution is much easier. Likewise, this gemstone can help you be a better listener and partner in a relationship.

Physical uses Dioptase is good for improving your eyesight and is beneficial for heart health. This stone is also useful for balancing your digestive organs—gallbladder, spleen, pancreas, and liver.

Divine guidance Are you paying attention to your diet? Are you absorbing all that goes on around you? Are you seeing your life clearly? Perhaps you have all the information you need for your projects, relationships, and life, but somehow you've had a hard time processing information. It's time to listen with your heart, gain mental clarity, and be a better listener.

About the stone:
Dioptase is a copper silicate and crystallizes in the trigonal system. Crystals are formed in clusters and are translucent to nearly opaque in darkly colored specimens.

DOLOMITE
Think Outside the Box

COLOR:	pink or peach-pink
CHAKRA(S):	heart, crown
PLANET(S):	Venus, Uranus
NUMBER(S):	2, 11
ELEMENT(S):	water
MOHS SCALE:	3.5–4
ASTRO SIGN(S):	Aquarius, Taurus, Libra

Affirmation My ideas are fresh and creative. I easily manifest my artistic thoughts. My heart is open to accepting assistance from others. It is easy for me to comfort myself when I am out of sorts. I relax my body, mind, and spirit to meditate regularly.

Spiritual uses Dolomite's comforting nature and calming vibrations improve the meditation experience. Use this stone with the intention of creating new pathways of consciousness by opening up to unexplored avenues for raising your awareness. For example, instead of a sitting meditation, try a moving meditation such as tai chi, a walk in nature, or you can explore lucid dreaming and shamanic journeywork to expand your spiritual horizons.

Mental uses Dolomite facilitates abstract thinking. As you gaze at this stone, open your mind to original thoughts and ideas that don't necessarily fit a predetermined mold. With this stone as your ally, bounce ideas off others or participate in a think-tank to come up with innovative approaches to whatever task is at hand, personal or professional.

Emotional uses With its gentle peachy-pink vibrations, dolomite is a stone of comfort and ease. With this stone in hand, you can balance your emotions through self-nurturing and open your heart chakra. This stone activates the ability to receive love, nurturing, and comfort in your life from yourself and others.

Physical uses The composition of dolomite is high in calcium and magnesium. With this vibration, it is good for your bones, teeth, hair, and blood circulation. Use this stone with selenite and calcite to create a grid for realigning your spine and any challenges you may have with your body's foundational structure.

Divine guidance Have you wanted to do something creative? Are you feeling artistic? Let your inspiration flow and generate your insight into manifest reality. It doesn't matter what it is—it could be a nice meal, a pretty garden, a beautiful photograph, or a detailed sewing project. Now is the time to produce and create; your project will bring you fulfillment and purpose.

> *About the stone:*
> Dolomite is a calcium magnesium carbonate that crystallizes in the rhombohedral system. Dolomite is also found as a rock in massive form, which is used for carving.

DUMORTIERITE

Harmony

COLOR(S)	blue, brown, green, violet, and pink
CHAKRA(S)	throat, third eye
PLANET(S)	Jupiter
NUMBER(S)	0
ELEMENT(S)	metal, earth
MOHS SCALE	7–8.5
ASTRO SIGN(S)	Sagittarius

Affirmation I am organized. I am in harmony with all life. I see life from a positive perspective. I magnetically attract peaceful, thoughtful people into my circle. My friends and family are supportive and happy for the good in my life. I am prosperous and successful. I am grateful.

Spiritual uses Dumortierite is a tool to help you hear, sense, or know divine intervention and information from angels, spirit guides, and devic forces. Inner peace is found within the quiet center of the third-eye chakra, associated with this stone. Use it to realign your inner sight and when you are developing your spiritual awareness and psychic intuition. It is also beneficial to help you objectively observe your behaviors, tendencies, or challenging issues with clarity. Being objective enables you to make a positive shift toward more enlightened behaviors and actions.

Mental uses Dumortierite enhances mental acuity. Employ this gem as an instrument to keep you focused on achieving your goals. Be it for business acumen or academia, this stone boosts your brain power.

Emotional uses Dumortierite grounds your goodness so it can be seen, felt, experienced, and enjoyed. It enables you to find the bliss within. This stone also reminds you that all is well when you know your truth and can speak and live it.

Physical uses Dumortierite helps calm inflammations throughout the body. Keep this stone on hand if you are experiencing any inflammatory reactions to an illness or allergy; hold it and concentrate on calming the inflammations.

Divine guidance Are you consciously aware of everything going on around you? Start paying attention to the subtle. Wake up completely, use your full mental capacity. It's time to meditate and focus on the positive.

About the stone:

Dumortierite is an aluminum borosilicate. The mineral crystallizes in the orthorhombic system, although it is usually found in fibrous or columnar massive form.

EMERALD

Abundance

COLOR(S)	green
CHAKRA(S)	heart
PLANET(S)	Venus, Jupiter
NUMBER(S)	4
ELEMENT(S)	water
MOHS SCALE	7.5–8
ASTRO SIGN(S)	Taurus, Cancer, Gemini

Affirmation I am grateful for my prosperity. I am healthy, whole, and complete. I am successful in all of my pursuits. My actions have beneficial results for everyone. I am fortunate. I have excellent business skills. I earn unlimited income doing what I love. I attract kind and courteous people.

Spiritual uses Emerald is the stone for connecting with the angels of healing, amplifying your link to Archangel Raphael, whose name is translated as "he who heals." Emerald is also the stone of Archangel Chamuel, the angel of healing relationships. This precious stone also represents spiritual generosity. Share your spiritual connection with others without proselytizing. With emerald energy, you can be a fountain of spiritual calm, wisdom, and strength to those around you. Emerald is associated with Vishnu and is sacred to the goddess Venus. Ancient Greeks wore emeralds to honor Aphrodite.

Mental uses Emerald has been known to enhance memory and mental clarity. This precious gem especially helps with mental acuity relating to business transactions.

Emotional uses Emerald is useful for healing emotions with an infusion of love. Gaze into this gemstone and imagine Divine love enveloping you. Embrace your emotions and allow the green rays of this gemstone to open your heart fully to love. Allow the love to flow through you, so that it can recalibrate your emotions and return them to balance.

Physical uses Emerald is a stone of abundance and healing. Its green vibrations help you understand that at the deepest level, everything is whole and well. Use this precious gem to focus on well-being and all that is good. Emerald is the stone of extreme wealth. With your health and vitality intact, use this stone to attract financial success through focused action.

Divine guidance Are you embarking on a new venture? Do you wish to increase your wealth to obtain more financial security? Trust that you have the ability to be successful and prosperous in a loving and healthy way. Simply activate your inner entrepreneur through focused study. Use your acquired knowledge to reach your goals.

About the stone:

Emerald is the green variety of the mineral beryl. Beryl is a silicate mineral containing aluminum and beryllium. It forms six-sided crystals in the hexagonal system. Other beryl varieties include heliodor, aquamarine, and morganite.

EPIDOTE
Above and Below

Color:	pistachio-green, green, yellowish-brown, brown, or sometimes blackish-brown-green
Chakra(s):	heart, solar plexus
Planet(s):	Mercury
Number(s):	3, 8
Element(s):	air
Mohs scale:	6–7
Astro sign(s):	Capricorn, Libra

Affirmation My thoughts and actions create beneficial results. I am healthy and abundant. All that I need is available to me. I am happy for other people's good fortune and blessings. I have an open heart. I am truly blessed. I am grateful for all the blessings still to come.

Spiritual uses The natural tetrahedron structure of epidote provides a deeper understanding and connection to the concept of "as above, so below." Employ this stone as a tool to tap into your sacred heart, that part of you that is aligned with divine love. This stone also provides an abundance of spiritual energy.

Mental uses Epidote increases your mental capacity to integrate the true meaning of love and abundance into your understanding of the world. Think from your heart with this stone in hand, and the truth will be yours. Use this heartfelt truth to make your decisions.

Emotional uses Epidote aligns you with parallel realities in which you already know how to love freely. This stone awakens the realization that there is plenty of love to go around. It is a good stone to improve relationships in which jealousy tends to be an issue.

Physical uses Epidote reminds you that there is plenty for everyone, including good health, sufficient income, and unconditional love. This stone assures you that all your basic needs are met with an abundance left over to share with others. It helps you relax into the knowledge that nothing is lacking. Use of this stone helps increase good health, abundant wealth, and the ability to love fully and completely.

Divine guidance Do you need a reminder that there is plenty for everyone? Are you a bit jealous of someone's blessings, or is someone envious of your good fortune, perhaps? Remember, good fortune and blessings are often the result of years of good thoughts and deeds, hard work, and an open heart. It takes many years to become an overnight success! Develop your capacity to love. Expand your knowledge. Work diligently toward your goal, and put your attention on your own life. Practice gratitude.

About the stone:
Epidote is a calcium aluminum silicate with varying amounts of iron. The more iron, the darker the color. Epidote crystallizes in the monoclinic system with prismatic crystals rarely exhibiting distinct terminations.

FLUORITE
Simply Genius!

Color(s)	green, purple, clear, yellow, and blue
Chakra(s)	crown, third eye, throat, heart, solar plexus
Planet(s)	Mercury
Number(s)	3, 8
Element(s)	water
Mohs scale	4
Astro sign(s)	Gemini, Virgo

Affirmation I am an intelligent being with the ability to focus on complex tasks. I enjoy learning new things. I am smart enough to realize that I can always discover new information. I am organized. I create the perfect space to learn.

Spiritual uses Fluorite is the ultimate stone for focus, making it ideal for meditation practices. It aids in releasing the "monkey mind" (in other words, it clears out the unnecessary chatter), thereby facilitating a "no mind" state of consciousness. With this stone in hand, practice calming your thoughts, and they will float away, one by one. Fluorite is also a beneficial tool in crystal grids. (See page 389 for more on crystal grids.)

Mental uses Fluorite is the genius stone. It supports the brain in thinking through complex problems. It's especially helpful to have nearby while working on computers. Some say it helps deflect the electromagnetic fields (EMFs) from computer equipment and other electronics. The natural configuration of fluorite resembles a motherboard in a computer, so it helps you think more like a computer in situations where more brainpower is needed.

Emotional uses Fluorite teaches you how to go with the flow and embrace challenging emotions. Use the green energy in this stone to feel with your heart, the purple energy to feel with your spirit, the blue energy to be at peace with your mind, and the yellow energy to maintain courage and self-confidence to move through challenging feelings.

Physical uses Fluorite is beneficial when kept close by during physical exercise. Whether you are dedicated to Pilates, yoga, running, muscle training, or the like, this stone is a great companion to help you stay on course with your fitness plan and garner strength and endurance. Use this "focus stone" to help you maintain a discipline.

Divine guidance Have you been feeling somewhat dull lately, perhaps unable to focus on and/or resolve complex tasks or situations? Know that you are an intelligent being and that you can lovingly accomplish whatever you put your mind to. Develop your inner genius. Seek to educate yourself in areas you feel your knowledge may be lacking.

About the stone:
Fluorite is calcium fluoride and crystallizes in the cubic system, often seen as well-formed octahedrons. Fluorite may be found in a large variety of colors; bi-color and parti-color varieties are often found.

Fossil, Ammonite
Spiraling into the Center

Color(s)	shades of brown
Chakra(s)	all
Planet(s)	Mars
Number(s)	3
Element(s)	water
Mohs scale	4–5.5
Astro sign(s)	Aries

Affirmation I know the truth in the center of myself. All the answers lie within. Ancient knowledge and wisdom are available to me. I recall my dreams when I wake and use them as tools to guide me in my waking life.

Spiritual uses Ammonite is a fossil from an extinct group of invertebrate marine animals. The spiraling structure of this fossil provides a tool for spiraling into the center of your own consciousness through various means like dream work, meditation, spiral dance, and walking a labyrinth or a medicine wheel. Used as index fossils to determine geologic time periods, it can help you establish time lines during past- or present-life regression sessions. Because of this fossil's association with snakes or serpents, ammonite has been associated with healing and oracular abilities.

Mental uses Ammonite assists you in reaching in to examine the deeper recesses of your mind. Gaze at this fossil, follow the spirals to encourage your mind to go within, find answers, uncover truths, and deepen your connection with your own consciousness. It is helpful for resolving problems or issues by getting to the center of the challenge.

Emotional uses Named for a Greco-Egyptian deity named Ammon, who was associated with rams, ammonite assists you when it is necessary to simply charge ahead and delve into the past to uncover the source of emotional trauma. With this fossil on hand, bring challenges into the light, observe them, and allow the light to transform and transmute stuck emotions and feelings holding you back from achieving your full potential.

Physical uses Ammonite carries the vibration of safety in open waters and is a useful companion if you partake in a water-related sport or profession, such as swimming, fishing, boating, or scuba diving. This fossil is helpful for clearing out the intestinal tract, visualizing the healthy spiraling action of your own physical body.

Divine guidance Are you going round and round in circles? Are you trying to find the answers to a problem in your life? This stone signals a time to stop, go within, and allow yourself to step into the deep recesses of your mind and emotions to uncover the truth. It can be helpful to go to the ocean or a body of water to take the time to reflect.

About the stone:
Ammonite fossils are usually found as spiral- or ram-horn-shaped calcite fossilized shells. In some localities, the ammonites have an iridescent quality formed by a nacreous layer of aragonite with other impurities.

Fossil, Orthoceras
Get to the Point

Color(s)	black, white, and gray
Chakra(s)	root, navel, third eye, crown
Planet(s)	Mars, Jupiter
Number(s)	10/1
Element(s)	water
Mohs scale	6–6.5
Astro sign(s)	Aries

Affirmation My mind is completely clear. My focused intent aligns me with my highest purpose. I use past experiences as valuable lessons, allowing me to propel forward in life with ease. The way to my future is clear and bright.

Spiritual uses The ancient energy of orthoceras provides a deeper understanding of oneself through enhanced memory retrieval of previous incarnations. This fossil is ideal for use during regression therapy and afterwards capitalizing on memories of past experiences and lessons learned through them. With this fossil in hand, meditate on remembering your mission.

Mental uses Working with orthoceras promotes clear thinking. Use this fossil to help you maintain focused intent and to get in the habit of using a to-do list. An impression of an ancient animal, this fossil holds the vibration of forward movement, propelling you ahead in the direction you need to go.

Emotional uses Orthoceras helps you get in touch with your subconscious and the deep inner feelings you have for yourself and others. This is a perfect fossil to fully comprehend the old adage "what goes around comes around" on an emotional level. Through awareness, you can stop the repeating patterns in your life that cause you emotional distress.

Physical uses Orthoceras is beneficial for healing intestinal disturbances, for promoting proper absorption of nutrients, and for keeping the body hydrated. This fossilized mollusk is also useful for alleviating diseases that require balanced electrolytes in the body.

Divine guidance Are you on the precipice of remembering your soul's purpose? Is it on the tip of your tongue, so to speak? It is time to clear away your unhealthy repetitive patterns. Use your talents and focus instead on establishing peace and fellowship, starting with yourself, family, friends. Extend your community. You have a special spiritual mission. This fossil assures you that things are making a turn for the better. Maintain a positive outlook.

About the stone:
Orthoceras fossils are elongated shells generally fossilizing in limestone.

FOSSIL, PETRIFIED WOOD
Been There, Done That

COLOR(S)	shades of brown, clay-orange, green, blue, or black
CHAKRA(S)	root
PLANET(S)	Neptune
NUMBER(S)	12/3
ELEMENT(S)	water, earth
MOHS SCALE	5–7
ASTRO SIGN(S)	Pisces

Affirmation I am grateful for the years of experience that have molded today's success. My expertise is valued. I enjoy financial abundance. Everything I need to know is stored within me. I easily tap into my inner wisdom and knowledge.

Spiritual uses Petrified wood teaches you that much of what you need to realize, understand, remember, or know is buried deep within your body, mind, and soul. On a spiritual level, uncovering the layers of years of processing can be achieved through spiritual healing practices like yoga, tai chi, rebirthing (conscious connected breathwork), past-life regression therapy, meditation, and shamanic journeywork. Use petrified wood to connect with Archangels Auriel, Seraphiel, and Zadkiel.

Mental uses Petrified wood reminds you that all the knowledge and wisdom you need is available in the recesses of your mind. These fossilized pieces assist you in the process of clearing out the clutter that no longer serves you. It supports you as you remove the extraneous from your life and uncover the previously hidden information you need.

Emotional uses Petrified wood brings embedded feelings in your subconscious to the surface to remove unnecessary limits on your potential. This fossilized wood assists you in letting go of these unhealthy emotions.

Physical uses Petrified wood is an ally for organic gardeners. It supports the transformation of compost into rich fertilizer due to its stabilized vibration and ability to endure through time. This fossil holds a vibration that helps you tap into your body's ability to regenerate and rejuvenate. This stone is also good for supporting the cellular structure of your physical body.

Divine guidance What's buried deep within your consciousness? Is something so stagnant within your belief systems that you can't break out of the mold? Are you petrified about something? Step outside yourself and observe ancient patterns that have been in your ancestral history for many generations. Weed out what no longer serves you, embrace what does. Are you ready to be prosperous? Use the knowledge you've gained from the work you've been doing for the past ten to ten thousand years as the foundation for your success.

> *About the stone:*
> Petrified wood is a chalcedony pseudomorph in which the organic molecules of a tree or plant are replaced slowly with quartz (silicon dioxide), retaining the wood's structure.

FOSSIL, SHELL
Innate Wisdom

COLOR(S)	brown, tan, gray, and black
CHAKRA(S)	root, crown
PLANET(S)	Neptune
NUMBER(S)	12
ELEMENT(S)	water
MOHS SCALE	3-4 to 6.5–7
ASTRO SIGN(S)	Pisces

Affirmation Wisdom is stored in my cells and bones. I am conscious of my intelligence. I tap into ancestral knowledge. Meditation comes naturally to me. I go within for guidance every day. I integrate and process all I perceive with ease. My ability to telepathically send and receive messages improves daily.

Spiritual uses Fossilized shell is a good tool for connecting with your inner wisdom. The snail-shell structure is a reminder to spiral inward to understand your dreams and visions. Shell fossil is a record-keeper stone. All fossils provide the vibration of the wisdom of our ancestors and others who have walked on this path before us. The energy associated with this stone is like Owl Medicine. Owls have the ability to see in the dark, know what others don't, read between the lines, and connect with higher wisdom. Use the stone to activate Owl's vibration within you.

Mental uses Shell fossil helps you get to the source of the incessant chatter in your mind. This fossil helps train your mind to recognize the repetitive nature of thoughts. When you become aware of your thoughts, they will dissipate, and peace will ensue.

Emotional uses Fossilized shell is useful for entering the deeper layers of your emotions. With the wisdom of the fossil and the watery vibration of the seashell, this stone is excellent for gaining personal acceptance of your past. It is also useful for letting go of outdated belief systems.

Physical uses Turritella shell is beneficial for intestinal health as well as the proper elimination and easy removal of toxins. It also helps you enter the recesses of your mind to tap into the wisdom of your ancestors for guidance on new ventures.

Divine guidance Are you ready to uncover memories or wisdom stored within your consciousness? Recognize the value of the past and use those experiences as stepping stones for the future. You have much wisdom inherent with in you. Use it!

About the stone:
Shell fossils are formed by chalcedony or calcite replacement of organic material; when an abundance of shells and organic materials accumulate, they may transform into a sedimentary carbonaceous rock like limestone. Under the right conditions, whole fossils may still be found intact.

Fossil, Trilobite
Ancient Filtering System

Color(s)	shades of browns, gray and black
Chakra(s)	all
Planet(s)	Mercury, Neptune
Number(s)	9
Element(s)	water, air
Mohs scale	2
Astro sign(s)	Virgo, Gemini

Affirmation I easily accept the things that happen in life. I readily absorb life experiences. I see with my physical eyes as well as my spiritual eyes. My digestive system functions optimally. I gratefully and clearly receive guidance from my ancestors.

Spiritual uses Trilobites are marine creatures that flourished around 526 million years ago and have been extinct for over 250 million years. Their fossils are a spiritual aid, allowing the crown chakra to open up to receive wisdom from all ages past. A trilobite fossil is a good tool to help you turn off your personal filter so channeled messages aren't warped by your personal experience, instead remaining pure from the ancient records. In addition, trilobite's filtering system can keep unwelcome energies from interfering with the process so you can be a pure channel. Work with this fossil to become a highly sensitive intuitive.

Mental uses Trilobite is useful when you need support dealing with life's minutiae. With its ability to help you sort through what's important and what isn't, it is especially beneficial for anyone who works in any capacity with details and scheduling or organization.

Emotional uses Trilobite is a perfect tool for sorting out your emotions. This fossilized ancient marine creature helps you determine which feelings are yours and which have been imposed upon you by society or other individuals. It is a good fossil to use while journaling to sort out your feelings.

Physical uses Trilobite energy supports triage departments in an ER or in any situation where it is crucial to determine the order in which things need to take place. Engage the vibration of trilobite to help heal your kidneys, liver, and spleen, so they work at maximum capacity as a healthy filter for your body. This fossil is also good for the digestive system; with its exoskeletal structure, it is also beneficial for maintaining strong bones, joints, and muscles. It also supports eye health.

Divine guidance How are your filters? Are you able to discern what's really important to you? Do you need to improve your ability to deal with your emotions? It's time for you to figure out what stays and what goes—in any or all parts of your life. Discern what's best for you, and choose to be strong and aligned with your highest good. Your ability to see and know the truth is exceptional.

> ### About the stone:
> Trilobite fossils have been found worldwide in marine rocks, the most common of which is limestone. Thousands of extinct species have been identified through fossil studies. Trilobites had an exoskeleton, large head shield, and the body had three lobes, hence their name.

GALENA
The Silver Lining

COLOR(S)	metallic silver-gray
CHAKRA(S)	root
PLANET(S)	Uranus, Mercury
NUMBER(S)	17/8
ELEMENT(S)	earth, air
MOHS SCALE	2.5–2.75
ASTRO SIGN(S)	Aquarius

Affirmation I'm grounded, focused, and tuned in to the universe. I stay on task in my current projects. Challenging situations are transformed and the good is revealed. I'm a channel for creative energy. My creative projects bring me prosperity and abundance.

Spiritual uses Galena amplifies your ability to channel, and it assists you when you are studying to increase your psychic abilities or connect with any of the intuitive arts. Due to its conductive qualities, this stone sharpens your ability to "tune in to the right channel" while simultaneously providing a protective shield. It wards off psychic attacks and serves as a constant reminder to maintain protective sacred energy around you at all times.

Mental uses Galena is perfect stone to rub or keep nearby while you study. This stone helps you stay focused and on task so you can more easily integrate the study material into your consciousness, making it readily available when you need to retrieve it.

Emotional uses Galena engages your inner strength, prompting you to overcome feelings of vulnerability and empower yourself. Allow this mineral to garner your inner emotional strength by focusing your intention on self-love and stable foundations. It helps you find the foundation you need to stabilize your life, whatever that may mean for you.

Physical uses Galena is a natural semiconductor that enhances the financial gains associated with work in the production or sale of electronic gadgets, such as cell phones, televisions, and GPS devices. This stone supports eye health, especially in cases where bright light is uncomfortable.

Divine guidance Do you need to focus? Are you having trouble seeing the silver lining? Are you worried about finances? The time has come to put your nose to the grindstone and focus on what you really want. Channel all your energy with strong intention, and watch the prosperity roll in!

About the stone:
Galena is a lead sulfide often containing other impurities crystallizing in the cubic system. Well-formed cubic or octahedral crystals are common.

GARNET
Passion for Living

Color(s)	black, green, orange, brown, yellow, red, purple; the meanings listed here are for red garnets
Chakra(s)	root
Planet(s)	Mars
Number(s)	16/7
Element(s)	fire
Mohs scale	6.5–7.5
Astro sign(s)	Aries

Affirmation I have plenty of energy and plenty to share. I am vital and strong! I live a full passionate life. I am determined. All my needs are met. I am healthy to the core of my being. My body naturally heals itself.

Spiritual uses Garnet is the stone of awakening. Its fiery nature inspires enlightenment and activates kundalini energy—a sleeping, dormant force holding all of human potential. This energy is naturally coiled at the base of the spine and is quite powerful when activated. When working with garnet to uncoil this energy, do it with care through serious yoga practice. Garnet can be used to invoke the energy of Archangels Ariel, Camael, and Uriel. Some myths link garnet to Persephone of Greek mythology, the queen of the underworld and wife of Hades.

Mental uses Garnet keeps you focused on your creative power. Carrying the vibration of passion and determination, this red gem helps you to follow through on your goals. Use it when you need to stop procrastinating and get motivated. It also helps you to maintain balance, preventing anger and frustration.

Emotional uses Garnet reminds you to honor yourself and charges you to set boundaries with others. Because of its tendency to create a strong charge, avoid this stone when you are agitated or angry. Instead, use it when you simply want to state your case and claim your space.

Physical uses Garnet is a good stone to work with when you are in the process of manifesting. This semiprecious stone is directly connected to the vital life force, your blood flow, the circulation of other fluids throughout the body, and the alignment of the spinal column and fluids. A fertility stone, it also helps improve your libido and your love life.

Divine guidance Do you find that you live life passionately? Are you determined and focused on achieving your life goals? You probably have plenty of energy and some to spare. You are committed to yourself and others. You are self-empowered. It is easy for you to take charge of a situation and make things happen.

> **About the stone:**
> Garnet is a group of minerals all crystallizing in the cubic system. The most common form of garnet is iron-aluminum silicate (almandite); however, magnesium, calcium, and chromium can be found in other varieties. The garnets intermix in chemical composition and are found in a host of colors including black (andradite), green (tsavorite and demantoid), orange to brown (spessartite), yellow to orangish red, and red to purple (pyrope, rhodolite).

GOLDSTONE
Stellar!

COLOR(S)	blue, green, or red
CHAKRA(S)	third eye (blue); root, navel, and solar plexus (red); heart (green)
PLANET(S)	Venus
NUMBER(S)	4, 7
ELEMENT(S)	air, earth
MOHS SCALE	5–6
ASTRO SIGN(S)	Taurus, Libra

Affirmation I am energetic and vibrant. I shine my light brightly. I live my life passionately with determination. I am creative. I am abundant. I'm an amazing manifester! I have plenty of energy to get everything done. I am a mover and a shaker. Abundance is mine. I have what I need.

Spiritual uses Goldstone is very useful during meditation practice for focusing on its associated chakras—the third eye, root, and heart. Focus your attention on the sparkles within goldstone to activate your imagination. Visualize the gold flecks within your own aura. Feel your energy field magnified from the brilliance that stems from within.

Mental uses Goldstone helps you stay focused on happy thoughts. It is a "feel-good" stone that carries the good vibrations of well-being and joy. When used with conscious intention, this stone can increase your self-confidence and self-esteem.

Emotional uses Regardless of its color, goldstone is a stone of self-worth and self-motivation. It is an excellent mood stabilizer. The brilliant sparkles within the stone help remind you of your magnificence and encourage you to shine your light brightly with confidence.

Physical uses Goldstone is useful for giving you the physical energy required to maintain your personal ambition and drive. Green goldstone specifically is useful when you are healing from a heart problem or you need a reminder to eat dark green leafy vegetables for overall well-being.

Divine guidance Do you need some motivation? How is your self-confidence? It's time to remember all your good qualities and use them for the entire world to see. This is a time of good fortune. You are available to receive blessings and prosperity in your life. You just need to be aware that you deserve this good fortune!

About the stone:
Goldstone is a manmade glass containing crystallized copper.

HELIODOR
Beaming

Color(s)	translucent white, gold, or pale green
Chakra(s)	crown, solar plexus
Planet(s)	Sun
Number(s)	10/1
Element(s)	fire
Mohs scale	7.5–8
Astro sign(s)	Leo

Affirmation I process everything that is happening around me with ease and understanding. Mentally, I am clear and focused. I visualize my goals and aspirations effortlessly. I am self-assured, and I step forward in life with confidence and purpose. I am joyful. I have courage.

Spiritual uses Heliodor is a tool for visualizing a golden halo of light surrounding the crown of your head. Use this stone to set the intention of increasing your connection with the Divine and to maximize your intuitive skills, including the sensory gifts of clairvoyance, clairaudience, claircognizance, and clairsentience. This stone is a reminder of the miracle worker within you.

Mental uses Heliodor provides you with mental clarity. It helps you discern the thoughtforms, or the mental energy, circling in your mind. As you become consciously aware of your thoughts with the help of this stone, you can discard the outdated thoughts and replace them with thoughts focused on the life you want to live.

Emotional uses The fiery vibration of heliodor helps burn away negative emotions by shining a bright light into the darkness. Use this stone to improve your personal self-worth and increase your self-esteem. It is a good stone to support relief from depression.

Physical uses Heliodor is helpful for digestive issues. As a solar plexus stone, it helps with proper absorption of nutrients and foods through the digestive process. When used with conscious intention, this stone is beneficial for the healthy functioning of the spleen, pancreas, liver, gall bladder, and the small intestine. This stone is a reminder to eat the right foods for your body, and to stay focused on your goal.

Divine guidance Are you having digestive issues? Is something happening in your life that you find difficult to swallow? Are you feeling self-confident and clear, or are you down in the dumps and feeling confused? It's time to embrace all that you are and recognize your magnificence. Imagine the sun shining brightly at your solar plexus, rejuvenating your self-esteem and courage. You are a bright light with a clear, focused mind.

About the stone:
Heliodor is the yellow variety of beryl (aluminum silicate) and crystallizes in the hexagonal system. Other varieties of beryl include emerald, aquamarine, and morganite.

HEMATITE
Grounded

COLOR(S)	metallic black to steel gray
CHAKRA(S)	root
PLANET(S)	Earth, Mars
NUMBER(S)	4
ELEMENT(S)	earth
MOHS SCALE	5.5–6.5
ASTRO SIGN(S)	Taurus, Capricorn

Affirmation I am calm and peaceful. All is well, and life is good. My roots absorb goodness from the all-giving, bountiful earth, which fills me up and brings me serenity. I am love, and all that surrounds me is love.

Spiritual uses Hematite enhances meditation practice by using it with the intent to quiet the mind and to be in the nothingness state of consciousness. This widespread stone relaxes the physical body and worldly thoughts to enable quiet time for connection with the earth beneath you as you connect with the inner sanctums of your consciousness. Work with hematite to gain the assistance of Archangel Sabrael.

Mental uses Hematite removes scattered energy from your energy field and repels negative thoughts from your mind as well as from the minds of others.

Emotional uses Hematite works wonders in shifting negative feelings by calming and relaxing your attention on the source of the emotional challenge. With this stone in hand, imagine the metallic quality interrupting the connection between you and the source of your emotional discomfort.

Physical uses Hematite has calming vibrations that work wonders for those with high blood pressure or a hyperactivity disorder. This stone also prevents muscle cramping, balances the nervous system, and relieves insomnia. It is a useful tool for those with iron deficiencies by keeping iron-rich foods at the forefront of the mind. It is also a grounding stone that collects disjointed energy, providing you with the focus you need to provide yourself with a healthy income.

Divine guidance Do you have high blood pressure? Are you hyperactive in either body or mind? Is your brain on overdrive? Are you feeling physically hyperactive? Has restful sleep and/or relaxation been a problem for you? You may need to transform a negative situation in your life. Become grounded by focusing on peace, and breathe it in deeply as you feel your roots taking hold and expanding into the earth. Disquieting thoughts and excess energy drain away.

About the stone:
Hematite is iron oxide that when found in relatively compact form is hard enough for polishing. Hematite crystallizes in the trigonal system, with rhombohedral crystals or rosettes being rarely found. The material is usually found in massive form and sometimes with botryoidal growth.

HERKIMER DIAMONDS
Concrete Manifestations

Color(s)	transparent
Chakra(s)	crown, third eye
Planet(s)	Saturn
Number(s)	18/9
Element(s)	earth
Mohs scale	7
Astro sign(s)	Capricorn

Affirmation I am clear, energized, and connected. I embrace my dreams and move actively toward manifesting them. My dreams are filled with ideas and inspiration. I awaken with a clear memory of my dreams and easily interpret them. The insights I receive from dreams bring clarity and understanding to my life.

Spiritual uses The Herkimer diamond lends a hand in dreamtime. It is the number-one tool to use for lucid dreaming, shamanic journeywork, and vision seeking. It heightens your consciousness and awareness as if you are turning on a light in a dark room. Use this stone to improve your spiritual sight and clairvoyance. You can use a Herkimer diamond to ask for assistance from Archangels Gabriel, Metatron, and Raziel.

Mental uses Herkimer diamonds assist in retaining information. As you study, read, or research, keep this stone nearby with the intention that you will be able to recall information you've acquired exactly when you need it. This stone also helps sharpen your focus and mental ability, and it awakens your desire to learn new things.

Emotional uses Herkimer diamonds help you to understand why you feel a certain way. They uncover and reveal the little pockets of stored memories that were buried long ago. With this stone in hand, you can begin healing these previously hidden memories and release them to make room for positive energy and new experiences.

Physical uses Associated with vim and vigor, a Herkimer diamond improves your ability to endure rigorous physical activity. This stone provides you with plenty of vivacious energy so you can perform amazing feats.

Divine guidance Are you able to recall your dreams? Dreams can be your internal psychologist or your spiritual advisor, so be sure to record them when you wake for later contemplation. If you do not recall your dreams, take the time before going to sleep to form the intention to remember your dreams upon waking. Dreams are powerful tools for self-healing, personal awareness, and spiritual growth.

> **About the stone:**
> Not actual diamonds, Herkimers are doubly terminated quartz (silicon dioxide) crystals found in and around Herkimer County, New York. Good specimens are brilliantly clear, free of most inclusions.

Hiddenite
Composed Calm

Color(s)	pale yellow to emerald green
Chakra(s)	solar plexus, heart
Planet(s)	Chiron, Moon, Neptune
Number(s)	49/4
Element(s)	fire, water
Mohs scale	6.5–7
Astro sign(s)	Gemini, Cancer, Pisces

Affirmation I am calm. I am at peace. My intuition is strong. It is easy for me to feel, sense, or know how others feel. I am compassionate and kind. I attract thoughtful, loving people. I create a financially successful life. I am a money magnet. I am wealthy and abundant.

Spiritual uses Hiddenite improves intuitive insights by aiding you in psychic development and training. Use this stone to provide a buffer during times when you are extremely sensitive to the thoughts, feelings, physical challenges, and emotions of others. This stone is an excellent tool to relieve your mind of the incessant chatter when you meditate.

Mental uses Due to the lithium content within, hiddenite aids you in releasing worrisome and repetitive thoughts. Use this stone to bring mental peace and serenity. This stone helps you shift your intention to what is truly important in your life. With hiddenite in hand, focus your attention on your dreams, wishes, goals, and desires.

Emotional uses Hiddenite enhances balance between your mind and your emotions. It helps you release feelings that have a strong emotional charge, thereby reducing overreaction to life situations. This stone improves self-love and allows nurturing from others. It aids with diplomacy and emotional control in both business and personal pursuits. It also boosts your magnetic vibration to attract romance, love, and committed relationship, such as marriage.

Physical uses Hiddenite helps with weight control, specifically to avoid weight gain. With hiddenite in hand, you will be able to overcome cravings, binging, and overindulgence. Use this stone to shift your entrepreneurial skills to a determined drive to succeed. It helps you attain all of which you are capable. This is a stone of great wealth and material success.

Divine guidance Have you been dreamy? Do you have many theories and ideas without plans for actualizing them? Are you lacking the will to move forward due to incessant thoughts which create blocks to your success? Regardless of your goal, it's time to overcome the thoughts, feelings, and emotions blocking you from being all you can be. Commit to loving yourself more; allow a life filled with success, joy, and love.

> **About the stone:**
> Hiddenite is the green variety of the mineral spodumene, lithium aluminum silicate. It crystallizes in the monoclinic system.

HOWLITE
Purity

COLOR(S)	white with pale-gray webbing (natural form) or turquoise (dyed)
CHAKRA(S)	crown
PLANET(S)	Ceres, Moon
NUMBER(S)	2
ELEMENT(S)	water
MOHS SCALE	2.5–3.5
ASTRO SIGN(S)	Cancer

Affirmation Blessings flow through me like a healing river. I am fluid. I am pure and clear. I take the time I need to relax in a pool, bath, or body of water. I drink the right amount of water to maintain a limber, healthy body.

Spiritual uses Howlite is a reminder to connect with the moon, its cycles, and the spiritual benefits derived from the moon's receptive vibrations. Use this stone to open to your intuitive skills. Focusing on this gem can deepen telepathic, psychometric, and visionary intuition. With this stone in hand, turn your attention toward Native American teachings of Buffalo Medicine and White Buffalo Calf Woman. Learn the lessons of mindfulness to Great Spirit and respect of all humankind. This stone reminds you to pray and respect your elders as well as the environment, taking no more than you need.

Mental uses Howlite, with its white energy, helps you clear your mind of chatter. Draw on the energy of this stone to stay focused; concentrate your efforts on a task or job at hand. It improves upon your ideas or the ideas of others by replicating them with a slightly different twist or enhancement.

Emotional uses Howlite is helpful for cooling heated emotions and regaining emotional balance. The calming white energy of this stone relieves intense pressure during potentially explosive situations. This stone also has a cleansing vibration. It provides you with a higher understanding of the source of emotional stress, giving you a new, lighter perspective.

Physical uses Howlite is beneficial for muscles, bones, teeth, and nails. This stone is a reminder to drink plenty of water for optimal health. It can signal that you need to sit in a tub and soak away your worries, toxins, and stress. This stone is also aligned with the breasts, breast milk, and nursing babies. The Divine Mother brings the healing value of nurturing to the forefront of any physical ailment.

Divine guidance Are you drinking enough water? Do you take time to immerse yourself in healing waters, such as a bath or a refreshing pool? Water purifies your body and mind. Hydrate yourself inside and out to maintain fluidity at all levels of consciousness. Allow the natural flow to detoxify your body, mind, and emotions.

About the stone:
Howlite is a calcium silicoborate forming an opaque material which is white with black matrix. Howlite is often dyed to imitate turquoise or lapis.

INDOCHINITE TEKTITE
Expect the Unexpected!

COLOR(S)	black
CHAKRA(S)	root, third eye, crown
PLANET(S)	all
NUMBER(S)	1
ELEMENT(S)	earth, air, fire, water
MOHS SCALE	6–7
ASTRO SIGN(S)	all

Affirmation I easily handle the unexpected. I stop, breathe, observe, and move forward with grace. Blessings come into my life seemingly from out of nowhere. I have unlimited potential and my possibilities are endless.

Spiritual uses Indochinite tektite is a meteoric glass that activates telepathic abilities. Used during meditation, this stone open the third eye center. It increases intuition as well as the ability to foretell potential realities concerning a situation. This is a good stone for channeling information from other realms. This stone helps you fuel your way to new spiritual understanding. It ignites the unlimited potential of your spiritual growth into dimensions not yet explored.

Mental uses Indochinite tektite is useful when you are trying to understand metaphysical concepts. It opens you up to otherworldly thinking and possibilities, allowing you to see things from an entirely new perspective. This is the tektite that will help you realize you can create a wrinkle in your reality by choosing to look at things differently, thereby changing your situation. This tektite opens you up to thinking outside your personal universe.

Emotional uses Indochinite tektite gives you an objective perspective on your emotional reactions to life circumstances. With this stone in hand, emotional charges dissipate, and attachments or expectations drop away. Use this stone to help you remove expectations you have of others. If you release your expectations, you will not be disappointed.

Physical uses Indochinite tektite helps heal old injuries. While holding this stone, make an intention to release the memories stored in old physical injuries—scars that hold the energy of what was happening at that time in your life when the injury occurred. Indochinite tektite is good stone for glass blowers, artists, visionary leaders, explorers, pioneers, inventors, and and people who use creativity in all areas of life.

Divine guidance Have you been noticing that things seem to happen unexpectedly? Are you surprised frequently in your life? Or perhaps you are working on a divinely inspired project and trying to make a splash with its presentation. Now is the time to have the courage to present your project to the world. Realign yourself through your intention to be in flow and acceptance. Be in a place of allowing and enjoy what life has in store for you.

About the stone:
Tektites are natural glass objects thought to be associated with meteoric activity, with local rock or sediment fusing into glass upon impact. They are comprised mostly of silica. Indochinite is named for the region this tektite was found in, namely the former French colonies of Indochina (Laos, Cambodia, and Vietnam).

IOLITE
Eloquent

Color(s)	violet-blue, blue, violet, or yellowish-gray
Chakra(s)	third eye
Planet(s)	Mercury, the asteroid Pallas
Number(s)	4
Element(s)	earth
Mohs scale	7–7.5
Astro sign(s)	Virgo

Affirmation I have good communication skills. I see clearly and navigate my way through life with ease. I observe and clear detrimental patterns and habits. I have healthy, balanced relationships. Meditation comes naturally to me.

Spiritual uses Iolite is a perfect gem for meditation. The indigo blue variety is a third eye stone to activate your ability to quiet your mind, slow down your thoughts, and relax. Use this stone to help you navigate through the dimensions of spiritual realities. It helps align you with the ability to receive communication from loved ones on the Other Side, spirit guides, and Ascended Masters.

Mental uses Iolite is a stone for writers, teachers, and anyone in the field of communications. This is a stone of focus that also helps you organize your thoughts. Employ this sparkling blue gem to improve your ability to find the right words to express yourself clearly and succinctly.

Emotional uses Through the use of your intellect in combination with this stone, you have an opportunity to find hidden patterns and repetitive events that cause emotional disturbances. Through contemplation and meditation you find the source of what disables you from connecting with others in healthy relationships. This discovery of self also relieves aggressive tendencies. Iolite is the perfect gem to help you stay focused on this goal.

Physical uses Iolite is helpful to improve the eyesight. Additionally use it to help you if you are directionally challenged. Use it when you are trying to find your way—like a compass showing you the way. Iolite deflects the electromagnetic waves from cell phones, TVs, and computers. Keep one on you if you are constantly around electronics.

Divine guidance Do you find that the same pattern repeats itself in your life? Are you trying to find your way—mentally, physically, spiritually or emotionally? Embrace your inner genius as you use your mind to find direction and clarity. See the options clearly and calmly. Express your truth in your words, actions, and thoughts.

> **About the stone:**
> Iolite is a silicate of magnesium and aluminum, with some of the magnesium often being replaced with iron and manganese. Iolite crystallizes in the orthorhombic system and has a characteristic inky blue or violet color.

JADE
Good Fortune

COLOR(S)	shades of green, white, gray, black, yellow, orange, and violet
CHAKRA(S)	heart
PLANET(S)	Venus, Jupiter
NUMBER(S)	3
ELEMENT(S)	air
MOHS SCALE	6–6.5
ASTRO SIGN(S)	Libra

Affirmation I am healthy, happy, and prosperous. I am extremely lucky. Good health is mine. I am grateful for all of the gifts that come into my life. All is well. I am joyous. Life is good. I pause for a moment of gratitude!

Spiritual uses Due to its strong association with ancient China, jade is the perfect stone for connecting more deeply with Eastern philosophies and cultures for spiritual development. Also revered by the Mayans, jade is a useful stone during rituals, ceremonies, or as an altar piece for prayer and meditation.

Mental uses Jade is historically associated with good luck and beneficial results. Use this stone to change your mind, when necessary, about anything. It reminds you to think positively and stay focused on good outcomes. It is also helpful for visualizing ideas and beneficial results.

Emotional uses Jade can assist you to uncover the source of emotional eating. These varying tones of jade guide you to uncover why you want to eat when emotionally upset. Employ jade in amulet form to discover of the source of the feelings and learn to embrace and accept yourself exactly as you are.

Physical uses Jade's association with cures for the loins and kidneys dates back to use by various Native American peoples; some used it as a cure for kidney ailments. On a physical wealth level, this royal gem has been used in Chinese culture as a symbol of wealth and high rank dating back to 3000 BCE.

Divine guidance If you are drawn to jade, it's time to uncover the part of you that knows how to manifest good results. Believe in luck, good fortune, and prosperity. An attraction to this stone can also signal a time to connect with the spiritual practices of the ancient Mayan culture or Buddhist practices.

> *About the stone:*
> Jade is a name for two minerals with similar toughness and appearances. Jadeite is the more highly prized harder mineral, while nephrite is more prolific and softer. Jadeite is a sodium aluminum silicate composed of granular crystals, while nephrite is composed of interlocking fibrous crystals of calcium magnesium silicate with the presence of iron.

JASPER, COBRA
The Power of Animals

Color(s)	shades of brown
Chakra(s)	root, navel, solar plexus
Planet(s)	Pluto, Ceres
Number(s)	7
Element(s)	earth
Mohs scale	6.5–7
Astro sign(s)	Scorpio

Affirmation Nature nurtures me. Animals and other creatures bring me messages that guide me in my life. My connection with Mother Earth provides vital energy. I am focused and grounded. I remember and act on the wisdom of my ancestors. I am always divinely protected.

Spiritual uses Composed of fossilized snail shells and palm, cobra jasper offers your consciousness a deeper understanding of your ancestors. This stone helps you get you in touch with qualities developed in previous lifetimes. Use this stone to strengthen your connection with the animal kingdom and the power of animal medicine. An excellent stone for shamanic journeywork, it amplifies your relationship to your power animal and enhances the visions within the journey. It's also helpful for the practice of rebirthing.

Mental uses Cobra jasper is a grounding stone that also helps you stay focused. It gathers your thoughts and synchronizes them, and thereby you, with the rhythms of the earth. Use this stone to become aware of mental patterns or repetitive thoughts to determine if they are in alignment with the vision you have for your life.

Emotional uses Cobra jasper enables you to delve deep into your emotional body through the inner-journey process. This stone makes the journey easier to explore what might be otherwise uncomfortable. With this stone in hand, heal the part of you that is heartbroken, and give birth to the new you.

Physical uses Cobra jasper supports fertility, pregnancy, and the birthing process. Physical exercise through gardening is helpful for healing the physical body of many ailments, and this stone is a perfect ally to aid you in growing a beautiful garden or crop.

Divine guidance Have you been getting outdoors enough? Are you feeling stagnant? It is time to reconnect with nature. Get out there and put your hands in the earth. Garden, walk in nature, play with animals, and allow the earth beneath your feet and the sun above your head to nurture and realign you.

About the stone:
Cobra jasper is also known as calligraphy stone, Indian script stone, and elephant skin jasper, but it's currently not clear whether this stone is, in fact, a jasper (micro-crystallized silicon dioxide). The stone consists of a reddish brown opaque matrix containing multiple yellow inclusions of a harder, fossilized material. It is found in India.

JASPER, DALMATIAN
Loyalty and Unconditional Love

Color(s)	off-white with tan and black mottling
Chakra(s)	crown, root
Planet(s)	Venus
Number(s)	2
Element(s)	air
Mohs scale	6.5–7
Astro sign(s)	Libra

Affirmation I attract loyal people into my life. I cultivate and maintain meaningful relationships. I am a loyal and faithful person to all. My life is balanced. I trust myself fully. I know when to take action or remain still and quiet. I embrace the masculine and feminine energy within me.

Spiritual uses Dalmatian jasper is a tool for deepening the meditative state, helping you to maintain peace within your inner being. It helps you understand the duality of life. On planet Earth there is darkness, and there is light. This stone helps you stay focused on the light while embracing the darkness. This division into two mutually exclusive, opposed, or contradictory groups—light and darkness—is a point of contemplation. With this stone in hand, you can uncover what that means, and how to find the fine balance between the opposing forces.

Mental uses Dalmatian jasper is a helpful tool when you are working on becoming aware of your thoughts. Use this stone to determine what you are saying to yourself. Use it to gain clarity through contrast and clear delineation between black and white. This stone is perfect for helping you trust yourself and develop feelings of self-loyalty.

Emotional uses Dalmatian jasper is a stone of relationships. It holds the energy of Dog Medicine, which teaches us about loyalty and unconditional love. This stone is a reminder that the love, adoration, and companionship of a dog is healing and nurturing. With this stone in hand, focus on being loyal to yourself and loving yourself unconditionally.

Physical uses Dalmatian jasper supports your body's physical balance. This is a good stone for those who participate in the martial arts, tai chi, or chi gung. Its strong association for balancing the yin-yang energy creates a vibration that helps you capture the essence of this art for health and well-being. This is a good stone for a veterinarian, animal communicator, or anyone who works with animals.

Divine guidance Is your or someone else's loyalty in question? Are you building relationships with trustworthy and reliable people? Take a look deep into yourself to check in on your own level of fidelity and dependability. Do you have a strong association with animals? You can benefit through a connection with an animal companion for overall well-being.

About the stone:
Jasper is micro-crystallized quartz (silicon dioxide) heavily colored by iron and other impurities. The material is opaque. Dalmatian jasper is named for its resemblance to the breed of spotted dogs.

JASPER, KAMBAMBA
Soothe Your Nerves

Color(s)	green and blue
Chakra(s)	heart
Planet(s)	Saturn
Number(s)	9
Element(s)	earth
Mohs scale	6.5–7
Astro sign(s)	Capricorn

Affirmation I am calm and relaxed. The nourishing green energy of nature soothes my body, mind, and spirit. I am connected with the wisdom of my ancestors. Only goodness and love are allowed in my space. I am protected from negative influences.

Spiritual uses Kambamba jasper is a mystical stone that aligns you with inner peace inherent in your true nature. This stone opens you up to allow more love, calm, and tolerance into your consciousness. Hold it in the palm of your hand during meditation while you focus and breathe deeply. This mysterious-looking stone can be a tool to uncover karmic lessons brought forward from other lifetimes as well as this one.

Mental uses Kambamba jasper is beneficial when you are setting the intention to release yourself from negative or toxic thoughts, especially those that have been part of your consciousness seemingly forever.

Emotional uses Kambamba jasper calms and soothes emotional upsets. This stone is good for opening your heart, helping to increase prosperity, reduce inflammation, and improve your ability to give love and receive love. Its green energy opens your heart to loving yourself and others more fully and completely. It is also a good stone to keep nearby during regression therapy. The stone contains stromatolites, which are among the oldest fossils on earth, considered to be over 3 billion years old, which provides it with the energy to help dislodge any stored information that is causing a repetitive pattern in your emotional consciousness.

Physical uses The blue-green algae fossilized within Kambamba jasper carries the vibration of assistance, which is useful when you are releasing and removing toxins from your physical body. It helps when you are aiming to replace essential vital nutrients in your body. It also assists in the assimilation of vitamins and minerals. The green energy of this stone activates your ability to increase prosperity and abundance. Use it with the intention of increasing the money flow in your life.

Divine guidance Have you made a conscious decision to rid yourself of negative thoughts, beliefs, and behavior patterns? It is time to focus on your goals and intentions. Feed your body, mind, and spirit with the soothing vibrations of this blue-green energy.

About the stone:
Jasper is micro-crystallized quartz (silicon dioxide) heavily colored by iron and other impurities. Kambamba jasper is a rare orbicular jasper from Madagascar thought to contain stromatolites, ancient fossilized algae.

JASPER, LEOPARDSKIN
Flexibility

COLOR(S)	shades of brown, green, and red with mottling
CHAKRA(S)	root, navel, solar plexus
PLANET(S)	Neptune, Pluto, Chiron
NUMBER(S)	5
ELEMENT(S)	water
MOHS SCALE	6.5–7
ASTRO SIGN(S)	Scorpio, Pisces

Affirmation I am flexible and adaptable. I objectively observe circumstances and seize new opportunities as situations naturally shift and change in my life. I bend and flex with the flow of life around me. There is no resistance, only willingness to go with the flow.

Spiritual uses Leopardskin jasper grounds your spiritual practice through earth-centered spirituality. This mottled stone is beneficial for use in medicine wheel ceremonies, drumming circles, or shamanic journeywork. This jasper grounds your spiritual practice and increases your flexibility in exploring different spiritual avenues. It helps you to stretch yourself beyond your comfort zone in spiritual matters, as you delve into the nagual (Toltec spirituality) energy of the big cats such as leopards, jaguars, and panthers. Make use of this stone to enter other-dimensional realities with the intention of personal transformation.

Mental uses Leopardskin jasper is the stone of self-observation. It allows you to fully recognize that your beliefs, thoughtforms, and mental energy, were imposed or established by others. This realization makes it possible to consciously decide to discard what is no longer appropriate and retain that which has a positive influence.

Emotional uses With self-observation as your intention, leopardskin jasper assists you in releasing emotional patterns. The Cat Medicine within this stone can be useful as you stalk your emotions to uncover the source of repetitive patterns in your relationships, career, or any aspect of your life with gentleness and ease.

Physical uses Leopardskin jasper is a stone of flexibility that provides support for your muscles and tendons. This is a good stone for yoga instructors and massage therapists. It is also good for the general well-being of your bones, teeth, hair, and blood circulation. Use this stone with selenite and calcite to create a grid in your exercise room.

Divine guidance Are people around you suddenly changing their tune? Have you decided it's time to change yours? Do you need to be more flexible like a leopard? Stalk yourself mentally, physically, spiritually, and emotionally. Observe yourself and those around you to be mindful of the predominant intention.

About the stone:
Leopardskin jasper is an orbicular jasper with spherical inclusions in animal-like colors. Completely opaque, it gives the impression of the spots seen on a leopard.

JASPER, MOOKAITE
Strength

Color(s)	shades of red, mustard-yellow, mauve, and purple
Chakra(s)	root, navel, solar plexus, heart, third eye, crown
Planet(s)	Saturn
Number(s)	4
Element(s)	water
Mohs scale	6–7
Astro sign(s)	Capricorn

Affirmation I am strong. My inner core is powerful. I am physically fit, mentally focused, and emotionally balanced. Vital life force flows vigorously through me, providing me with the endurance to remain strong in all areas of my life.

Spiritual uses Mookaite jasper has a twofold benefit: the purple-mauve shade realigns your physical chakras with the spiritual being you truly are, and the yellow shade is helpful for increasing the possibility of revelations and realizations during contemplative meditation practice.

Mental uses Mookaite encourages you to find a way to keep your mind stable. Use this stone as a tool to keep yourself focused and grounded. Mookaite can be used to soothe your mind, quiet distracting thoughts, and keep you on task to reach your goal. It is a good stone to keep on your desk or workspace to promote the aforementioned qualities.

Emotional uses Mookaite is found in creek beds, and as such, it inherently holds the vibration of going below the watery surface of your emotions to tap into the core issues that cause emotional upset. This stone can be found in a variety of color combinations. The yellow in this stone specifically is associated with the solar plexus chakra and your focus on self-worth, self-confidence, and the courage to be all that you can be.

Physical uses The red vibration specifically in mookaite is associated with the root chakra and the basic survival needs of food, shelter, and water— which translate into the foundation for prosperity. It is the stone of motivation and is a perfect antidote for procrastination. The vibrant red vibration promotes well-being and inner strength. The red energy also increases endurance. With this stone in hand, use water therapy to heal your physical body and the correct amount of fluid intake to maintain homeostasis.

Divine guidance Have you been procrastinating lately or avoiding some tasks? Perhaps you've avoided looking at an emotional issue that needs resolution. Take the time to find the root cause of emotional patterns. Remove challenges that have been entrenched in your emotional body and heal once and for all. Everything will fall into place.

About the stone:
Mookaite jasper is micro-crystallized quartz (silicon dioxide) heavily colored by iron and other impurities. The material is opaque and generally refers to jasper found in Australia's outback.

Jasper, Orbicular
Go with the Flow

Color(s)	generally white with spherical inclusions in a variety of colors; the meanings below focus on the green ones
Chakra(s)	crown, heart
Planet(s)	Mars, Neptune, Moon
Number(s)	0
Element(s)	water
Mohs scale	6.5–7
Astro sign(s)	Aries, Pisces, Cancer

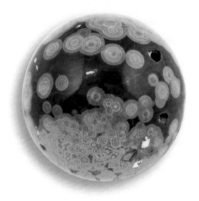

Affirmation I glide through life with balance and grace. I am mindful of my thoughts, words, and actions. I go with the flow. My emotions are stabilized. I manifest a happy, joyful life through the intentional creation of reality. I am conscious of the power of the Law of Attraction.

Spiritual uses The orblike inclusions of orbicular jasper provide a tool for focus during meditation and for getting to the center of yourself. This stone helps align you with All That Is. Use this stone for insight into your past lives so you can recall your spiritual lessons.

Mental uses Orbicular jasper aids in the understanding of the universal Law of Attraction and Reciprocity. Due to its spherical patterns, it holds the vibration of how thoughts, words, and actions interact in our world. This stone is a reminder of the circular flow of energy—how what you send out comes back to you. All thoughts travel in a circular direction, returning as manifest reality.

Emotional uses Found on the shores of the ocean, orbicular jasper holds the vibration of the tides of your emotions and the ebb and flow of your feelings. Use this stone as a tool to help you during times when you are working on emotional issues that seem to come and go—just as the tides of the ocean come and go. This stone is especially beneficial if your emotions are like bubbling lava in a volcano ready to erupt. This stone can ease you into a calmer state of being.

Physical uses Use this stone when you need to balance your sodium and iodine levels and relieve water retention for overall health. This stone is useful for getting the most detoxifying benefits from hydrotherapy and salt baths. Keep this stone close by when you need the energy of the seashore to regenerate and renew you.

Divine guidance Have you been yearning to return to or visit the ocean? Do stories of the legendary city of Atlantis pique your interest? It is time to visit the nearest ocean and rebalance yourself in the salty water. If you are unable to get to the ocean, go to the nearest body of water to find balance. Investigate the legends of mermaids and sirens to uncover another layer of understanding of yourself.

About the stone:
Orbicular jasper is a form of spherulitic chalcedony, micro-crystallized quartz (silicon dioxide) colored by oxides, iron, and other impurities. Quartz and feldspar form the spherical (orbicular) structures. Orbicular jasper from Madagascar with green, tan, and brown coloring is also known as ocean jasper; poppy jasper is a red and yellow colored orbicular jasper from California. *See also* jasper, leopardskin.

Jasper, Red
Manifesto Presto!

Color(s)	red
Chakra(s)	root, navel
Planet(s)	Mars, Saturn
Number(s)	4
Element(s)	fire, earth
Mohs scale	6–7.5
Astro sign(s)	Aries, Capricorn

Affirmation I am grounded and focused on the task at hand. I complete projects. I enjoy and share the result of my creative endeavors. I am motivated to accomplish all that needs to be done. I live life with vim, vigor, and vitality. My passion for living is dynamic.

Spiritual uses Red jasper holds a high vibration for spiritual discipline and therefore helps you clear your mind. It helps you to be mindful during prayer and contemplation and increases your endurance and focus during long spiritual ceremonies or practices. This red stone is a good reminder to stay focused when establishing a new spiritual discipline. Use red jasper to connect with Archangel Ariel.

Mental uses Red jasper helps you put an end to procrastination. Use this stone when you have a task at hand that requires focus and mental endurance for successful completion. As it is the stone of diligence, you can use it to maintain steadfast concentration to any goal.

Emotional uses Red jasper reactivates your passion for living when you've been feeling apathetic, unemotional, or spiritually defunct. Because of its red-hot vibration, this is not a stone for use when you are angry or agitated. Rather, employ this stone when you are feeling blue or bored to counteract the vibration of disinterest.

Physical uses Red jasper is the stone of endurance. Use it when you are focusing on developing your strength and improving your vital life force. This stone is useful for restoring, regenerating, and rejuvenating your passion and libido. A stone of fertility, this gemstone supports a healthy pregnancy and birth. Use this stone when healing blood-related diseases or imbalance.

Divine guidance Are you procrastinating? Are you feeling like you just don't have the energy to move forward? It is time to take action and complete what you have planned. Speak up for yourself. Follow through, and take the necessary steps to see your projects to fruition. Have confidence in your own ability to make things happen.

> **About the stone:**
> Jasper is micro-crystallized quartz (silicon dioxide). The material is opaque, and the color is formed by the oxidation of the iron present, in addition to other impurities.

JASPER, YELLOW
Inner Strength

COLOR(S)	mustard yellow
CHAKRA(S)	solar plexus, third eye, crown
PLANET(S)	Mercury
NUMBER(S)	40/4
ELEMENT(S)	air
MOHS SCALE	6–7.5
ASTRO SIGN(S)	Gemini

Affirmation I have a deep inner connection with the earth and the sun. I'm connected with the strength from within. My inner strength amplifies my self-confidence and courage. I act fearlessly. I am enthusiastic. It gives me pleasure to compliment and encourage others. Joy is a normal part of my life!

Spiritual uses Jasper has historically been used by medicine men and women for protection, and yellow jasper is specifically beneficial to deflect jealousy. This stone connects you with your inner strength and courage. It amplifies the potency of your solar plexus, keeping you protected during spiritual practices such shamanic journeywork and deep meditation.

Mental uses Yellow jasper enhances mental clarity. When something is "as clear as mud," hold on to a piece of yellow jasper and visualize your mind clearing so you can more accurately see the situation at hand. This stone aids in discernment and understanding. Use it when you need to set boundaries.

Emotional uses Yellow jasper is beneficial when you are trying to absorb and understand your own feelings. When you are having difficulty putting your finger on what you are feeling, this stone can help you recognize the emotions at play and assist in coming up with some ideas to help you feel better.

Physical uses Yellow jasper aids with digestion, specifically with the proper functioning of the gall bladder, liver, pancreas, spleen, and kidneys. This stone is useful for helping you to hone in on the clarity you need to make important changes to your diet (including your mental diet!) to maintain a healthy digestive process.

Divine guidance Are you having a hard time sorting out all the details of what's going on around you and within you? Do you need to gain some understanding to get clear on what direction you want to head? It is time to take a grounded approach and gather realistic solutions by taking the necessary time to examine yourself and the situation through quiet contemplation.

About the stone:
Jasper is micro-crystallized quartz (silicon dioxide). The material is opaque and the color is formed by the oxidation of the iron present as well as the presence of other impurities.

JASPER, ZEBRA
It's Black and White

Color(s)	black and white
Chakra(s)	crown, root
Planet(s)	Saturn
Number(s)	4
Element(s)	earth
Mohs scale	6.5
Astro sign(s)	Capricorn

Affirmation I stay focused on what I'm doing. My connection with the earth is strong. I feel safe and secure. I'm a self-motivated person. I get things done. I am very perceptive and discerning in all areas of my life. I see things from varying perspectives.

Spiritual uses Zebra jasper joins the heaven above you with the earth below you. Garner the vibes of this stone to enhance your yoga practice or when incorporating tai chi or chi gung into your life. This jasper further improves a grounded, spiritual life, keeping one's focus on practical paths rather than on unattainable ideals. It is also useful for shamanic journeywork or getting in touch with your animal totem.

Mental uses Zebra jasper is beneficial for a writer who is avoiding the process of writing. With this stone in hand, you are more apt to sit down and put pen to paper. This jasper carries the energy of mental clarity, giving you the ability to sort through all of the details of a project. When things don't appear to be black and white, this stone helps you sort through all the shades of gray.

Emotional uses Zebra jasper is an excellent stone to have on hand if you want to feel safe. Work with this black and white stone when you are feeling ambiguous about your emotions so you can get a handle on your own personal truth. Working with this stone also promotes balance in your life.

Physical uses Zebra jasper provides you with the physical endurance you need for staying focused on what needs to get done while maintaining the motivation to do it. It is a good stone to have on hand if you are easily distracted. It helps you concentrate on what you need to do in the moment rather than on every other thing that you need to get done later.

Divine guidance Do you see everything as either black or white? Is there no in-between for you? It is important to clearly define some things in your life while remaining open to possibilities—in other words, look for the common ground and that unique "in-between" point of view.

> **About the stone:**
> Jasper is micro-crystallized quartz (silicon dioxide). The material is opaque, and the color is formed by oxidized iron as well as the presence of other impurities. The name describes the appearance of the material.

JET
Cooling Fires

COLOR(S)	black
CHAKRA(S)	root
PLANET(S)	Pluto
NUMBER(S)	16/7
ELEMENT(S)	fire
MOHS SCALE	2–4
ASTRO SIGN(S)	Scorpio

Affirmation I am clear-headed. I'm aligned with my natural rhythms. Meditation is effortless for me, and I practice regularly. I am at peace. I am safe and sound. Divine protection always surrounds me. I am aligned and connected with this present moment.

Spiritual uses Jet is the mystic's stone. With the right intention, it can expand your consciousness to include the belief that spontaneous enlightenment is achievable. This grounding stone relaxes your consciousness into deep meditative practices by quieting the incessant chatter that often arises when your intention is on having "no mind." Jet is also useful for deflecting psychic attacks.

Mental uses Jet quiets your mind. Use it to decompress and release the pressure on your mind. With this stone in hand, you can release any anxiety you are feeling and allow your affairs to unfold with ease. It helps you ignite the fuel for your mind to conjure creative thoughts; it also provides solutions outside the norm.

Emotional uses Jet has a cooling effect on your emotions. With its peaceful vibration, this stone calms you when you are agitated and brings serenity to your consciousness. This stone is very beneficial during the grieving process, especially during the anger stage. When used with conscious intention, it helps reduce angry feelings.

Physical uses Jet is helpful for removing toxins in the body, especially in the case of food poisoning, drug abuse, alcoholism, and smoking. Use this stone during detoxification as a supportive aid. It is especially helpful for people recovering from overuse or abuse of drugs, foods, and alcohol. It is even useful during the process of becoming a nonsmoker.

Divine guidance Are you lacking focus? Do you feel unprotected or ungrounded? Are you grieving the loss of someone, something, or some aspect of your life that no longer applies? It is normal to grieve over the lost of something or someone who was part of your life for a very long time. You must now align yourself with the reality that this no longer exists in your everyday life. You will find the grounding and peace you need to move forward with calmness and serenity. You have the ability to have a great awakening.

About the stone:
Jet is a fossilized wood that has turned into coal. It is formed from driftwood that was deposited in stagnant water. Over time, a mix of chemicals, the decaying process, and intense pressure caused the material to harden. Jet was used in jewelry in England since before the Roman Empire, and it is considered an organic gem material.

KUNZITE
Miracles and Love

Color(s)	translucent, pale pink, or pale purple
Chakra(s)	heart
Planet(s)	Juno, Venus
Number(s)	13/4
Element(s)	air
Mohs scale	6–7.5
Astro sign(s)	Taurus, Libra

Affirmation I am love. All that surrounds me and all that is attracted to me is love. I look within and love myself exactly as I am. I attract love, joy, and happiness into my life. I am comforted. I am blessed! I have an entourage of angels and spirit guides.

Spiritual uses Kunzite is a reminder that love is the answer to all. Use this stone to radiate love in a wide circumference around your being. With the heart chakra being the center of your consciousness, love is who you truly are. This stone is useful in your meditation practice for expanding your sphere of love. Kunzite is associated with Archangels Chamuel, Gabriel, Haniel, and Metatron.

Mental uses Kunzite helps you maintain your focus and attention on your heart chakra and love. Use this stone to imagine that all that you are, all you do, and all you attract is love. This stone emanates love and well-being, so use this vibration to telepathically transmit loving thoughts to people, places, and things to make the world a better place. It is ideal to use in circumstances with discordant words and thoughts, transforming and transmuting them into harmonious interactions.

Emotional uses Kunzite helps you attract healthy romantic relationships as well as supportive loving friendships and good business colleagues. This stone encourages kindness, compassion, and tolerance. It also reduces stress and worry and helps relieve depression and anxiety. Use kunzite when you need to discover how to nurture yourself. This is the perfect stone to help you realize how you want to be loved and how to love yourself. When you learn these two things, you begin to attract others who will love you the way you deserve to be loved.

Physical uses With its loving energy, kunzite is good for supporting the health of your physical heart as well as your general health, as love heals all things. With kunzite in hand, imagine love vibrating in every cell, bone, and muscle in your physical body. This practice amplifies the degree of healing for yourself and others as well. This stone also helps relieve stress-related diseases. According to some sources, stress is the source of all diseases.

Divine guidance Are you looking for more love in your life? You are good at giving love and can open even more to receive loving supportive friends and family in your life. You are ready to increase the love in your life as well as the miracles that occur all around you. Determine how you want to be loved and start out by loving yourself in that way.

About the stone:
Kunzite is the pink to light purple to variety of the mineral spodumene, lithium aluminum silicate. It crystallizes in the monoclinic system.

KYANITE
Alignment

Color(s)	deep blue
Chakra(s)	crown, third eye, throat
Planet(s)	Earth, Uranus
Number(s)	7, 11
Element(s)	earth
Mohs scale	4–7
Astro sign(s)	Virgo, Aquarius, Pisces

Affirmation I am balanced. My body is calm and relaxed. I sleep well and rejuvenate my body, mind, and spirit through my actions. I receive divine guidance simply and clearly. I am one with all that is. My chakras are balanced. I am aligned with the Divine.

Spiritual uses Kyanite is the stone for activating your innate ability to communicate telepathically. The soothing blue shades of this stone align the spiritual being within you with the higher realms of consciousness, enhancing your ability to receive and transmit information on all levels. This stone teams up with selenite to align your energy centers so they are harmoniously working to provide a perfect vessel for communication with the higher realms, especially the Archangels Metatron, Michael, Sandalphon, Seraphiel, and Tzaphkiel.

Mental uses Kyanite is a good stone to have on your desk while studying or trying to figure out a solution to a problem. Use this stone to support you when you are consciously transforming ideas into manifest reality. Selenite amplifies its ability to help you consciously create desired circumstances.

Emotional uses Kyanite calms the emotions. Its blue energy helps to balance an aura that has too much red energy—in other words, it brings a calming energy to anyone suffering from anger or other inflammatory emotions through faulty perceptions. This is a stone with many useful qualities. It can be used to align the chakras, and it strengthens feelings of peace and serenity.

Physical uses The blue vibration of kyanite automatically assists the physical body in balancing inflammations when used in conscious conjunction with deep relaxation, improved eating habits, and adequate, refreshing sleep. The calming vibration of this stone adds a holistic component to the treatment of inflammation-related disease. Kyanite is beneficial for healing and aligning the spinal cord and the overall skeletal structure.

Divine guidance Have you been feeling off-kilter? Are you confused? Does life seem chaotic? Focus your intention on balance and consciously align your chakras. As you regain your center, you can connect with higher wisdom and use your intuition as a daily part of your life. Take the time right now to stop, quiet your mind, and go into a contemplative state.

About the stone:
Kyanite is an aluminum silicate that crystallizes in the triclinic system. Bladed crystals are often splintered due to perfect cleavage; the hardness is directional. The material is much softer in the direction of the crystal's length.

LABRADORITE
Wide-Angle Lens

COLOR(S)	reflective shades of green with blue hues
CHAKRA(S)	heart, third eye, crown
PLANET(S)	Neptune
NUMBER(S)	7
ELEMENT(S)	water
MOHS SCALE	6–6.5
ASTRO SIGN(S)	Pisces

Affirmation My inner light shines brightly for all to see. I am a shining star. I am love. My intuition is strong. I perceive life from a higher perspective. I take time for reflection. I observe how the world around me is a mirror of the world within me.

Spiritual uses Labradorite helps you reflect on your inner light. It also helps you recognize the varying effects that light, color, and sound have on your consciousness and spiritual practices. This makes it a good stone for metaphysicians or those interested in New Age thought. This is a useful stone for meditation, lucid dreaming, psychic development, and spiritual awareness. It expands the awareness of the heart and mind.

Mental uses Labradorite is the philosopher's stone, helping you to examine the recesses of your mind. Use this stone to shine light on the knowledge and wisdom within you. A good study aid, it helps you increase your intelligence. It is also helpful for contemplation and amplifies your ability to perceive life through a wide-angle lens. Gaze into this stone, allowing light to refract off it, while you imagine or visualize the answers to whatever you search for arising in your awareness.

Emotional uses Labradorite guides you toward understanding the "mirrors" in your relationships, helping you to better see your relationship with yourself. It also enables you to see through the various layers of your emotions. It is ideal for when you are in the process of reinventing yourself. It supports you through the cycle of getting to know previously hidden aspects of yourself, and it helps you recognize features and characteristics that were eclipsed behind old preconceived notions.

Physical uses Labradorite is beneficial for general health of the eyes, nerves, brain, bones, and spinal cord. This stone assists when you need to rebalance the distribution of chemicals in the brain, especially for those challenged with multiple sclerosis, cerebral palsy, Parkinson's disease, optic neuritis, retinal problems, and psychotic episodes. Use this stone in the material world of commerce to pick up on the subtleties of the marketplace and to make shrewd adjustments to business plans.

Divine guidance Have you been reflecting on your life lately? Is it time to contemplate what is truly important? Use the many tools you have available to you to focus your intention on understanding the inner workings of your heart and how you relate to others. Make the necessary adjustments to realign your material and physical selves, as well as your mental, emotional, and spiritual selves.

About the stone:
Labradorite is a member of the plagioclase series of feldspars composed of a varying mixture of sodium aluminum silicate and calcium aluminum silicate. Labradorite crystallizes in the triclinic system; however, it is usually found in massive form with characteristic iridescence. The variety mined in Finland is known as spectrolite and displays an even greater range of iridescence.

Lapis Lazuli
Intuition

Color(s)	deep dark blue with metallic gold flecks
Chakra(s)	third eye, crown
Planet(s)	Jupiter
Number(s)	3
Element(s)	fire
Mohs scale	5–6
Astro sign(s)	Sagittarius

Affirmation I am focused. I see, sense, feel, and know the truth. I follow my intuition. It is easy for me to meditate. My entourage of angels orchestrates my life. I receive messages all the time and follow my internal guidance system. Sage wisdom is innate within me.

Spiritual uses Lapis lazuli opens the third eye and the intuitive senses when used with conscious intent. This is a good stone for helping you remember your dreams and promoting clarity during dreamtime. Use this stone to channel the Other Side, for mediumship, and to access the Akashic Records (the cosmic library). Use lapis lazuli to invite assistance from Archangels Camael, Metatron, and Michael.

Mental uses Lapis lazuli is a grounding stone that helps you focus on your studies. It improves your concentration and focus, and it can be used while taking a test to align with the higher knowledge accessible to all. This stone is especially beneficial for integrating the more complex, scholarly subjects of higher education.

Emotional uses The deep blue vibration of lapis lazuli calms feelings of frustration, agitation, and anger. With this stone in hand, you can find ways to deal with the emotional turmoil resulting from abuse—physical, mental, or emotional—to heal and find inner peace. The calming energy of lapis lazuli is useful for issues related to inner child work, alcohol, and drug addictions as well as sex addiction. The deep blue color of this stone helps heal anger and rage.

Physical uses Like all stones that carry dark-blue energy, lapis lazuli can assist in calming inflammations. The cooling vibration of dark blue reduces the effects of inflammatory diseases. Use this stone after surgery or when healing from a sprain or strained muscle or ligament. When used with conscious direction, this stone also improves eyesight. Since calcite, sodalite, and pyrite are often found within lapis lazuli, refer to each of these stones' pages to gain a deeper understanding of this gemstone.

Divine guidance Have you noticed that you are very intuitive lately? Are you listening to your inner guidance? Perhaps it's time to let go of the extra stress you've taken on, and just relax. Let go of anger and frustration. Listen to that still, small voice within to find the answers you seek.

About the stone:
Lapis lazuli is considered a rock because it is composed of several minerals, including hauynite, sodalite, noselite, and lazurite, along with the presence of calcite and pyrite. Hauynite causes the blue color, while the calcite is responsible for the white inclusions. These minerals and impurities may be present to varying degrees.

LARIMAR
Oceans of Loving Communication

COLOR(S)	varies from white to light-blue to green-blue to deep blue
CHAKRA(S)	throat
PLANET(S)	Neptune
NUMBER(S)	11, 12
ELEMENT(S)	water
MOHS SCALE	4.5–5
ASTRO SIGN(S)	Aquarius, Pisces

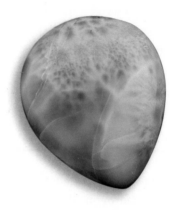

Affirmation I listen and really hear what others are saying. Others listen to me and understand what I am communicating. I am in touch with my emotions. I breathe in life completely. It is easy for me to relax into the ebb and flow of life. I am balanced, whole, and complete.

Spiritual uses Larimar is ideal for telepathic communication, which is transmitted from heart to heart and translated from mind to mind. Associated with Dolphin Medicine, use this stone to align you with interspecies communication to hear and know messages from other realms of consciousness. This stone is good for animal communicators, as well as a good one to use to experience rebirthing. With larimar in hand, connect with Archangels Muriel and Thuriel.

Mental uses Coupled with the power of breath, larimar can help you gain more clarity in your life. This stone helps you identify and ask for what you need and want. It also reminds you to pay attention to your words and thoughts and what they are creating in your life.

Emotional uses Larimar helps you get in touch with your emotions in a balanced way, filling your awareness with sunshine and love. Using this stone is almost like relaxing on sandy beach on a beautiful day. This is the stone of loving and clear communication and the healing that accompanies it from a higher realm.

Physical uses Larimar supports the general health of those who live or work near the ocean or otherwise have a strong attraction or need for the ocean. Use this stone to remind you to spend time near the salty spray of the ocean. Because this stone is found in the saltwater of the Caribbean, larimar's salt vibration also helps rebalance the thyroid and iodine levels.

Divine guidance Do you have an affinity for dolphins? Have you found that you feel so much better after spending time at the shore? It's time to spend some time by the ocean. Connect with the healing, salty energy of the seawater and its cleansing properties to support both your physical and emotional health. If you can't get to the ocean, take the time to enjoy a salt bath.

About the stone:
Larimar is a greenish-blue to blue variety of pectolite, a sodium calcium silicate. Though pectolite has been found in many locations, this blue variety has only been found in the Dominican Republic.

LEPIDOLITE
Balance Emotions

COLOR(S)	shades of lavender, sometimes with pink inclusions
CHAKRA(S)	solar plexus, third eye, crown
PLANET(S)	Neptune
NUMBER(S)	3
ELEMENT(S)	water
MOHS SCALE	2.5–3
ASTRO SIGN(S)	Pisces

Affirmation I embrace my emotions. Nurturing energy surrounds me. My emotional body is aligned. I recognize the love within me. I attract loving, balanced friends and family into my inner circle. I am calm. I am serene. Tranquility and peace are mine.

Spiritual uses Lepidolite helps to hone psychic skills, including channeling and mediumship, while fostering a reasonable hold on this reality. It helps you open up neural pathways in the brain to access higher realms of consciousness as well as information from other realms of existence.

Mental uses Lepidolite encourages a healthy, detached outlook on situations. The pink tourmaline inclusions are a reminder to maintain a loving force. This stone is good to hold on to when you are feeling mentally unstable or vulnerable. It helps you tap into another level of understanding and to see things from a greater perspective.

Emotional uses Lepidolite carries the vibration of lithium, which is used medically to balance the emotions and limit or eliminate extreme mood swings, while the vibration of the pink tourmaline is beneficial for opening the heart center. With this stone in hand, open your heart to love, feel the nurturing vibration, and restore balance in your life.

Physical uses The lithium contained within lepidolite holds the power to rebalance brain function and neurological functions. This stone is beneficial for depression and mental illness stemming from mood swings. Use this stone while in the process of healing neurological associated diseases. Employ it to overcome economic slumps, personally or in commerce, as it helps you maintain equilibrium even when the marketplace is acting like a roller coaster with funds. It can help you maintain a positive outlook when financial markets seem instable.

Divine guidance Have you been feeling depressed? Do you have mood swings? It is time to restore your well-being. A joyful outlook on life can be yours. Take the necessary steps to shift your focus from that which troubles you to that which brings you joy. Recognize that life flows in circles and all cycles shift and change. Focus on how you want your reality to manifest.

About the stone:
Lepidolite is a silicate containing lithium, aluminum, and potassium. It is often found with other lithium minerals such as tourmaline. Lepidolite crystallizes in the monoclinic system; however, it is usually found in massive form.

LODESTONE
Magnetized

COLOR(S)	grayish-black
CHAKRA(S)	root
PLANET(S)	Saturn
NUMBER(S)	8
ELEMENT(S)	earth
MOHS SCALE	5.5–6
ASTRO SIGN(S)	Capricorn

Affirmation I am a magnet for all of the good things in life. I attract loyal and trustworthy acquaintances and colleagues, and positive situations. I ask for what I need, and receive it with an open heart. I take the action necessary to attract financial success, good relationships, and safe surroundings.

Spiritual uses Ideal for grounding and protection, lodestone can be used to improve your connection with the earth. When used with intention, it points toward safe and protected spiritual directions. It is beneficial for use in deep meditative states and shamanic journeywork. Use this stone to aid you as you delve into the world of power animals, nature spirits, and interspecies communication.

Mental uses Lodestone's magnetic qualities draw to you whatever you think about and focus on. With this stone in hand, you can create a happy and healthy life by clearing negative thoughts and replacing them with positive thoughts and belief systems. This stone helps improve spoken and telepathic communication. It aids in reading between the lines to truly grasp what is being said or written.

Emotional uses A stone of good luck, lodestone helps you focus your attention on creating a world filled with good fortune for yourself and your loved ones. When you are unsure of how to proceed with your life, it also helps you find direction. Use this stone to maintain a positive outlook using the energy of magnetism inherent within the stone.

Physical uses Lodestone supports your efforts at improving your physical health. This stone can be used as a talisman during travel based on its historical use for navigation. It is also beneficial for eyesight and childbirth. With its vibration of good fortune, you can also use it conjure up money or other things of a material nature that you are trying to manifest in your life.

Divine guidance What are you magnetizing in your life? Are you happy with all that you are manifesting? Remember that your thoughts and beliefs create reality, so change your thoughts, stop worrying, and create the life you really want! Have courage and faith as you navigate your way through life. Telepathically send out the message of all that you wish to be and that you wish to create and then believe in your ability to magnetize it into your life.

About the stone:
Lodestone refers to the mineral magnetite when found with natural magnetism.

MAGNESITE
Release, Relax, Renew!

COLOR(S)	white
CHAKRA(S)	crown
PLANET(S)	Moon, Ceres
NUMBER(S)	2
ELEMENT(S)	water
MOHS SCALE	3.5–4.5
ASTRO SIGN(S)	Cancer

Affirmation I release muscular tension. My body is completely relaxed. I allow troublesome thoughts and worries to be released from my consciousness. I have renewed clarity. My creative nature supports my ability to renew myself at any stage of life and at any time. I go with the flow!

Spiritual uses Magnesite expands your intuition during channeling or other psychic practices to allow information to flow more easily through your consciousness. This puffy-looking white stone allows you to integrate or translate the messages from Ascended Masters, spirit guides, and loved ones on the Other Side. It takes the edge off what otherwise might seem like an agitating insight.

Mental uses Magnesite is a perfect rock to relax your mind and release the tension of negative thoughtforms or mental energy. Use this stone to remind you to allow yourself to move into the place of "no mind."

Emotional uses With its calming energy, magnesite balances your emotions so that you can get in touch with your true feelings. This stone helps you to clear out old emotional patterns. With this stone in hand, relax your emotional body, and move into a more accepting place.

Physical uses With its high magnesium content, magnesite is a soft stone and carries the vibration of that softness. This white chalky stone must often be stabilized with other components to keep it together, so it is a reminder that it is okay to rely on others. Use this stone for muscle relaxation, healthy evacuation of the large intestine, and ease of absorption and digestion of food.

Divine guidance Are you pushing for new insights or understanding? Are you trying to force the information through your consciousness? Relax your body, mind, and spirit, and allow your subtle bodies to absorb what is truly important.

About the stone:
Magnesite is a magnesium carbonate crystallizing in the trigonal system.

MAGNETITE OCTAHEDRON
Charisma

COLOR(S)	metallic gray or black
CHAKRA(S)	root, solar plexus
PLANET(S)	Uranus, Jupiter
NUMBER(S)	9, 12
ELEMENT(S)	earth, air
MOHS SCALE	5–6
ASTRO SIGN(S)	Sagittarius, Aquarius

Affirmation I am a magnet for all of my heart's desires. I magnetically attract anything I truly need. I am nurtured and protected by the Divine. All of the energy and thoughts I send out into the world return to me multifold. As above, so below.

Spiritual uses The structure of magnetite octahedron aligns you with the vibrational energies of bringing heaven to earth. It is a reminder of "as above, so below," meaning you can dance with the Divine while still residing on the planet. This stone can also help you to develop a charismatic vibration that aligns you with the manifestation of miracles for yourself and others.

Mental uses Magnetite octahedron's triangles help you sort out your thoughts so you can get organized. Gaze at this stone when trying to make order out of chaos. Allow it to move you away from unimportant information or distractions so that only the highest and best come through you.

Emotional uses Magnetite helps you sort out feelings regarding your relationships. Whether the relationship is romantic or professional, this stone helps you gain clarity regarding decisions you need to make about the people in your life. It also assists you in stepping courageously into your inner strength to be a balanced, healthy partner in your relationships. It is a good tool for amplifying self-confidence.

Physical uses With its high iron content, magnetite offers support to those who are challenged by iron deficiencies or overall physical weakness. Hold or gaze at magnetite as you set the intention to strengthen your vital life force energy. Use this stone to improve overall circulation, healthy lymph function, and good vascular health.

Divine guidance Are you suddenly finding yourself attracted to someone or something? Are you finding that people are suddenly attracted to you? You have a magnetic personality and can attract exactly what you need when you need it. Have faith in your charisma, and put it to good use.

About the stone:
Magnetite octahedron refers to the mineral magnetite when it crystallizes and forms octahedrons. Magnetite is an iron oxide and may contain varying amounts of magnesium, zinc, manganese as well as lesser amounts of manganic, aluminum, chromium, and vanadium.

MALACHITE
Bull's Eye

Color(s)	dark green with lighter and darker green and blue-green bands
Chakra(s)	heart, solar plexus
Planet(s)	Saturn
Number(s)	8
Element(s)	earth
Mohs scale	3.5–4
Astro sign(s)	Capricorn

Affirmation I focus on my heart center. I treasure the lessons I learn being in relationships. I find balance within. I feel love for myself and all beings. Love swirls into my life. I recognize repetitive patterns. I choose patterns of love, compassion, and kindness.

Spiritual uses Carrying the vibrations of the heart, malachite's swirling shades of green represent the lessons the heart must go through during its lifetime, effectuating healing not only in this lifetime but also in past lives. These patterns are lessons that you can use to further your spiritual evolution. Call on Archangels Chamuel, Melchizedek, and Raphael using malachite.

Mental uses Malachite can help you get clear when you have many thoughts going round and round in your head. If you are experiencing repetitive thoughts you are unable to release, use this stone to realign your mind with your heart, and use your heart as your center of thought.

Emotional uses Malachite is a stone that helps you get to the heart of a matter. This stone reminds you that patterns that repeat in relationships again and again contain a lesson to be learned. This stone helps you grow emotionally, mentally, and spiritually as you recognize emerging patterns.

Physical uses Malachite helps you connect with life's sweetness. It is a good stone if you have diabetes or are healing from pancreatic issues or digestive challenges. This copper carbonate mineral aids those suffering from the symptoms of arthritis as well.

Divine guidance What patterns in your life do you keep repeating? Are you ready to emerge from the maze you've created? Walk the labyrinth, and find the higher spiritual purpose for all of your challenges and lessons. As you discover which patterns no longer serve you, remove them and replace them with new patterns. Look for the emerging patterns of joy, harmony, and inner peace. Embrace them and continue forward in your evolutionary spiral upward.

About the stone:
Malachite is a copper carbonate. It is found as botryoidal or stalactitic masses with the deposit of dissolving copper ores causing its characteristic banding.

MOLDAVITE TEKTITE
Out of This World

COLOR(S)	olive green or dull green
CHAKRA(S)	heart, third eye, crown
PLANET(S)	Venus, Neptune, Earth
NUMBER(S)	5
ELEMENT(S)	water, fire
MOHS SCALE	6.5–7
ASTRO SIGN(S)	Taurus, Pisces

Affirmation My consciousness is awake. I am aware. I feel the limitless nature of all life. I believe in unlimited potentials and possibilities. I am creative and prosperous. I fully embrace extraordinary wealth. My heart is open to giving and receiving love.

Spiritual uses Moldavite is a tool for channeling otherworldly beings. It also helps you contemplate the vastness of the cosmos and the part you play in the vast scheme of life on Earth. This naturally formed green glass can help you remember your soul's contract and how to complete it while remaining focused on love, peace, and harmony. Moldavite is associated with Archangels Raphael, Sandalphon, and Zadkiel.

Mental uses Like most other tektites, moldavite can help expand your mind to enable you to think beyond the ordinary. Tektites are natural glass rocks formed by the impact of meteorites on the earth. This quality helps you in all areas of life, including your ability to see the greater perspective.

From a distance or in hindsight, you can grasp the greater reality and touch upon increased self-knowledge as well as tolerance for others with moldavite in hand. This stone can also stimulate a lazy mind into activity or increase intelligence as needed.

Emotional uses Moldavite opens your heart as well as your mind, enabling you to find inner peace, harmony, and joy. This stone can help you release your watery emotions, especially unreasonable feelings of despair that result in crying fits. Use it to help you shed tears and heal pain to improve your emotional health. Find unique ways to release your pent-up feelings.

Physical uses Moldavite is useful when healing from heart surgery. Moldavite is a perfect amulet for an inventor or anyone who creates something entirely new, be it machinery, artwork, medical research, or technology and beyond. The green energy of this stone promotes prosperity while keeping you focused on the greater good for all. This is a good stone for inventors, cardiologists, heart surgeons, neurologists, and visionaries.

Divine guidance Do you have an interest in space, astronomy, astrology, or extraterrestrials? Do you enjoy scholarly activities or mind-bending projects? It is time to embrace concepts that at first glance may seem far out. You have a brilliant mind that craves stimulation. Take time to explore beyond the outer limits of your own core belief systems.

About the stone:
Tektites are natural glass objects thought to be associated with meteoric activity, with local rock or sediments fusing into glass upon impact. Moldavite contains approximately 75 percent silica, 10 percent alumina, and smaller quantities of iron oxides, lime, soda, potash, magnesia, titania, and manganese oxide; it is found in central Europe, mainly in the Czech Republic.

Moonstone
Extraordinary Awareness

Color(s)	milky white, transparent reflective white, beige, gray, brown, peach, or black
Chakra(s)	crown, third eye, solar plexus, navel
Planet(s)	Moon
Number(s)	13
Element(s)	water
Mohs scale	6–6.5
Astro sign(s)	Cancer

Affirmation I am consciously aware of my belief systems and thoughts. I am extremely intuitive and perceptive. I awaken my consciousness and become aware of what thoughts, people, or situations need to be shifted or realigned in my life.

Spiritual uses Moonstone is a perfect tool for increasing your intuition and trusting the process of becoming an intuitive. Psychic awareness includes the ability to use the six sensory gifts, or "clairs"—clairvoyance, claircognizance, clairaudience, clairsentience, clairolfaction, and clairgustation. Use moonstone to connect with the archangels of the Divine Feminine—Auriel and Tzaphkiel. This pearly stone is beneficial for rituals involving the Divine Feminine, the Goddess, the moon, and all mythological goddesses. Moonstone, also known as hecatolite, is associated with the ancient Greek moon goddess Hecate. This is also a good stone to connect with the year's thirteen moons and the women and teachings of the International Council of the Thirteen Indigenous Grandmothers, goodwill ambassadors from Alaska, North, South, and Central America, Africa, and Asia with a mission of world peace.

Mental uses Moonstone promotes dreaming. Dreams provide tools for self-knowledge and help bring mental clarity. With moonstone under your pillow, use the messages of dreamtime to restore mental balance.

Emotional uses Moonstone helps restore emotional balance. This is a good stone for cleansing negative energy from your energy centers, or chakras. This is also a stone of reflection, helping you to look within using the powerful tool of self-observation for self-improvement and spiritual growth. With this stone in hand, watch your actions and reactions to others without judgment. Black moonstone specifically is a reminder that all is created from the void, the great mystery, and the emptiness.

Physical uses Moonstone is the stone most associated with female fertility, and the associated menses, premenstrual syndrome, and menopause. The Divine Feminine works through this stone to help assist women in all the joys of womanhood—maid, mother, and wise woman. This stone helps you embrace the constant ebb and flow of female hormones.

Divine guidance Are you aware of life's cycles? Do you notice changes with the moon's phases? Have you been feeling sensitive? Are you extremely intuitive? Trust your intuition, and step into your personal power. Go within using prayer, meditation, and contemplation. Observe the intentions behind the "buttons" to gain further clarity and understanding about your life and the lives of those around you.

About the stone:
Moonstone is an orthoclase feldspar which is potassium aluminum silicate. Moonstone crystallizes in the monoclinic system and displays the unique gemological phenomenon called adularescence, the blue or white billowy light or schiller seen when the stones are cut correctly.

MORGANITE
Irresistible Love and Spiritual Affluence

Color(s)	translucent pink or peach
Chakra(s)	heart, solar plexus
Planet(s)	Venus, Jupiter
Number(s)	17/8/88
Element(s)	air, fire
Mohs scale	7.5–8
Astro sign(s)	Libra, Sagittarius

Affirmation All that I need is always within my reach. I am grateful for all I have. Extraordinary love and amazing wealth are always available to me. The time is now! I have an abundance of spiritual helpers ready to assist me in all areas of my life.

Spiritual uses Using the pink vibration of morganite helps you connect with spiritual affluence. There is an abundance of spiritual helpers—master teachers, loved ones on the Other Side, saints, angels, goddesses, muses, and so on—available at your beck and call. Appeal to your guardian angel and Archangel Metatron with this gem in hand. Hold or gaze at morganite to attract spiritual riches. Be of service to others spiritually and the benefits will return to you multifold.

Mental uses Morganite gives you a pair of rose-colored glasses when you need them the most. This stone helps you shift from a negative outlook to a positive one—the great transition from the half-empty glass to a full glass (notice that it is not just half-full).

Emotional uses Morganite has the power to pull you out of the doldrums. The nurturing pink energy wraps you energetically in a blanket of love to help you work through tough feelings. With this stone in hand, allow the love in to melt away the roughness. Melt into this stone's loving vibration and be healed.

Physical uses Morganite supports healthy skin. This stone, with its pink vibration, is good for skin regeneration and rejuvenation. It allows the healthy flow of blood through the epidermis. It is helpful to improve healthy blood circulation and prevents vascular disease and imbalances. This is a good stone for estheticians, dermatologists, and vascular doctors.

Divine guidance Are you ready to attract the best of everything? Do you believe the best is yet to come? Make a clear decision to manifest the good now in this moment. Don't wait until tomorrow. You are being called to experience spirituality in everyday living. See the love in everything.

About the stone:
Morganite is the pink variety of beryl, a silicate with aluminum and beryllium. Beryl crystallizes in the hexagonal system with six-sided prisms. The color often contains yellow along with the pink and is thought to be caused by the presence of manganese, cesium, and rubidium. Other varieties of beryl include heliodor, aquamarine, and emerald.

Muscovite
Shimmering Light

Color(s)	shades of gray, brown, green, or yellow; rarely violet or red or silvery-white; also can be transparent or translucent
Chakra(s)	all
Planet(s)	Moon
Number(s)	11
Element(s)	water
Mohs scale	2–3
Astro sign(s)	Cancer

Affirmation I am in touch with my feelings. I honor my emotions. It is easy for me to reflect on the blessings and challenges in my life as an objective observer. My observations strengthen my spiritual nature and improve my inner foundations for knowledge and wisdom.

Spiritual uses Muscovite's shimmering protective energy reminds you that where there is love, there can only be goodness and well-being. Its silver energy lends itself to helping you with your link to your innate receptive and intuitive nature. This is an instrument for self-observation and self-reflection.

Mental uses Muscovite is found as crystalline material in tablet-like formations. It carries the vibration of good transmission of knowledge. Symbolically, this stone reminds you to make use of books, reference materials, or the Internet to research what you need to know. You can use it when you are in the midst of researching for better retention.

Emotional uses A stone that facilitates honoring your feelings, muscovite can help you sort out your thoughts and emotions to enable you to express your truth. It also helps you open your ears and senses—right down to your nerve endings—to be able to hear and grasp what others are communicating. This stone can be a rock-sized relationship counselor, since good communication is a key ingredient in all types of relationships.

Physical uses Due to its potassium-rich content, muscovite supports nerve cells and can help improve neurological dysfunctions. Use this stone to improve hearing. Muscovite is beneficial for improving recovery from stroke, lowering blood pressure, relieving anxiety and stress, improving muscular strength, revving up metabolism, and helping heal heart and kidney disorders. This stone also helps fight fatigue and muscle weakness.

Divine guidance Are you feeling mentally, physically, or spiritually fried? Do you need to recapture your essence down to the very cells of your being? Pay attention to the signs and symptoms of overwork, lack of nutrition or rest, and reenergize yourself. Take time for inner reflection and self-observation to expand your spiritual foundation. Allow yourself to listen well and communicate eloquently with the important people in your life—and likewise, your spirit guides and angels.

About the stone:
Muscovite is a potassium aluminum silicate that crystallizes in the monoclinic system. It usually forms as rocks, although tabular crystals with hexagonal outlines are found. Other elements, usually metals, are found as impurities in this mineral belonging to the mica group.

OBSIDIAN (APACHE TEARS)
Feel Your Feelings

COLOR(S)	translucent smoky brown to black
CHAKRA(S)	root, navel
PLANET(S)	Pluto, Chiron
NUMBER(S)	0
ELEMENT(S)	fire
MOHS SCALE	5–5.5
ASTRO SIGN(S)	Scorpio

Affirmation I completely embrace my feelings and allow them to come to the surface. Feelings of anger, sorrow, and grief will pass as I release them from my body. I open myself up to the healing energy of the love and prayers people send me.

Spiritual uses Apache tears support all types of grieving processes, but they are especially sympathetic when trying to cope with the grief associated with suicide. Turn to Apache tears to give you strength as you experience an array of emotions, from guilt, anger, blame, shame, and confusion to relief, despair, betrayal, abandonment, and acceptance. Apache tears can connect survivors with departed loved ones who chose to die as they gain the necessary spiritual understanding to cope with their decision.

Mental uses Apache tears help to ground you and keep you focused. Use this stone to keep your mind on the task at hand. It is also beneficial for maintaining a positive outlook, keeping negative thoughts at bay. Use it to deflect negative energy.

Emotional uses Apache tears support you during periods of grief and mourning. Although there is an inconsolable aspect to missing someone close who has passed, this volcanic black glass reminds you that you can turn to others for support while allowing your feelings of grief to take their normal course, which can be very rocky at times.

Physical uses Apache tears can help you with the physical ache that often comes with grief. The stress associated with sorrow can cause physical pains in your bones and muscles. On the other hand, physical tears are physiologically beneficial. If you are having a hard time letting yourself cry, regardless of whether or not it is grief associated, this stone can help prime the pump of your tears.

Divine guidance Are you in need of a good cry? Are you feeling sad over a loss? There are so many reasons to allow ourselves to grieve the passing of a loved one, a job, a way of life, or anything that has changed from one way of being to another way of being. Acknowledge the angst and move through it; embrace the possibility of a happy life again.

About the stone:
Apache tears are small pieces of decomposed obsidian, natural glass composed of two-thirds silica or more, formed during the cooling of volcanic lava. They are commonly found in the American Southwest.

OBSIDIAN, BLACK
Great Void, Great Mystery

Color(s)	black
Chakra(s)	root
Planet(s)	Venus, Pluto
Number(s)	5
Element(s)	fire
Mohs scale	5–5.5
Astro sign(s)	Libra, Scorpio

Affirmation I am focused. I am responsible. I stay with matters until they are settled or reach completion. I accomplish whatever I set out to do. I pay attention to what is going on around me and within me. I am attentive.

Spiritual uses Black obsidian draws you inward to the center of yourself, to the place of truth. In Native American teachings, it is likened to the Great Void or the Great Mystery from which all things are created. It is a stone for spiritual dreaming and creating, best used in the western quadrant of the Native American medicine wheel. Black obsidian can be used to request the aid of Archangels Melchizedek and Sabrael.

Mental uses Black obsidian is perfect for grounding and keeping you focused. If you have a tendency to be easily distracted or off-center, use this stone to keep your mind on the task at hand. It is also beneficial for maintaining a positive outlook by keeping negative thoughts at bay. Use it to deflect negative energy.

Emotional uses Black obsidian helps you dredge up emotions that are buried deep within yourself. This stone reminds you that negative emotions can play havoc on your life by broadcasting an unconscious program that perpetuates negative patterns. This volcanic glass supports you while you search the darker recesses of your emotional body.

Physical uses Black obsidian helps you avoid ingesting toxins by keeping you focused on healthy eating. It realigns your energy so that you can make proper food choices. It also supports you during the process of breaking bad habits, such as smoking, overeating, overdrinking, or using drugs, or putting an end to habitual patterns that no longer serve your higher self.

Divine guidance Have you been feeling scattered lately and unable to focus on what's important? Look deep inside, and you will see a reflection of all that is going on around you. Prioritize your intentions, and focus on one thing at a time. Grounding yourself is important now so that you can accomplish your goals with sincerity and purpose.

About the stone:
Black obsidian is a natural glass, composed of two-thirds silica or more, formed during the cooling of volcanic lava. As a glass, it has no innate crystalline structure.

Obsidian, Golden Sheen
Inner Wisdom

Color(s)	black with a reflective golden sheen
Chakra(s)	root, navel, solar plexus
Planet(s)	Pluto, Neptune, Chiron
Number(s)	5
Element(s)	fire, water
Mohs scale	5
Astro sign(s)	Scorpio, Pisces

Affirmation I am safe. I live in the present. I use the lessons learned in the past to empower me. I am wise today because of the knowledge gained from previous experiences. I experience visions. I trust my inner spiritual sight and act accordingly.

Spiritual uses Use this golden variety of obsidian to achieve grounded interaction with the earth while connecting with the cosmic forces of the universe. The golden sheen activates the golden flecks of light that naturally sparkle in your energy field. Use this stone to remember your golden halo of light emanating in all directions around you. This stone will help keep you safe from unwanted psychic influences, removing the hook of negativity from your energy field.

Mental uses Use gold sheen obsidian to sharpen your mental aptitude so you can enter deeper meditative states and tap into higher forces for the good of the community. With focus, you can also use this stone to deflect dark forces from interfering with the higher good of humankind.

Emotional uses Golden sheen obsidian assists in balancing and healing abuse from the past that is still being carried around in the emotional field. Gaze at this reflective gemstone to awaken memories, and contemplate how these memories are currently affecting your life. Acknowledge repetitive patterns, and make a clear decision to remove the obstacles that keep such patterns in motion.

Physical uses Golden sheen obsidian keeps the physical body prepped for energetic focus and reflection. With this stone in hand, accept the gift of health, and release old memories that interfere with your ability to be healthy. Use this stone while going through a physical cleansing process.

Divine guidance Is your mind carrying around toxic memories? Are you ingesting unhealthy foods that contain disease-causing toxins? It's time to take the necessary steps to clean up your diet and rid your mind of toxic energy. Use your powers of intuition to find the guidance you require.

> **About the stone:**
> Golden sheen obsidian is a natural glass composed of two-thirds silica or more, formed during the cooling of volcanic lava, with gas bubbles causing the sheen.

OBSIDIAN, RAINBOW
Remembering

COLOR(S)	iridescent black
CHAKRA(S)	all
PLANET(S)	Neptune
NUMBER(S)	7
ELEMENT(S)	fire, water
MOHS SCALE	5
ASTRO SIGN(S)	Pisces

Affirmation Energy freely flows through my energy centers, and the rainbow body within me is enlivened. I am highly aware on all levels—mentally, emotionally, physically, and spiritually. I look inward to remember and know. The past makes me stronger.

Spiritual uses Rainbow obsidian points you toward the rainbow body of your soul. It is a reminder that you are a luminescent being carrying the full spectrum of light. Use this stone as a tool for meditation and inward reflection. With this stone in hand, if you look hard enough and remember deep enough, you can see, sense, or know the internal rainbow body, even in this dense human form.

Mental uses Rainbow obsidian is a good stone to use when you need to trigger your memory. Use it as a tool for focus while studying, doing rituals, or engaging in any other activity requiring focus and memory from deep within the recesses of your mind. This stone helps you dispel negative thoughtforms (mental energy).

Emotional uses Black obsidian is a tool for understanding how to use traumatic experiences of the past as lessons today to help you become a better person. It is never pleasant to re-experience the deep emotional wounds and trauma of the past, but the rainbow energy of this stone supports you in this endeavor so the hooks keeping you attached to those trying memories can begin to disintegrate.

Physical uses The rainbow reflection within black obsidian is a perfect tool for all kinds of health challenges. This stone contains the hopeful message that if you can find a rainbow within a dense black rock, you certainly can find a cure within your consciousness and the worlds of traditional and non-traditional medicine to help you reclaim your health and balance. With this stone in hand, reclaim your rainbow body on all levels—physically, spiritually, mentally, and emotionally.

Divine guidance Are you in touch with all the levels of your being? Are you looking for ways to find balance? Are you seeking a spiritual connection? Remember that there is always a rainbow to be found even in the most difficult challenges. This rainbow is part of you and can be found within.

About the stone:
Rainbow obsidian is a black obsidian that displays rings of iridescence when cut and polished properly.

Obsidian, Snowflake
The Light Within

Color(s)	black with moss-like white spots
Chakra(s)	root, crown
Planet(s)	Moon
Number(s)	13
Element(s)	water
Mohs scale	5
Astro sign(s)	Scorpio

Affirmation I courageously see through the darkness of adversity to make positive changes. There is always light at the end of the tunnel. I am aligned with the light. I see myself, situations, and others clearly. I easily transform the negative to the positive.

Spiritual uses Snowflake obsidian can open new pathways of spiritual thought and connection. The white flecks in this stone emphasize the enlightening nature it generates when the right intention is set. This stone demonstrates that within your consciousness is the opportunity for realization. With focused purpose in your spiritual practices, be it a meditation technique, a yogic posture, or a dream practice, this stone can increase the spiritual benefits. Use snowflake obsidian to tap into these sources during sacred circle ceremonies.

Mental uses Snowflake obsidian is ideal for assisting you with accepting change and transformation in your life. This stone helps you note any unyielding thought patterns that need to be altered or crystallized ideas that must be shattered.

Emotional uses Snowflake obsidian helps you find the benefits in emotional challenges. It is useful as a catalyst to uncover how your emotional upsets are simply predecessors to change. This stone is a reminder that challenges or upsets in your life are the precursors to a better way of life or an improved way of looking at life.

Physical uses Snowflake obsidian eases the problems associated with the menstrual cycle. It is useful for balancing hormones through every stage of a woman's life. This is an excellent stone for doulas, maternity nurses, pregnant mothers, nursing mothers, and, of course, new fathers as well.

Divine guidance Are you afraid of the dark? Do you fear the unknown? Do you feel vulnerable? Remember, there is always darkness within light. Darkness accentuates brightness so that we can clearly see situations, people, and circumstances for what they are. Embrace the darkness to enhance the clarity in your life.

> **About the stone:**
> Snowflake obsidian is a natural glass composed of two-thirds silica or more, formed during the cooling of volcanic lava, that displays white snowflakelike inclusions of the mineral cristobalite.

ONYX
Endurance

Color(s)	black, white
Chakra(s)	black (root), white (crown)
Planet(s)	Saturn
Number(s)	4
Element(s)	earth
Mohs scale	6–7
Astro sign(s)	Capricorn

Affirmation I am focused and grounded. I am persistent. I stay with the task at hand until it is complete. I am able to handle challenges. I am always safe and protected. My business is a great success and endures all economic cycles with ease.

Spiritual uses Black onyx is beneficial to establish a protective shield when offering spiritual counseling, tarot card readings, channeling, automatic writing, and any other modality that opens you up to psychic influences. The white variety of this stone amplifies telepathic connection with your own higher consciousness and helps you tap into the Akashic Records (the history of the cosmos). Use it when you intend to obtain messages from the angelic realm to open your intuitive ears.

Mental uses Black onyx is a perfect stone for your desk or wherever you perform your work—be it a carpenter's workstation, an aircraft mechanic's toolbox, or a daycare provider's pocket. This stone helps provide mental focus, grounding, and the ability to stay on task. Use black onyx to deflect negative thoughtforms.

Emotional uses Use this stone as a grounding tool and feel safe in its presence. Place a black onyx next to your bed if you have nightmares or night terror. Make it your intention that the stone will guard against any negative influences while you sleep peacefully. Black onyx specifically is beneficial for releasing any type of fear.

Physical uses Black onyx amplifies your financial strength and ability to stay focused and to achieve financial goals. This is a perfect stone for an entrepreneur and helps the self-employed gain confidence and endurance to stay in business. It promotes longevity in business.

Divine guidance Have you been feeling a bit scattered? Are you trying to reach a goal(s) but keep getting pulled off course? Perhaps some fears are keeping you from moving forward with your life or career. Have the courage to embark on your journey to fulfill your dreams and desires. Identify your fears, and use the tools at your disposal to conquer them so you can bravely move toward your goals.

About the stone:
Onyx is a form of chalcedony which is usually black and white. This material is frequently dyed to a black color and used in jewelry.

OPAL
Diffraction

Color(s)	opalescent white, gray, red, orange, yellow, green, blue, magenta, rose, pink, slate, olive, brown, and black
Chakra(s)	all
Planet(s)	Saturn, Ceres, Neptune, Venus
Number(s)	8
Element(s)	water
Mohs scale	5.5–6
Astro sign(s)	Pisces, Libra

Affirmation I am incredibly intuitive. I have the gift of insight. I accumulate information the way a sponge absorbs and holds water. I am receptive. I nourish myself through a close connection with pools and baths. I drink plenty of fresh water throughout the day.

Spiritual uses The watery vibration of opal makes this stone a perfect tool for connecting with the devic forces of water, including all the devas of the undine family of which merfolk and water sprites are but a few. Connect with blue-green energy to assist in interspecies communication with dolphins and whales for expanded spiritual awareness. Atlantean mysteries can be recollected through channeling or automatic writing while using this stone. Ancient Greeks believed the opal had the power of giving foresight and the light of prophecy to its owner.

Mental uses Opals are supportive when encountering mental obstacles. Use this stone to gain the perspective needed to make the shift from distraction to action.

Emotional uses With its high water content, opal is excellent for shifting your emotions through self-awareness. This stone also helps protect you from too easily absorbing other people's energy, feelings, or thoughts. Because opal produces its colors through interference and diffraction, allow this stone to run interference for you when encountering challenging people, places, or things that affect your emotions or hurt your feelings.

Physical uses Opal is beneficial for the health of your eyes, kidneys, and skin. This stone is helpful if you are challenged by dehydration or water retention. Use it to balance your body's water content. This is a good stone for those who work in or around water, such as a physical therapist who employs hydrotherapy.

Divine guidance Have you been emotional or on the verge of tears lately? Is other people's energy affecting your well-being? You are a highly intuitive person. Find solace in the water—a bath, swim, or walk along the water's edge will help clear away energy that isn't yours and replenish your energy field.

About the stone:
Opal is hydrated silicon dioxide, sometimes containing the minerals cristobalite and tridymite. As an amorphous, water-containing stone, it does not crystallize. Opal comes in many colors with or without the play of color, which is caused by silica spheres of varying size being closely packed together. As the solidification of a silica gel, it is generally found in seams or veins, but more rarely it is found in massive form exhibiting botryoidal growth, in stalagmitic form, or as a replacement pseudomorph in fossils.

PEACOCK COPPER
Vibrant!

Color(s)	blue, purple, turquoise, copper-red
Chakra(s)	all
Planet(s)	Sun
Number(s)	3
Element(s)	fire
Mohs scale	3–3.25
Astro sign(s)	Leo

Affirmation I am full of vigor! I am authentic and loyal. I confidently show my true colors to others. My life is dynamic and full of vibrant energy. It is a fabulous feeling to be all that I can be! I am full of life-enhancing joy and goodness.

Spiritual uses Peacock copper offers support as you learn to express yourself within the realm of angels, spirit guides, and Ascended Masters, especially when varying shades of blue are the predominant colors. The archangels associated with this stone are Sandalphon and Uriel. This stone helps you remain grounded as you tap into these higher frequencies. It also helps you translate information as it is "downloaded" to your consciousness.

Mental uses Peacock copper activates your creative energy and helps you see things from a new and colorful perspective. This stone is perfect for helping you raise your self-esteem, and it encourages the development of a happy optimistic outlook. The many colors increase your ability to be enthusiastic and spread sunshine and happiness.

Emotional uses Peacock copper helps cool your anger. If you need a bit of anger management, this stone can be your constant companion until you rebalance your emotions. It can also help you crack through the crust covering the source of your emotions so you can unearth the real issues and heal them once and for all.

Physical uses Peacock copper is useful for those with arthritis or other inflammatory diseases. It is also good for resolving iron deficiencies and improving water absorption in the large intestine. This stone improves your vital life force energy. This is the stone for artists, actors, public speakers, or for anyone in the spotlight.

Divine guidance Are you in touch with your magnificence? Have you been living your life in full splendor? If not, find ways to bring more joy into your life. It's time to be aware of the source of your emotional challenges or perceived blocks so you can release them. Get in touch with your inner radiance, and shine your light brightly.

About the stone:
Peacock copper is a sulfide of copper and iron. The outside of the stone oxidizes to produce an iridescent display of red and purple. It is also known as peacock ore or bornite.

PERIDOT
Heal the Healer

Color(s)	olive green or chartreuse
Chakra(s)	heart, solar plexus
Planet(s)	Pluto
Number(s)	22
Element(s)	fire
Mohs scale	6.5–7
Astro sign(s)	Leo, Virgo, Capricorn

Affirmation I am genuinely happy for the good fortune of others. My friends, family, and colleagues are happy for my good fortune. I know that good fortune is the result of good thoughts and energy. I send out positive vibes and look forward to meeting them again in the future.

Spiritual uses Peridot is a stone of transformation that helps you rise above addictions. Even more importantly, this stone serves as your guide as you facilitate healing processes that assist others going through what you have already overcome. This is the stone of the wounded healer. Use it as a tool to increase the benefits of Reiki sessions. Peridot is ideal to gain the assistance of Archangels Sabrael and Zadkiel.

Mental uses Peridot is beneficial when you are going through a rite of passage or ritual. This stone helps you transcend any challenge presented through inner strength, connection to higher realms of consciousness, and divine will. It also assists you in thinking outside the box by opening your mind to unlimited possibilities.

Emotional uses Peridot is helpful for transforming negative emotions like self-sabotage, jealousy, agitation, and impatience into lighter emotions such as love, compassion, acceptance, and gratitude. It is also beneficial to assist you in digesting life—accepting your world as it is and then transforming it with clear intention to create the reality you wish to have.

Physical uses Peridot supports the digestive system. It can be used to support the optimal functioning of the gall bladder, liver, pancreas, and spleen. This olive-colored stone also supports the proper assimilation of nutrients of food, drink, water, and light.

Divine guidance Are you feeling jealous of someone's good fortune? Do you perceive that others are jealous of you? Stay focused on the goodness in your life. Remove your attention from other's good fortune and focus on the blessings in your own life. Step away from people who are resentful of your destiny.

> **About the stone:**
> Peridot is a magnesium iron silicate that crystallizes in the orthorhombic system. Crystals are typically not very well formed flattened prisms with vertical striations.

PETALITE
Oneness of Mind and Heart

Color(s)	transparent, translucent pink/white, or pale pink
Chakra(s)	heart, crown
Planet(s)	Mercury, Venus
Number(s)	4, 7
Element(s)	water
Mohs scale	6.5
Astro sign(s)	Aries, Leo

Affirmation I am in constant communication with my higher consciousness, guides, and angels. I listen intently with my heart. I have a balanced mental perspective. I stay on task. Clarity and compassion are abundant within me. I am grateful for all the blessings in my life.

Spiritual uses Petalite helps you align your head with your heart while you are learning to balance your emotions. When communication does not feel as strong, use this stone to reactivate your connection with the angelic realm. It stimulates the link to higher consciousness and facilitates communication from Ascended Masters and other spiritual guides. With this stone in hand, listen to the messages from angels with your heart.

Mental uses Petalite helps you to maintain a balanced state of mental consciousness. Use this stone to think clearly and keep your perspective on reality. This stone facilitates creating calm, peace, and serenity. It calms people with hyperactivity when held with focused intention.

Emotional uses With its mood-supporting lithium content, petalite helps balance the emotions by keeping mood swings at bay, especially in romantic relationships. Let this stone remind you to invite and invoke angelic assistance to feel safe and secure.

Physical uses Petalite supports you when the chemicals in your brain are out of whack and you are going through a manic period. With this stone in hand, set the intention to balance your brain physiology.

Divine guidance Have you been feeling moody lately or perhaps a little scattered? Have you forgotten to employ the aid of your angelic helpers and spirit guides? Take time to meditate on your heart center to know your truth. Call on your spirit guides and angelic guardians to help you through any challenging situation.

About the stone:
Petalite is a lithium aluminum silicate that crystallizes in the monoclinic system. Crystals are rare and the material is usually found in massive form.

PICASSO STONE
The Writing on the Wall

COLOR(S)	black, brown, and/or yellow with dark, branchlike inclusions
CHAKRA(S)	root, navel, solar plexus
PLANET(S)	Venus
NUMBER(S)	6
ELEMENT(S)	earth
MOHS SCALE	4–5
ASTRO SIGN(S)	Taurus

Affirmation The path of enlightenment is revealed to me daily. I clearly see my way through life. The experiences of the past give me the wisdom to recognize the way of the future. I know truth from deep within myself.

Spiritual uses When trying to find your individual path to enlightenment, Picasso stone can help you map out your upcoming journey and guide you in the manner in which to step forth. With this stone in hand, ask that your personal spiritual path be revealed to you.

Mental uses The grounding qualities of Picasso stone help you sort out the many choices available to you. When mental confusion arises, contemplate the lines mapped within this stone. Use it as a tool for focus. This stone's lines are created due to pressure in the earth. You, too, may have been under pressure from life challenges that have affected you deep within. These pressures have transformed your life. This stone promotes stability.

Emotional uses Picasso stone is a tool for transforming your emotions, resulting in life-enhancing self-transformation. Like a gemstone GPS, it guides you along the emotional path that will provide you with the transformational experience that will most benefit you in your life.

Physical uses Picasso stone helps get you up and moving. The physical activity it inspires is beneficial if you are trying to lose weight. With its mapping vibrations, you can use the energy of this stone to follow your heart to the treasure of motivation to get your body moving for overall health and well-being.

Divine guidance Are you in the process of transforming your life? Or perhaps you are trying to find your way. Delve deep within yourself to access the knowledge and wisdom you've gained from life's experiences. Use this inner knowing to help you to clearly see which path to travel.

About the stone:
Picasso stone refers to a variety of jasper (microcrystalline quartz) also known as Picasso jasper or Picasso marble due to its resemblance to abstract paintings.

PIETERSITE
Courage

COLOR(S)	varying hues of brown, blue, red, and gold
CHAKRA(S)	root, navel, solar plexus, third eye
PLANET(S)	Jupiter, Mercury
NUMBER(S)	7, 2
ELEMENT(S)	fire
MOHS SCALE	5-6
ASTRO SIGN(S)	Gemini, Virgo, Sagittarius

Affirmation I am grounded, focused, and courageous. I am willing to take chances and try new things. Illusions fall away in front of me. I see through appearances and bravely follow my intuition without hesitation.

Spiritual uses Pietersite serves as a grounding force while you take spiritual steps to develop your third eye and intuitive skills. Its iridescence and swirling fibrous segments combined with the stabilizing force of this stone increases your ability to bring forth inspired self-awareness. This is a good stone to enhance the sensory gift of clairvoyance, or psychic sight.

Mental uses Pietersite helps you gain mental clarity. Its chatoyancy (the optical reflectance most commonly seen in cats' eye gems) creates an effect that helps you go within to reflect but also notice the reflections from outside yourself. This stone provides an avenue to clearly see through illusions and deception, beyond mirrors of distraction.

Emotional uses Pietersite strengthens your personal power and the ability to shine. This stone is useful for improving your self-esteem, joy, enthusiasm, and courage. Use this stone to have confidence in your perceptions in the mirrors life presents you. It's a tool for healing emotional issues involving personal interactions.

Physical uses Pietersite encourages the proper functioning of the pituitary gland and the regulation of the other endocrine glands so the proper amount of hormones for growth, sex, metabolism, blood pressure, and body temperature are produced. This stone is also beneficial for eye health.

Divine guidance Do you need more courage to set boundaries? Are you aware of everything that is going on around you? Take the time for some inner reflection. Improve your ability to notice when people are true to their word—or not. Have confidence in your intuitive sight.

About the stone:
Pietersite is a quartz jasper variety containing mineral fibers that give it a chatoyancy similar to tiger's eye. It develops in a massive form under pressure and metamorphic activity and has only been found in the Hunan province of China and Namibia. Pietersite is also known to contain limonite.

PRASIOLITE
Get Your Verve Back!

Color(s)	translucent pale green
Chakra(s)	heart, root
Planet(s)	Saturn
Number(s)	4
Element(s)	earth
Mohs scale	7
Astro sign(s)	Capricorn

Affirmation I am a determined person with the strength to follow through to the next best thing. My body, mind and spirit are strong, healthy, and unwavering. Vitality and energy are mine. I am filled with vim and vigor—mentally, physically, and spiritually.

Spiritual uses Prasiolite carries the vibration of protection and helps to strengthen your auric field. It also amplifies your ability to sit in meditative states for long periods. The pale green stone opens pathways in your consciousness to accept the challenges of spiritual fortitude. Use this stone for rebirthing or any spiritual practice that uses the breath for transformation and enlightenment.

Mental uses Prasiolite is an excellent tool to improve your ability to stay focused and see a task to its completion. This stone is especially useful to have by your side or in your pocket when you have long hours of mental activity ahead of you. It adds to your mental strength and perseverance.

Emotional uses Prasiolite strengthens your heart's abilities to accept emotions and emotional challenges. It is beneficial when you are feeling stuck in a relationship and need to make a shift either through accepting your change of heart or by giving yourself the permission and courage to talk the situation out to reach resolution and deeper states of intimacy.

Physical uses Prasiolite helps reduce blood pressure, rebalance the blood, and relieve muscle cramping. Use it with intention to improve energy after experiencing constipation or diarrhea to restore your energy and normal, healthy processes. It can also be used to ward off germs and viruses. Work with this stone to improve iron deficiencies and rebalance yourself when dealing with health challenges due to iron deficiencies. It is beneficial for strength and endurance via improved muscle strength.

Divine guidance Are you feeling weakened in body, mind, and/ or spirit? Are you depleted and need a bit of determination and strength? Spend some time in meditation to help you recapture your endurance and your vigor for life on all levels. Take time to find and eat the right foods to provide the core nutrients your body is craving.

About the stone:
Prasiolite refers to a green quartz (silicon dioxide). Most prasiolite on the market is obtained by heat-treating amethyst, although natural occurrences do exist.

PREHNITE
All That Is Good

COLOR(S)	translucent pale green
CHAKRA(S)	heart, solar plexus
PLANET(S)	Earth
NUMBER(S)	13
ELEMENT(S)	earth
MOHS SCALE	6–6.5
ASTRO SIGN(S)	Virgo, Capricorn, Pisces

Affirmation I am open and receptive to all that is good. I have the support of good friends. My friends and colleagues see the good within me. I am well respected. I embrace new opportunities and new friendships. Great happiness is normal in my life.

Spiritual uses Prehnite is a perfect stone to help integrate the spiritual teachings of the impermanence of all things into your everyday life. It aligns you with the vibrations of peace and renewal inherent in the constant changes of the universe and releases the feeling of being challenged by them. Use it for meditation practice to contemplate the impermanence of life and the cycles of creation and destruction.

Mental uses Prehnite helps you stay awake and alert when you feel mentally weary. Use this stone to help you stay focused and renew your attention on the matter at hand. This is a perfect stone to help you release the incessant chatter within your mind. It helps you sort your thoughts, helping you understand what is truly important.

Emotional uses Prehnite assists in dealing with feelings of unrest during times of constant change. This stone of transformation can help you see and feel how the end of certain conditions can be beneficial for the evolution of your body, mind, and spirit. It opens your awareness to see the good in all things.

Physical uses Prehnite is useful for supporting the health of bones, teeth, hair, and nails. It amplifies the ability to endure physically stressful situations over long periods of time when one might otherwise feel weathered and weary. Prehnite is beneficial for careers involving extreme attention to details like accountants, editors, surgeons, nurses, seamstresses, and tailors.

Divine guidance Have you been upset about how life is changing? Perhaps you've been feeling worn out by rigid thought patterns. Now is the time to be open to fresh new ideas, new people, and great happiness as you release old, worn-out life situations and perspectives. Be open to new opportunities, and enjoy riding the wave of change!

> *About the stone:*
> Prehnite is a hydrated calcium aluminum silicate that crystallizes in the ortho-rhombic system. Usually this mineral is found in massive form, often exhibiting botryoidal growth.

PYRITE
Golden Opportunities

COLOR(S)	silvery or brassy metallic gold
CHAKRA(S)	root, navel, solar plexus
PLANET(S)	Sun
NUMBER(S)	5
ELEMENT(S)	fire, air
MOHS SCALE	6.5–7
ASTRO SIGN(S)	Leo

Affirmation My confidence is rock solid. I focus on my intentions and take positive action to manifest my goals. I am prosperous and experience abundance in all facets of my life. I enjoy the many favorable opportunities presented to me.

Spiritual uses Pyrite reminds you of the golden flecks in your halo. With this stone in hand, visualize an energy field around your whole body that is especially luminescent around your head. Within this field, see, sense, or feel the sparkling golden pyrite activating and expanding your energy field.

Mental uses The golden vibration of pyrite assists you in remembering your magnificence. You are powerful—use this gemstone to remember who you truly are, and watch your self-esteem increase. Growing in block formations, it is inherent within the stone to offer a strong foundation to improve some of your core beliefs about yourself.

Emotional uses Pyrite helps strengthen courage and self-confidence. Use this stone when you need the guts to set boundaries and stand up for yourself. It helps you feel empowered. This golden gem offers the opportunity to allow the reflection and expansion of your positive qualities.

Physical uses Pyrite is a stone of financial abundance. Use this stone with intention when you are trying to improve your financial status. Draw on its gold energy while you take action to increase your monetary wealth. This stone also provides physical protection by deflecting negative energy or situations.

Divine guidance Are you worried about having enough money? Can you accept prosperity? You can earn unlimited income doing what you love. You have the skills necessary to follow your dreams. Have confidence, and believe in yourself and your ability to be prosperous.

About the stone:
Pyrite is iron sulphide and crystallizes in the cubic system. This iron mineral often crystallizes in the form of cubes with striations running at right angles to the adjoining faces. Pyrite may also form with twelve five-sided faces known as a pyritohedron. Pyrite also occurs as a replacement mineral in the formation of fossils.

QUARTZ
Clarity

Color(s)	transparent
Chakra(s)	all
Planet(s)	all
Number(s)	11, 22, 33, 44, 55, 66, 77, 88, 99
Element(s)	all
Mohs scale	7
Astro sign(s)	all

Affirmation I am a clear channel of love, light, and well-being. All is well in my life. I have great mental clarity, balanced emotions, and financial abundance. All of my heart's desires are realized now! The way is always evident and effortless.

Spiritual uses Clear quartz carries within it the full spectrum of light. It transmits and transduces energy. Use this stone for any and all spiritual pursuits including meditation, connecting with your guardian angel, channeling, higher knowledge and wisdom, shamanic journeywork, spiritual-healing modalities, and energy work. Clear quartz assists when aligning with Archangels Haniel, Michael, and Sandalphon. This stone is easily programmable, too: just hold the quartz and think of the desired thought, words, or action that you want infused into the crystal. Always program the stone with love and well-being, and all will work out for the highest good.

Mental uses Clear quartz helps you stay focused on the goal at hand. It's a perfect companion for students of all ages and all teachings. Use clear quartz while you study or work on projects. This gemstone is helpful for memory recall, so employ it when taking exams or any type of test.

Emotional uses Clear quartz helps you clarify the real source of your emotional upset. Pay attention to your feelings and emotions while holding clear quartz, as it amplifies whatever you are focused on. Be sure to intend that working with the clear quartz will help you uncover whatever you need to realize or understand to relieve your emotional upset. Clarity and understanding often alleviates disturbing feelings.

Physical uses Clear quartz is a crystal that essentially supports your overall well-being. As with its emotional use, whatever you intend or focus your attention on while holding clear quartz will amplify it. It extends a hand of support to increase your ability to be successful in all endeavors and areas of life, including financial security, fertility, creativity, family blessings, a happy home, a healthy body, and much more.

Divine guidance Is there something you're having trouble understanding? Are you missing the point? Have you been trying to remove the chaotic energy from your life? It is time to gain clarity and have a clearer picture of what is truly going on within you and around you. Can you see the bigger picture? Get focused and stay focused! Take the time to meditate and try to see the greater perspective from varying points of view.

About the stone:

Quartz is a prolific mineral composed of silicon dioxide and is found in several forms. Quartz is in the trigonal system and it exhibits piezoelectricity, a phenomenon wherein electricity is created when pressure is applied to the crystal. It is this unique characteristic that enables quartz to be used in electronic equipment such as transmitters, radios, and clocks. The varieties that crystallize are known as amethyst, citrine, smoky quartz, rose quartz, and rock crystal quartz, depending on their color.

QUARTZ, CATHEDRAL
Love, Light, Wisdom, and Knowledge

Color(s)	translucent, yellow (citrine), purple (amethyst)
Chakra(s)	all
Planet(s)	Earth
Number(s)	33
Element(s)	earth
Mohs scale	7
Astro sign(s)	Aries

Affirmation I am light and love. It is easy for me to see the bigger picture. I access higher wisdom and knowledge any time I need it! I am grateful for all the wise spiritual beings who guide my path.

Spiritual uses Cathedral quartz aligns you with higher wisdom as its crystals reach up to the heavenly realm to contact God, the Great Spirit, and the wisdom of the ages. Gaze into this stone and project your intent to be an instrument of the higher will. Use this stone to access the Akashic Records (the history of the cosmos). This type of quartz provides a direct link to the Council of Light, the Ascended Masters, the archangels, and all higher realms of consciousness.

Mental uses Cathedral quartz assists you in tapping into your intelligence. This stone helps you focus on your goals with the underlying and overlying intention of allowing the highest good for all to manifest.

Emotional uses Cathedral quartz invokes the angels, spirit guides, and any spiritual master to be by your side whenever your emotions are raw. Employ this stone to help you rise above the situation and be the "bigger person" in emotionally charged situations.

Physical uses The many spires and multiple terminations in cathedral quartz assist in the manifestation of your physical goals, whatever they may be. Use this stone to help you remember to keep your mind open to the many opportunities and perspectives available to you. It supports those who work with modern technology such as smartphones and computers.

Divine guidance Are you ready to align with the Divine? Do you believe you can be your own mystic? Now is the time to acknowledge your own direct connection with higher wisdom and knowledge. You are an amazing being of light, and it's time to be a light worker. Allow yourself to see things from a higher perspective and take on the role of the wise one with confidence.

> **About the stone:**
> Cathedral quartz is a formation of silicon dioxide crystals with multiple terminations that resemble a cathedral's spires.

Quartz, Channeling
Divine Inspiration

Color(s)	transparent
Chakra(s)	crown
Planet(s)	Jupiter, Venus
Number(s)	7, 3
Element(s)	air
Mohs scale	7
Astro sign(s)	Pisces

Affirmation I am divinely inspired. I use the information and wisdom delivered into my consciousness for the good of all. I take positive action using the wisdom of those who have walked this path before me. I am a channel of love, light, and well-being.

Spiritual uses Channeling quartz connects you with your angels and spirit guides. It aligns you with trust so divine inspiration becomes evident. This quartz helps you put your awareness in direct contact with the seven chakras and the body, mind, and soul, allowing you to receive and interpret insights and information to use in your daily life. Use channeling quartz to create divinely inspired artwork, write a book, create a dance routine, and anything you want to be able to "download" from the Divine.

Mental uses Channeling quartz helps bring your mind into focus. This quartz crystal point can be used as you would use a radio knob to tune it into the right channel. Channel quartz aids you in sorting out issues and thinking things through. Use this stone when studying for a test or figuring out a solution to a problem. This quartz point brings things into perspective by helping keep your mind clear.

Emotional uses Channeling quartz can help you reconnect with an emotional part of yourself that you've lost, hidden, or buried, such as your inner child, your inner mother, your inner genius, or your inner wise woman. With this stone in hand, allow yourself to open your consciousness to realign your feelings and emotions from within as well as from the assistance of the ones who watch over you from the heavenly realms.

Physical uses Channeling quartz is a stone for the performer or anyone on stage. It is also the stone of travel, especially long-distance travel, which provides the opportunity to experience different cultures. The three-sided face of this quartz is the stone of productivity and manifesting in the physical world. Use the energy of the seven-sided face on the point of this crystal to follow through on your good business ideas. This is a good stone for yoga instructors, astrologers, numerologists, metaphysicians, archeologists, travel writers, entertainers, psychic investigators, and researchers.

Divine guidance Do you need inspiration? Do you often feel inspired? You can be an instrument and a channel of knowledge and wisdom. Take the time to clear and align your chakras. Make it your intention to gain clarity in your life. It's time to sort out what's truly important in your life and clear away the challenges. Solutions are always available. Ask your angels for understanding or clarity, and then be ready to receive the inspiration.

About the stone:
Channeling quartz refers to a silicon dioxide crystal that has a seven-sided face and a three-sided face on the point or termination of the crystal.

QUARTZ, CHLORITE PHANTOM
Earth Steward

Color(s)	transparent with green chlorite inclusions
Chakra(s)	heart
Planet(s)	Earth
Number(s)	4
Element(s)	earth, water
Mohs scale	7
Astro sign(s)	Taurus

Affirmation I am a steward of the earth. It is easy for me to "think green." I reduce the amount of waste produced in my household. I reuse and recycle everything I can. I will leave our planet in better condition than it was before I arrived.

Spiritual uses Chlorite phantom quartz holds the vibration of nature. Just as you would use chlorophyll-rich green drinks and foods to cleanse and detoxify your body, the same is true with cleansing your aura or energy field by using this stone. The spiritual wisdom of the plant kingdom and the devic forces of the plants can be accessed by working with this quartz. It opens a doorway so you can meet fairies, gnomes, and elves.

Mental uses Chlorite phantom quartz gives you a peek into a microcosm of life, helping you to gain better perspective on that level while opening your mind to the macrocosm. The inner structure of the stone provides a "green-print" to help you engineer new ways of planetary stewardship. This stone inspires green building and green living. And it is a reminder to reduce, reuse, and recycle to make it possible to live in harmony with nature.

Emotional uses Chlorite phantom quartz helps you embrace the perceived negative emotional challenges of your past so you can use it as fertilizer or foundational nutrition for your future experiences. Use the green energy of the phantom's display of periods of growth to integrate the teachings of those past emotional lessons.

Physical uses Due to its rich green content, chlorite phantom quartz carries the vibration of abundance and prosperity. It also helps you connect with nature and sparks an interest in herbs, aromatherapy, and natural healing alternatives. This stone contains inclusions of green minerals that outline and display old growth. It is supportive during the process of a physical cleanse and helps you maintain a clearer conscious connection with your physical being.

Divine guidance Do you have a green mindset? Do you follow through with that mindset in your everyday choices? Do you know what kind of footprint you are leaving on Mother Earth? It's time to think green and step into your role as a steward of the earth. This planet depends upon you to reduce, reuse, and recycle. Take the time to look at what needs to be cleared away and renewed in your life. You may have a knack or affinity for the therapeutic use of essential oils, herbs, and other forms of naturopathy.

About the stone:
Chlorite phantom quartz refers to the presence of a mineral from the chlorite group occurring inside a clear quartz crystal. During the crystallization process of quartz crystals, a chlorite mineral can cause coloring of the phantom images of crystal faces. Usually green, this coloration can be of a variety of colors depending on the mineral's makeup. Phantoms are caused by a pause in the growth of the crystal due to a lack of mineral-rich liquids forming the crystal or a change in the mineral content of these liquids.

QUARTZ, ELESTIAL
Angels, Angels … Everywhere!

Color(s)	transparent, brown, or black
Chakra(s)	all
Planet(s)	Chiron
Number(s)	11, 22, 33
Element(s)	water, earth
Mohs scale	7
Astro sign(s)	Scorpio, Aquarius

Affirmation I am grateful for the angelic orchestration in my life. Angels provide guidance to me all the time. Angels light my path. All is well. I allow angels to work through me to provide healing for myself and others. I am a conduit of the Divine.

Spiritual uses Elestial quartz is ideal for angelic communication. Legend has it these geometric treasures were brought through the ethers by the heavenly realm, which is why this skeletal quartz often looks singed. If you are an Angel Messenger Practitioner or you work with angels, divination cards, or other modalities like Integrated Energy Therapy (IET), a focused healing energy to clear energy blocks that have accumulated in the body, elestial quartz is a good addition to your toolbox. Use it to help you channel angels, Archangel Sandalphon, Ascended Masters, and saints.

Mental uses The geometric formation of elestials helps align your mind with anything having to do with numbers: mathematics, geometric, formulaic equations, or electronic configurations. For those whose work involves information technology, this stone can assist with finding a solution to the problem when an impasse has been reached.

Emotional uses Elestials help heal old emotional wounds. They also are great to give you a boost when you need to figure out what emotions are buried in your consciousness. If you need to "uninstall" an emotional program, work with an elestial while you dream, journal, cry, emote, or process your feelings. You'll find you have support from the angels and can clear away unneeded emotional baggage.

Physical uses Elestial quartz, especially the smoky quartz variety, is helpful for stress-related aches and pains. Hold this stone in the palm of your hand or place it on the part of your body that is challenged. Visualize the stone amplifying your intention to relax and release the source of the discomfort. This stone is beneficial for your bones, muscles, and skeleton.

Divine guidance Are you a messenger? Do you receive messages from angels? If you aren't already aware of the messages angels are bringing you, then being attracted to this stone alerts you to listen and pay attention to all the signs and symbols around you that give you clues to make your life easier.

About the stone:
Elestial quartz crystals are composed of silicon dioxide with multiple terminations, etchings, inclusions, and extrusions, creating a skeletal look.

QUARTZ, GIRASOL
Shimmering Lights

COLOR(S)	translucent milky white
CHAKRA(S)	crown
PLANET(S)	Moon
NUMBER(S)	0
ELEMENT(S)	water
MOHS SCALE	7
ASTRO SIGN(S)	Cancer

Affirmation I objectively observe myself in my interactions with others. I increase my self-awareness as I watch my words and actions from various perspectives. I continue to work toward self-improvement at every opportunity. I notice the mirrors and projections around and within me without judgment or preconceptions.

Spiritual uses Girasol quartz aligns you with the moon phases, the Divine Feminine, and your intuition. Its reflective qualities enhance meditation practice and deepen contemplation. Use this stone to amplify dream recall and the ability to interpret your dreams for personal growth and spiritual awareness. Use girasol quartz to call on the assistance of Archangel Auriel.

Mental uses Girasol quartz enhances your ability to visualize and to use your imagination. Both visualization and imagination are the keys to the creative powers of manifestation. Use the refractive and reflective qualities of this stone to manifest your dreams. Stay focused on what you want, and release your focus on what isn't working or what you don't want.

Emotional uses Girasol quartz has an opalescent quality that mirrors everything around you to help you observe yourself. If you are pointing fingers at others, take a moment to observe yourself to see if there is an aspect of yourself that resembles those challenging qualities you are pointing at! If not, then step away from the situation, person, place, or thing, and move into your own personal truth.

Physical uses Girasol quartz is a good stone for mothers. This quartz carries the energy of mother's milk, which is also representative of the nurturing energy required to raise balanced, healthy children. This stone is beneficial for supporting the mammary glands and the womb, as well as for balancing hormones for both sexes.

Divine guidance Have you noticed that people and situations are reflecting your feelings or thoughts? Pay attention to the messages these mirrors provide. It's time to go within and take stock of what work you need to do to improve your self-awareness and personal growth. Pay attention to the moon cycles, and learn how you can use the energy of the moon to improve your life.

About the stone:
Girasol quartz is a semi-transparent form of quartz (silicon dioxide) with a silk (microscopic fiberlike inclusions) that sometimes exhibits asterism or a bluish glow. This could be due to the presence of sillimanite, an aluminum silicate, in the quartz.

QUARTZ, ISIS POINT
Impermanence

COLOR(S)	transparent
CHAKRA(S)	all
PLANET(S)	Pluto, Uranus
NUMBER(S)	45/9
ELEMENT(S)	air
MOHS SCALE	7
ASTRO SIGN(S)	Scorpio, Cancer

Affirmation I accept life's impermanent nature. I easily adapt to my changing environment. Change is good. I assist people who are challenged by change. I embrace transitions as they exist within life. I embrace the grieving process.

Spiritual uses The Isis crystal carries the vibration of acceptance and understanding change and transitions. It activates the visionary vibration of your consciousness to allow the evolution of your ideas and your faith, and the manifestation of potential realities. This particular quartz formation helps improve your spiritual sight and knowing (clairvoyance and claircognizance). Use these crystals to help spirits and disincarnate entities find their way to the light or the Other Side. Give it as a gift to those who are mourning the death of a loved one; it will help the grieving fully release their dear departed into the light.

Mental uses The Isis crystal helps you with communication and telepathic linking. It can help you out of a rut when you've become too set in your way of thinking, opening your mind to other possibilities. This in turn helps you increase your chances of enjoying a favorable outcome. This stone is also a reminder that anything is possible with strong will and intention.

Emotional uses The Isis crystal supports you through any kind of transition. It is especially helpful for hospice caregivers and the loved ones of a family member as they transition to the Other Side. Use this crystal when there is a conflict between your emotions and your common sense. It helps you accept when old friends depart your life and new alliances and networks form.

Physical uses The Isis crystal helps you maintain all parts of your body as whole. It aligns you with recognition of how all your thoughts, feelings, words, and actions affect your physical health. It is also a perfect stone to assist you in accessing your intuition to know how to recapture your physical health—to once again become whole and complete.

Divine guidance Are you trying to change your life? Start by changing the way you look at things. Open your mind to the unlimited possibilities of the seen and the unseen. You are a visionary. Use your intuitive skills to open up your potential realities.

About the stone:
An Isis point is a silicon dioxide crystal that has a five-sided face or facet on the termination of the point.

Quartz, Laser Wand
Limitless Focus

Color(s)	transparent
Chakra(s)	third eye, crown
Planet(s)	Saturn, Sun
Number(s)	65/11
Element(s)	earth
Mohs scale	7
Astro sign(s)	Capricorn

Affirmation I focus easily on the infinite wisdom of the ancient ones. Fine-pointed clarity resides in my heart and mind, bringing me all the knowledge I need. It is with clear intentions that I move forward—self-assured and confident.

Spiritual uses Quartz laser wands, which are wider at the base of the crystal and then narrow to a laser-like point at the tip, are often used for psychic spiritual healing. The hieroglyphic-like etchings and markings on the sides of the quartz crystal are conducive toward helping you retrieve the wisdom of the ages. This type of clear quartz point helps maintain focus during meditation. Real laser wands will sing or make a tingling sound when two or more gently touch each other, which help to align your consciousness through sound much like you would use a singing bowl. They are sometimes known as singing crystals.

Mental uses Laser wands hone your ability to stay focused, helping you be more systematic and organized in your approach to things. Working with this stone helps you reach your goals. Keep this stone nearby to help you attract influential people who can help you achieve your desired outcome.

Emotional uses A laser wand can help you heal from relationships or situations that were based in selfish material pleasures and outcomes. This wand fine-tunes your ability to observe yourself objectively and make the necessary corrections to your behavior and patterns.

Physical uses Laser wands are beneficial for the overall health of the kidneys and the adrenals, and help relieve stress-related disease. From a financial perspective, this stone helps you focus on the direction you should take to create abundance in your life.

Divine guidance Are you trying to get to the point of the matter? Have you learned from past experiences? Look back as a tool for understanding and self-growth. Allow yourself to move forward with confidence. Open yourself up to making new friends, developing new relationships, and establishing networks for both personal and financial gain.

About the stone:
Laser wands are quartz crystal points (silicon dioxide) appearing as long, thin crystals with distinct terminations.

QUARTZ, PHANTOM
Patterns of the Past

Color(s)	clear quartz with phantom inclusions
Chakra(s)	crown, third eye, solar plexus
Planet(s)	Pluto, Neptune
Number(s)	13
Element(s)	earth
Mohs scale	7
Astro sign(s)	Scorpio, Pisces

Affirmation I embrace the hard-earned lessons of the past to catapult me into a bright and positive future. I love to learn new things every day in all areas of my life. Opportunities constantly present themselves to me. I recognize opportunities and take immediate action.

Spiritual uses Phantom quartz crystals appear as if they have a crystal "ghost" inside them. This "apparition" helps you remember who you truly are and where you are about to go. These crystals help you realize you have much more to learn and opportunities from which to grow. Because phantoms within crystals aren't always extremely obvious, they help you with spiritual sight and the ability to use your peripheral psychic sight. This is also a perfect amulet for ghost hunters who investigate reports of ghosts with the goal to detect the energies of the unseen forces. It is also helpful for remembrance of past lives to learn from the past and grow into the future.

Mental uses A phantom crystal is beneficial for grounding your energy when you begin to think that you are a more advanced being than others, without squashing your self-esteem and positive energy. This stone helps you look deeper and keeps you in touch with the awareness that there is much more to know and learn. With this awareness, this stone can then activate your courage to proceed to your next level.

Emotional uses Phantom quartz helps you gain clarity on repetitive emotional patterns throughout the various stages of your life. It is helpful for uncovering the cyclical nature of how you engage in relationships so you can break recurring themes and move forward in a healthy way. This is a stone of transformation and change. It helps release the ego's attachment to behaviors and situations.

Physical uses Phantom quartz supports recovery from the habitual use of drugs, alcohol, or any other overused substance. A stone of purification, it is also helpful during a physical cleanse for overall health.

Divine guidance Have you ever caught a glimpse of spirit in your peripheral vision? It's time to develop your intuitive skills and receive guidance from many realms of consciousness. Are you going through a mutual growth spurt in your life? Take a look at where you've been and realize there is so much more you can do and learn. Release patterns of your past, and heal the issues once and for all.

About the stone:
Phantom quartz is silicon dioxide with outlines or ghost-like images of crystal faces inside the crystal, caused by a pause in the crystal's growth due to a lack of mineral-rich liquids forming the crystal or a change in the mineral content of these liquids.

Quartz, Record-keeper
Accessing the Akashic Records

Color(s)	clear, smoky brown, black, and yellow
Chakra(s)	all
Planet(s)	Sun
Number(s)	9
Element(s)	water, air
Mohs scale	7
Astro sign(s)	Leo

Affirmation I am divinely guided. All wisdom and knowledge are stored within my consciousness. I listen to the guidance that flows through me. Angels and high spiritual beings guide me in my daily life. I'm grateful for their guidance. I only ask for assistance and the information or path is revealed.

Spiritual uses Record-keeper crystals, crystals with naturally formed triangular etchings, hold records of the past, present, and the potential realities of the future. In using a record-keeper, you have a chance to tap into the information stored within your cells, bones, muscles, and DNA, as well as an opportunity to access the Akashic Records (the history of the cosmos). When you meditate with a record-keeper crystal, you will be open to a download of information. However, you may not know specifically what information has been downloaded in that moment. The information is retrievable when you need it.

Mental uses The stone of ancient wisdom, a record-keeper crystal is ideal when studying or working on a project that requires access to universal wisdom. This is a perfect totem stone for the writer, musician, or artist. The record-keeper will send what you need to know or integrate into your knowledge base. Though you may not be aware that the "download" has occurred, the information will be retrievable when required.

Emotional uses Record-keeper quartz is beneficial during periods of change and transition. It can help you access the higher purpose for these changes. At a very deep, intuitive level, record-keeper quartz can answer that eternal question, "Why is this happening?" With the understanding gained through meditation with this stone, you can forge ahead with greater ease and emotional balance.

Physical uses Record-keeper quartz aligns energetically your body, mind, and spirit. It is a perfect stone for healing through holistic means. It also promotes success in any type of visionary business such as yoga studios, metaphysical stores, and spiritual publishing houses. It is also a good stone for librarians or anyone in the business of keeping records.

Divine guidance Are you paying attention to your thoughts—the ones that seem divinely inspired? Take action on those thoughts, and watch how events in your life unfold in a favorable way. Are you using the information and wisdom stored within you? It's time now to share and teach what you know to help others on this planet.

About the stone:
Record-keeper quartz crystals are silicon dioxide with naturally formed triangular etchings on one or more of the faces of the termination.

Quartz, Relationship Crystals
Relationships

Color(s)	transparent
Chakra(s)	heart, solar plexus
Planet(s)	Venus, Juno
Number(s)	6
Element(s)	earth, air, fire, water
Mohs scale	7
Astro sign(s)	Libra

Affirmation I attract healthy, harmonious relationships into my life. My colleagues, friends, and family respect me. They see my magnificence and accept me exactly as I am. It's wonderful to be liked and loved so much by such wonderful people!

Spiritual uses Relationship crystals are ideal for fostering palpable relationships with your angels, animal totems, and spirit guides. Just as you cultivate friendships, business relationships, family relationships, and romantic relationships, it is beneficial to realize that the relationship with your guides and angels is just as real. Allow this stone to guide you toward amplifying the reality of the relationship you have with your guardian spirits.

Mental uses A relationship crystal—two crystals growing together—can represent relationships in your life. Choose the stone carefully, as some relationship crystals have one point that is substantially larger or taller than the other. A crystal with this configuration is beneficial for a parent-child or teacher-student relationship. Look for specimens with equally sized crystals to represent a more balanced relationship. This stone helps you concentrate on the positive qualities you want to foster in that relationship and steers your thoughts away from what isn't working.

Emotional uses A twin crystal is a relationship crystal in which the height of the two crystals is equal, making this stone ideal for a business partnership, platonic friendship, or a romantic relationship. Use a twin crystal with the intention to maintain a balanced and healthy relationship. A family crystal is a relationship crystal with two points equal in size representing the parents plus one or more smaller crystals representing the children. These clusters of crystals help balance emotions and improve confidence within relationships, They also provide a reminder that when there are no expectations or assumptions, there are no disappointments.

Physical uses Relationship crystals are useful for significantly improving your business and financial success. Use this cluster of quartz for communication and understanding in any type of relationship. This stone is a reminder that good communication involves truly hearing what another person is saying and capturing the essence of the feelings associated with the message. When we truly hear what is being said, we have a better chance of understanding.

Divine guidance Are you ready to meet the love of your life? Would you like to reignite your soul-mate connection with your partner? Maybe you are ready to start a family. Cultivate and nurture the loving relationships presently in your life, and change your mindset to think as "we" rather than "me" to attract or renew more love into your life.

About the stone:
Relationship quartz crystals are silicon dioxide with two terminations at the point or two crystals growing together side by side.

QUARTZ, ROSE
Compassion, Kindness, and Love!

COLOR(S)	pink
CHAKRA(S)	heart
PLANET(S)	Venus
NUMBER(S)	6
ELEMENT(S)	water
MOHS SCALE	7
ASTRO SIGN(S)	Taurus, Libra

Affirmation I am tolerant and accept the differences between my beliefs and those of others. I am nurturing. I accept nurturing from others. I am compassionate and kind. I give love to others and readily accept theirs in return.

Spiritual uses The pink vibration of rose quartz activates the bridge between the upper three chakras and the lower three. This is significant because this bridge helps connect your human existence as a grounded individual on this planet with your spiritual one. This stone aligns your consciousness with Divine love, compassion, mercy, tolerance, and kindness. It calls the energy of the angels, including Archangels Chamuel and Haniel, to surround and protect you.

Mental uses Rose quartz adds the element of love to the thoughts you hold in your consciousness. With this stone in hand, practice thinking through your heart. Put your attention and focus on your heart when you try to think things through, and you will find a peaceful loving solution to whatever you are contemplating.

Emotional uses Rose quartz is the perfect stone to help you attract romance and love into your life. It aids in attracting your soul mate. The soothing pink color of the rose quartz crystal is perfect for situations when you need to feel comforted and surrounded by unconditional love. Use it when you need to amplify your own feelings of unconditional love for others as well. It is a good stone for grief, loss of love, loss of friendships, and to make a better connection with babies and children.

Physical uses Rose quartz supports skin regeneration and skin rejuvenation. It can also help during a cancer-related healing process. Use this stone as a sleep aid and for healing the physical heart and any diseases or challenges associated with the heart.

Divine guidance Are you ready to allow healthy, loving relationships into your life? Or maybe you are ready to start or recharge a romantic connection. Gift yourself with time to rejuvenate your physical body and emotions. Allow yourself time for healing emotional wounds.

About the stone:
Rose quartz is the pink form of silicon dioxide with microscopic mineral inclusions that make it translucent to cloudy. Although rose quartz is usually found in massive form, it very rarely crystallizes; these crystals are sensitive to light and their color will fade. The color of stones cut from its massive form is stable, however.

QUARTZ, RUTILATED
Sparkling Golden Light

COLOR(S)	transparent with red and golden rutile inclusions
CHAKRA(S)	root, navel, solar plexus, third eye, crown
PLANET(S)	Sun, Venus
NUMBER(S)	6
ELEMENT(S)	fire
MOHS SCALE	7 (quartz), 6 (rutile)
ASTRO SIGN(S)	Leo

Affirmation I am energized, healthy, and strong. I am grateful that my vital life force provides me with the energy and motivation to live life to the fullest! Financial abundance is mine. My connection with the Divine is alive and well.

Spiritual uses Rutilated quartz represents the halo of light surrounding your head, or crown chakra. The golden light sparkling within the white energetic sphere of the auric field exemplifies the infinite connection to the cosmos, the Divine, and All That Is. Use this stone to improve your intuitive skills and your connection with guides, angels, and your higher self. With its ability to ward off negativity, this is a good stone for protection.

Mental uses The golden red energy in rutilated quartz promotes fine-tuned thinking. This stone is useful for tapping into higher thought and wisdom. By placing your attention on the rutile within the stone, you can better maintain focus and eliminate scattered thoughts.

Emotional uses Rutilated quartz is a self-empowering stone. Use it to find the shining light within you, and step away from the useless act of downplaying yourself. With its ability to boost courage, this stone is beneficial for improving your self-esteem.

Physical uses Rutilated quartz is a reminder to protect yourself from harmful ultraviolet rays. Use this stone to improve your energy level. The red and golden rutile inclusions enhance your physical endurance. It adds chi or life force to the body, mind, and spirit. Some legends say that this stone slows the aging process. With this stone in hand, visualize increased wealth and prosperity. Its golden energy will amplify your financial success and abundance.

Divine guidance Are you ready to move forward with your life? You have the courage within you to move ahead with your ideas by getting the wheels in motion to create your project or intention. Recognize the amazing, powerful person you are and shine on!

About the stone:
Rutilated quartz is silicon dioxide containing long, thin, hair-like rutile crystals, usually exhibiting a red or golden color.

QUARTZ, SMOKY
Grounded Protection

COLOR(S)	translucent brown or black
CHAKRA(S)	root
PLANET(S)	Pluto
NUMBER(S)	53/8
ELEMENT(S)	earth
MOHS SCALE	7
ASTRO SIGN(S)	Scorpio

Affirmation I am divinely protected. All is well, life is good. I easily refocus my efforts away from distractions. I honor my grounded connection with Mother Earth. I am free of emotional baggage. I fully appreciate this transformation and enjoy emotional balance. I am aware of my feelings.

Spiritual uses Smoky quartz is an especially good protection tool for use during spiritual ceremonies and rituals. Use this stone in crystal grids (see page 389) to maintain protective energy and deflect negative vibes. You can also use it to deflect the electromagnetic frequencies emitted by electronics. Grounding you and helping clear out the constant chatter of the mind, it is a perfect companion to meditation practice.

Mental uses Smoky quartz helps eliminate doubt and worry when you are faced with chaos and/or confusion. This stone helps you feel safe and sound. With focused intent, smoky quartz helps amplify your feelings of security. It is also an excellent tool for realigning scattered energy.

Emotional uses Smoky quartz is a wonderful healing tool following the energetic cord-cutting process. When emotional trauma has been released (emotional cords have been cut), place this stone on or near the areas of your body associated with the trauma. Visualize the smoky quartz cauterizing the emotional scar to prevent any further damage or repetition. This stone can also helps you get out of hot water when emotions are steaming.

Physical uses Smoky quartz is an excellent smoking cessation aid. It helps to eliminate the urge to smoke and also softens the anger and agitation associated with nicotine withdrawal and the detoxification process.

Divine guidance Are you trying to ward off negative thinking? Are you aware of your thoughts? Let go of your repetitive patterns. Focus on where you are going and manifest your best life. Do you feel that you've been scattered lately? Are you feeling confused? Find your connection and ground yourself. Stay focused on what is important in your life. Establish a circle of protection to keep you on course.

About the stone:
Smoky quartz is the light to dark brown variety of quartz (silicon dioxide). Its color is caused by impurities of aluminum and irradiation of the stone, naturally or artificially.

Quartz, Tabular
Mental Telepathy

Color(s)	translucent, brown to black, yellow, purple, lavender
Chakra(s)	all
Planet(s)	Mercury
Number(s)	2
Element(s)	air
Mohs scale	7
Astro sign(s)	Gemini

Affirmation When I speak, people listen and understand me. I communicate from my heart to the hearts of others. I visualize and send mental pictures as I express my ideas, visions, opinions, and matters of importance.

Spiritual uses Tabular quartz is the perfect stone to use when creating grids of light for purposes of increasing the vibration of love on this planet. "Tabbies," as they are colloquially known, are a perfect tool to amplify this matrix-like grid or energetic web that surrounds the earth. This stone is ideal for interdimensional connection and communication with spiritual beings, including angels, saints, guides, and Ascended Masters.

Mental uses Tabular quartz is ideal for communicating directly from your heart and mind to the heart and mind of someone you are speaking with through the use of mental images. Tabbies are good tools for speakers and teachers, as well as anyone whose work includes communications. This stone is also a good study aid as it stores the information until you are ready to retrieve it: simply rub the stone and hold the intention to recall the data.

Emotional uses Tabular quartz is the relationship counselor of the gemstone kingdom. This stone lends emotional support through the use of effective listening skills and communications skills. With this stone in hand, you are better able to transmit the feelings associated with the words you are speaking to improve communication with others. When a person is heard and understood, it prevents emotional upset and distress.

Physical uses Tabular quartz is beneficial for the eyes, ears, and brain.

Divine guidance Do people listen when you speak? Do you feel like you are not being heard? Think about what you wish to communicate until you know exactly what you need to say. Use visualization and imagination to telepathically convey your message through mental images from heart to heart and mind to mind.

About the stone:
Sometimes called "tabbies," tabular quartz are tablet-like silicon dioxide crystals in which two sides are much wider than the other four.

Quartz, Time Link
Unlimited Potential

Color(s)	transparent
Chakra(s)	third eye, crown
Planet(s)	Chiron, Pluto
Number(s)	10/1
Element(s)	air
Mohs scale	7
Astro sign(s)	Scorpio, Aquarius

Affirmation I imagine future potential realities. I manifest with my thoughts, words, and actions. I trust that the reality I create is wonderful. I have plenty of time. I complete tasks. I stay focused on the present. I relax and enjoy everything I do.

Spiritual uses The time link quartz crystal is a portal to the unlimited source of the no-mind, the Great Mystery, and the Great Void from which all things come forth. Use this crystal, a quartz point with a seventh facet that is a parallelogram, in contemplation and meditation to go deep within to the place of nothingness.

Mental uses A time link crystal opens your mind to unlimited potential future realities from which you can choose. Every future moment depends on your present thoughts and state of consciousness. With this stone in hand, you can become very aware of what you believe, release your limited beliefs and thoughts, and replace them with positive ones.

Emotional uses When a time link crystal point has a facet that angles to the left, it assists you in accessing a past life or earlier parts of this life, enabling you to heal and rebalance emotional and mental issues. It is a powerful tool to heal childhood trauma or imposed belief systems that no longer serve your highest good. Use time link quartz with a facet that angles to the right to visualize and imagine the unlimited potential realities available to you in your future.

Physical uses Time link crystals deepen your connection to many realms: the subconscious, the super-consciousness, and the various incarnations of your soul, supporting the healing of the physical body from any type of disease or imbalance. As you successfully heal your past, you will release outdated beliefs, balance karma, and delete negative molecular memories so that you may become healthy, whole, and complete.

Divine guidance Are you asking the question, "Why is this happening to me?" or "What did I ever do to deserve this?" Are you caught in a pattern in which you are experiencing the same situation over and over, but only the "cast" is different in the same play? Now is a good time to look into regression. Through regression, you can begin to uncover the original sources of the issues presently at play in your life.

About the stone:
Time link crystals are quartz crystal points (silicon dioxide) that have a seventh facet in the shape of a parallelogram.

Quartz, Tourmalinated
Energetic Connections

Color(s)	transparent with black sticklike inclusions
Chakra(s)	root
Planet(s)	Pluto, Mercury
Number(s)	5
Element(s)	air
Mohs scale	7
Astro sign(s)	Scorpio, Gemini

Affirmation I am mindful of the energetic connections between myself and others. I automatically sever unhealthy strings of attachment. I am grounded and focused. I relax in nature to regenerate and rejuvenate my energy field. My body easily deflects electromagnetic frequencies. I balance my life with fresh air and sunshine.

Spiritual uses The black tourmaline in tourmalinated quartz helps you integrate your spiritual practice into everyday life. The clear quartz amplifies the power of the black tourmaline, allowing you to go deeper into previously hidden aspects of your consciousness. The tourmaline deflects negative energy stemming from psychic attacks. The quartz brings clarity to help understand the source of the negative energy. It is beneficial during shamanic journeywork, and it can be worn as an amulet of protection and to help reveal deeper spiritual truths.

Mental uses Tourmalinated quartz helps you return to center when you feel out of balance. It helps you focus so you can continue to achieve your goals. This stone is also useful for clearing negative mental energy associated with jealousy, negative self-talk, confusing mental chatter, and general chaos.

Emotional uses Tourmalinated quartz helps draw out dark, negative emotions so they can be released. Use this stone when you overreact to a situation or a person and need to understand the reason for the negative reaction. With this stone in hand, locate the source of the emotional problem so you can begin to heal.

Physical uses Black tourmaline is useful for deflecting electromagnetic frequencies emitted from cell phones, computers, and other electronic devices. This stone helps you identify and heal sources of physical toxins by increasing your awareness of what needs to be cleared out in order to achieve and maintain good health.

Divine guidance Do you need to release the energetic cords attached to your ancestors and your past? Do you still have easily pushed buttons? Take the time to recognize the patterns you are repeating from your parents and other family members established by your upbringing. Once you identify the belief systems and habits that were instilled at a young age, you can release those ties to the past. Snip the wires that connect to your buttons.

About the stone:
Tourmalinated quartz is quartz (silicon dioxide) containing tourmaline inclusions, usually exhibiting a black color.

Quartz, Window
I See Clearly Now ...

Color(s)	transparent
Chakra(s)	heart, third eye, crown
Planet(s)	Sun
Number(s)	9
Element(s)	air
Mohs scale	7
Astro sign(s)	Aquarius

Affirmation I am awakening every day in many ways. I am conscious of my thoughts, words, and actions. I have great clarity. I meditate and contemplate. I am a catalyst to awaken awareness in all beings.

Spiritual uses With its perfect diamond-shaped face (usually a seventh facet), window quartz, the stone of the seeker, is a portal into your consciousness. Use this stone to practice self-observation. During open-eyed meditation, gaze into the diamond-shaped face on the point, forming the intent to explore the inner sanctums of your consciousness as you empty your mind of the regular chatter.

Mental uses Window quartz crystal helps you observe your thoughts, patterns, and behaviors, and it helps you be open to releasing whatever is no longer useful in realigning with a higher consciousness. This stone can play an important role in the evolution of your mind and your mental capacities. It helps you stay attuned to the realization that regardless of your intellectual acomplishments, you always have so much more to learn. It is most ideal for the eternal student.

Emotional uses A quartz crystal with a window facet aids in revealing the intention behind the intention, helping you to know your true essence beyond illusions and the masks you wear. This crystal helps you look inside yourself, and it magnifies your ability to see reflections from the people around you every day. This stone reminds you that you can learn many lessons about yourself by observing the actions of others and seeing them as a reflection of yourself.

Physical uses A window crystal is well suited for a nurse, doctor, or other healthcare professional who continues to search for new sources for healing. This is a good companion stone for researchers, inventors, or anyone searching for facts and knowledge. This stone can also be used to improve eyesight and any physical conditions relating to the eyes.

Divine guidance Are you searching for higher spiritual truths? Do you know that there is still so much more to learn in life and so much more room to grow mentally, spiritually, and emotionally? Research the various tools available to expand your knowledge and support your growth, and employ those that suit you best.

> *About the stone:*
> Quartz crystal points (silicon dioxide) with a perfect diamond-shaped face, usually a seventh facet.

RHODOCHROSITE
Inner Strength

COLOR(S)	pink, rose-red with white inclusion swirls
CHAKRA(S)	heart, solar plexus
PLANET(S)	Venus
NUMBER(S)	2
ELEMENT(S)	water
MOHS SCALE	3.5–4
ASTRO SIGN(S)	Taurus, Libra

Affirmation It is safe for me to be powerful in loving ways. I am magnificent! I have the strength to do anything I set out to do with loving intention. I am grateful for the courage to be all I can be! I am love.

Spiritual uses This optimistic gem provides a link to the Divine Feminine. With this stone in hand, connect with the female Ascended Masters, including Mother Mary, Kuan Yin, Isis, and Mary Magdalene, to acquire the qualities of the feminine Christ consciousness. This stone is also perfect to connect with Archangels Auriel, Chamuel, and Tzaphkiel. Rhodochrosite helps to align you with compassion, inner peace, tolerance, and love. It tells you to love yourself and others completely and wholly just as you are!

Mental uses Often found in silver mines, this gem is good for helping you see the silver lining within any situation. There is always something positive that can come out of even the most negative situations. It takes time and hindsight to see that silver lining, but rest assured it does exist.

Emotional uses The nurturing rose-red color of this gem provides a link between your heart and your solar plexus, helping you garner the courage to love yourself fully and completely. It's a good stone to remind yourself of your perfect magnificence. Rhodochrosite helps you overcome verbal, mental, and emotional abuse by jogging your memory to say a positive affirmation any time negative thoughts from the past arise.

Physical uses Rhodochrosite has been known to assist people in the process of healing from cancer. There is a gentle loving quality about this stone that elicits courage and strength during challenging times.

Divination Do you realize that you are magnificent? Believe in your magnificence and embrace your power. Know that you are strong enough to set boundaries with others and assert yourself in a loving manner. Allow yourself to be who you truly are: a loving and magnificent being.

About the stone:
Rhodochrosite is a manganese carbonate that crystallizes in the trigonal system. Usually the material is found in massive or stalagmitic form, although transparent, well-formed rhombohedral crystals are found. Lighter colors represent more calcium occurring with the manganese. *See also* calcite, pink.

RHODONITE
Restoration and Recovery

COLOR(S)	pink, pink-red, or pink-brown often with black inclusions
CHAKRA(S)	heart
PLANET(S)	Venus, Saturn
NUMBER(S)	15/6
ELEMENT(S)	earth
MOHS SCALE	5.5–6.5
ASTRO SIGN(S)	Capricorn, Libra

Affirmation My body is in a constant state of restoration and healing. My mental and emotional bodies are nourished and balanced. I find balance in my life through play, work, rest, exercise, and laughter. I easily nurture myself. I attract nurturing people into my life.

Spiritual uses Rhodonite is a stone that will help ground your spiritual practice. With this stone in hand, visualize and connect your heart with the energetic roots that grow from the soles of your feet. This stone reminds you to find ways to integrate your spirituality into everyday life so your heartfelt connection with the Divine becomes evident in your daily interactions with others. Make this your intention, and take delight in how charmed your life becomes.

Mental uses Rhodonite helps you to relax your mind enough so that you don't take everything so seriously. With this stone in hand, look for and appreciate the comical aspects of mental challenges, and allow the laughter that originates within to well up and relieve pressure and uplift you mentally as well as emotionally. Rhodonite helps you connect your heart and mind.

Emotional uses Rhodonite helps to restore balance to your emotional body after a period of grief following a loss or disappointment. This rosy gem also offers grounded support during times of heartache and sorrow. Allow the gentle pink energy to help you carry on as you journey through a period of unhappiness. Use this stone to feel love.

Physical uses Rhodonite is a good stone to assist you in healing and balancing your physical body. When you are going through physical healing, emotional balancing, financial reestablishment, or grief recovery, this stone reminds you that it is important to take the time to recover after you've been through the wringer, so to speak. Recovery time is necessary to restore your balance so it doesn't result in future disease or imbalances.

Divine guidance Are you in the process of healing after the loss of a job, relationship, pet, or loved one? It is important to reestablish your equilibrium—physically, mentally, and emotionally—after periods of intensity. Try this: look in the mirror, smile, and say, "I love you!" It's time to cultivate a deeper relationship with yourself. Uncover what you can do for yourself to increase your happiness.

About the stone:
Rhodonite is a manganese silicate usually containing calcite that crystallizes in the triclinic system. Rhodonite is usually found in massive form, pink with black veining. The black inclusions are caused by oxidized manganese.

RUBY
Vitality!

COLOR(S)	red
CHAKRA(S)	root
PLANET(S)	Mars, Sun
NUMBER(S)	10
ELEMENT(S)	fire
MOHS SCALE	9
ASTRO SIGN(S)	Aries, Leo

Affirmation Vital life force flows vibrantly through me. I am strong and healthy. I'm motivated to be productive. My tasks and creative projects are completed with ease. I am grateful for my energetic passion for life! I am abundant. I am safe.

Spiritual uses Ruby aligns you with higher consciousness. It helps you be aware of the spiritual and mystical experience that is the unity of the universe also called superconsciousness (yoga), objective consciousness (Gurdjieff), Buddhic consciousness (Theosophy), cosmic consciousness, God-consciousness (Sufism and Hinduism), and Christ consciousness (New Thought). Use this stone to experience spirituality in everyday living. Ruby is a good stone for connecting with a number of archangels, including Ariel, Camael, Melchizedek, and Uriel.

Mental uses Ruby increases your passion for life when used with conscious intent. This brilliant gemstone is a motivational tool for helping you complete tasks. If you've been procrastinating, this stone gives you that needed jumpstart to begin a task or project. Rub a ruby to get your mind wrapped around the idea that it is time to move forward and take action.

Emotional uses Rubies are helpful for getting you fired up when you have a blasé attitude about life. If you've been lacking enthusiasm and generally feel bored, the red energy of ruby will get your blood flowing. As with all red stones, avoid ruby when you are feeling angry, frustrated, or agitated until you get your emotions in balance again.

Physical uses Ruby's hardness and red energy align you with your inner strength. This gemstone revs you up with the fuel required to live life to its fullest. This is a good stone to keep on your person when healing from blood-related disorders or blood pressure challenges.

Divine guidance Do you need to add a little pizzazz to your life? Have you been feeling tired lately? It is time to take steps to improve your endurance and overall health. Get your energy centers recharged, and renew your passion for living a vibrant life!

About the stone:

Ruby is the red variety (orangish red to purplish red) of the mineral corundum, which is aluminum oxide. Pink or purple stones are known as pink or purple sapphires. Corundum crystallizes in the trigonal system. The color in a ruby is caused by the minute presence of chromic oxide.

RUBY IN FUCHSITE
Heartfelt Truth and Goodness

Color(s)	green with red-ruby inclusions
Chakra(s)	root, heart
Planet(s)	Venus
Number(s)	6
Element(s)	earth
Mohs scale	2–3 (fuchsite), 9 (ruby)
Astro sign(s)	Taurus

Affirmation I am love. Deeply and fully, I love all that is. I am grateful for romantic love in my life. I am healthy and balanced in every way. I am blessed with great friends, companions, and colleagues. I willingly share my love and my life with others.

Spiritual uses Ruby in fuchsite vibrates with the energy of spiritually aligned romantic love. Use it as a magnet to attract the perfect life partner. Allow it to help you open your sacred heart to a higher vibration of loving and being loved. This stone helps you have the courage to demonstrate your love and aligns you with heartfelt truth and goodness.

Mental uses Ruby in fuchsite's red energy moves the mind into action. Use this red energy when you are feeling lethargic or stuck on the same thought patterns. The ruby in this stone will move the energy enough to create a mental passion for life. The fuchsite shifts that energy into motion so thoughts that were once stuck or repetitive actually progress to complete a plan of action or intention.

Emotional uses Ruby in fuchsite is a reminder that you are capable of profound feelings of love and well-being. With this stone in hand, turn your attention back to your heart to heal hurt feelings and open yourself up to receive love. The soft green vibration of the fuchsite gently prods you toward accepting friendships and relationships, while the brilliant ruby energizes you to embrace relationships with open arms.

Physical uses Potassium-rich fuchsite combined with the blood-red ruby inclusions balance the cells of the heart as well as the transmission of the electrical impulses. With this stone in hand, use your intention and the power of visualization to attract a balanced, healthy state throughout your physical body. You can also use the stone with the intention to attract the right healthcare practitioners to help you with heart issues.

Divine guidance Have you been a bit shy about accepting overtures of friendship? Are you a bit timid about getting back into a romantic relationship—or rekindling an existing one? Make an effort to turn that reticent attitude into a more outgoing outlook and be willing to connect. Embrace your personal power, recognize your magnificence, and enjoy fulfilling interactions with others.

About the stone:
Fuchsite is a green chrome muscovite of the mica group, sometimes found with ruby inclusions.

Ruby in Zoisite
A River of Bejeweled Blessings

Color(s)	a green and black matrix with opaque red or pink ruby inclusions
Chakra(s)	heart
Planet(s)	Mars, Venus
Number(s)	1, 6
Element(s)	air, fire
Mohs scale	6.5–7 (zoisite), 9 (ruby)
Astro sign(s)	Aries, Libra

Affirmation I am willing to receive love. The door to my heart is open. Blessings flow into my life. I accept gifts, love, and attention with ease and grace. I am grateful for all that is bestowed upon me.

Spiritual uses Ruby in zoisite amplifies the love you give to others and aligns you with your sacred heart and the sacred heart of all beings. Your heartfelt love reaches all the corners of the earth. Use this stone to send healing vibrations to areas where the people and the earth have experienced suffering or disaster. With this stone in hand, amplify your loving prayers and focused intentions to contribute to world peace.

Mental uses Ruby in zoisite helps you shift your perceptions so you can see everything through the eyes of love. With this stone in hand, silence your thoughts, and look within your heart. If you are really disciplined, this stone will help you gain clarity on all that you want to know. It also helps you bring your thoughts to the forefront of your awareness and place them in your heart before you make a decision.

Emotional uses Zoisite with ruby amplifies the vibration of love. It is especially comforting to use during the grieving process, as it helps mend a broken heart. The red energy of the ruby activates passion. This stone helps you speak from your heart and allows the vibration of love to flow through you. It helps you receive love and attention.

Physical uses Zoisite with ruby is an excellent amulet for heart disease, lung disease, breathing challenges, and esophageal problems. This stone reminds you that whatever you need to know, no matter what it is, when you look within from a place of love, the answer will come. This stone also amplifies sexual and sensual energy combined with mature love. It also promotes a stable source of financial income from a loyal and enduring source, and it helps with altruistic efforts as well.

Divine guidance Do you give joyously but find it difficult to receive? It is safe to allow others to do nice things for you and to shower you with gifts. Permit blessings and love to pour into your open, receptive heart. It's time to receive with grace.

About the stone:
Zoisite is a calcium aluminum silicate sometimes found with ruby inclusions.

SAPPHIRE
Divine Wisdom

COLOR(S)	blue, green, orange, pink, purple, yellow, white; meanings listed here are for blue sapphires
CHAKRA(S)	third eye, crown
PLANET(S)	Mercury
NUMBER(S)	8
ELEMENT(S)	air
MOHS SCALE	9
ASTRO SIGN(S)	Virgo, Leo

Affirmation I am blessed with a deep understanding. I have a clear view of the truth. I am grateful that I have mental clarity. My spiritual life is full. I love to share my blessings with others! I have great poise and grace.

Spiritual uses A sapphire makes a good meditation tool, and it helps to train the mind for contemplation and understanding. A stone of wisdom and truth, it clears away distortions and brings forth spiritual knowledge. Use this gemstone to align with higher realms. With its royal associations, sapphire is a good stone for wise leadership. It also supports altruistic work that affects large populations.

Mental uses Sapphire helps you train your mind for single-pointed focus. Use it to reduce confusion and gain clarity and understanding. With its ability to sharpen mental capacity, this stone is helpful for better comprehension of written material, especially extremely dense scholarly texts. It helps you bring your attention to details and organize your materials.

Emotional uses Sapphire helps balance the emotions. It brings calmness to the mind and helps you understand feelings more clearly. Work with this stone to increase inner strength and improve self-esteem. With a greater sense of self-understanding and further self-exploration of your finer qualities, self-confidence increases and general happiness ensues. This calming stone also relieves anger and frustration.

Physical uses Sapphire is supportive when setting the intention to improve bone density and strength. For those who have undergone reconstructive surgery in which titanium has been used, this is an excellent stone to support good physical health; the blue energy calms inflammation and promotes postsurgical healing. Sapphires are helpful for people with dementia or Alzheimer's disease.

Divine guidance Are you feeling confused? Are you in search of wisdom and deeper spiritual insight? Engage in illuminating activities such as meditation, contemplation, and reflection to better understand and truly comprehend the nature of reality, which will illuminate spiritual truths.

About the stone:
Sapphire is the term identifying any color of the mineral corundum, which is aluminum oxide. Sapphire is found in a wide variety of colors, including colorless. The blue variety is colored by trace amounts of iron and titanium.

SARDONYX
Loyalty and Fortunate Life

Color(s)	bands of red, brown, black, and/or white; green (dyed)
Chakra(s)	heart, root
Planet(s)	Saturn, Jupiter
Number(s)	4
Element(s)	earth
Mohs scale	6.5–7
Astro sign(s)	Capricorn

Affirmation I attract good friends into my life. My friends and colleagues are people of integrity. I am grateful for the happy, loyal relationship I have with my romantic partner. I have extraordinary good fortune in all aspects of my life—especially in my relationships with others.

Spiritual uses Sardonyx is ideal to help you maintain a clear mind while meditating. Use this stone as your meditation partner to ward off distracting thoughts, sounds, and interruptions during your regular meditation practice. This is a stone of great discipline, and it is a good tool for a yoga, tai chi, or chi gung practitioner to amplify a stable practice.

Mental uses Sardonyx can be used to help you develop a more structured existence. If you have a tendency to be pulled in many different directions, this stone is a perfect tool to stay on one road at a time. It helps with mental focus and strong concentration. Keep this stone next to your to-do list to reinforce the discipline required to complete tasks.

Emotional uses Green-dyed sardonyx is the stone of good relationships. If you are challenged by the people you've attracted into your life, use this stone to help you make a clear decision to allow those challenges to fade away. As you do so, set another intention to attract into your life thoughtful, loving friends who honor you on all levels.

Physical uses Red and black sardonyx provide the stabilization and strength required to have the endurance, energy, and fortitude to create prosperity and good fortune based on good moral ethics. With its grounding vibrations, this stone helps you translate your energies into tangible results. This is a good stone for a builder, athlete, physical therapist, chiropractor, or massage therapist. Keep it nearby to increase business success in these occupations.

Divine guidance Do you have an inclination toward chaos? Are you easily distracted? If you have many things to care of or accomplish in a day, take steps that will help you to maintain focus on one thing at a time while also supporting your ability to multitask. A clear mind and focused intention provide a strong foundation for accomplishments.

About the stone:
Sardonyx is the brownish-red to orangish-red banded variety of chalcedony. The green variety is likely dyed.

SCOLECITE
On the Wings of Angels

COLOR(S)	translucent, white, and sometimes pink, salmon, red, or green
CHAKRA(S)	crown, third eye, throat
PLANET(S)	Neptune, Uranus, Mercury
NUMBER(S)	1
ELEMENT(S)	fire
MOHS SCALE	5–5.5
ASTRO SIGN(S)	Pisces, Aquarius

Affirmation I consciously request and accept the help of angels. My life flows easily with grace. The energy of healing, love, and well-being flows through me. Meditation is a normal part of my day. My crown, third eye, and throat chakras are balance and aligned. My intuition is intact.

Spiritual uses Scolecite amplifies your intention to remember your dreams. The ability of this stone to hold an electrical charge under pressure opens the portals residing in the crown, third eye, and throat chakras, allowing for receiving and processing of divine inspiration, healing light, and true wisdom. It is especially beneficial for guiding your higher consciousness to be a divine channel of God's love and to connect with Archangel Gabriel.

Mental uses Scolecite aids the ability to receive information from higher realms of consciousness. Use scolecite with conscious intent to conduct the incoming and outgoing wisdom, vibrations, and communication from the spiritual realms. Scolecite holds the vibration of helping you with your memory and focus. It also aids in your ability to transition from sleeping and waking states. Use this stone to awaken your spiritual consciousness.

Emotional uses Scolecite brings about behavioral adjustments when used with purpose. With this stone in hand, set your intention on rebalancing attitudes and responses. Through self-knowledge, understanding, and retention of information gained through contemplation on this stone, the manner in which you act and react is naturally regulated.

Physical uses On a physical level, scolecite helps with brain function, especially as it relates to the brain's plasticity. It aids in stress reduction, relieving pressure, calming inflammation throughout the body, and helping lower blood pressure. This stone is good for those who work as electricians or in the world of computers, electronics, and car repair.

Divine guidance Are you trying to process a lot of information? Do you find it challenging to fall asleep, and then when you finally get to sleep, it's already time to get up—and waking is a challenge? It's time to sort out what's happening in your life. Write in your journal before you go to bed in the evening, and make it your intention to remember your dreams. Record your thoughts and memories upon waking. Find peace as you process each nugget of information.

> **About the stone:**
> Scolecite is a hydrous calcium aluminum silicate that crystallizes in the monoclinic system, and it is usually found as fibrous crystals or masses.

SELENITE
Divine Connections

COLOR(S)	reflective milky white
CHAKRA(S)	crown
PLANET(S)	Moon
NUMBER(S)	7
ELEMENT(S)	water
MOHS SCALE	1.5–2
ASTRO SIGN(S)	Cancer

Affirmation I am aligned with the Divine. I am a spiritual being of divine love and divine light. My spine, bones, tendons, and muscles are healthy, strong, and aligned. I have access to the ancient wisdom stored within me.

Spiritual uses Selenite aligns you with higher consciousness. Associated with Selene, the Greek goddess of the moon, this gemstone is a heaven-sent tool that activates your connection with ancient wisdom and knowledge. Use it during meditation with the intention of aligning your awareness with spiritual master teachers, Ascended Masters, angels, and spirit guides. There are many archangels associated with this stone, including Auriel, Gabriel, Metatron, Sandalphon, Seraphiel, Tzaphkiel, and Uriel. It helps you tune into what your angels and guides want you to know.

Mental uses Selenite brings mental clarity and helps you maintain focus. This is a grounding stone that keeps your thoughts focused on your intention. With this stone in hand, allow your intuitive nature to meld with your intelligence, combining your knowledge with spiritual wisdom.

Emotional uses Selenite is a reminder that you are spiritually, physically, and mentally aligned. It is easy to keep your emotions in balance. This stone helps you detach from drama, thereby allowing you to gain a greater understanding of people and situations. Use this stone like a magic wand of love, light, and goodness to help dissipate any feelings of inadequacy, jealousy, doubt, fear, or any other type of negativity.

Physical uses Selenite is an excellent stone for massage therapists, chiropractors, and physical therapists—it can be used to amplify the benefits of their treatment. This stone also supports the proper care of muscles, bones, nerves, and tendons, helping to strengthen your core physical structure. Selenite's protective qualities and its ability to align you with only the highest good for all concerned helps you maintain loving vibrations when placed at the entrance to your home (inside and out).

Divine guidance Are you feeling out of balance or out of sync with the rest of the world? Do you need to take some time to seek spiritual fulfillment? Are you experiencing physical aches? Whether you answered yes to one or all of these questions, it's time to take care of yourself physically, spiritually, mentally, and emotionally. Take time to tune in to your own innate wisdom to realign your consciousness with love and well-being. Quiet your mind. Hear the ancient wisdom within. Listen to what your angels and guides want you to know.

About the stone:
Selenite is the form of the mineral gypsum that crystallizes in well-formed, clear points. Selenite (gypsum) is a hydrous calcium sulphate that crystallizes in the monoclinic system with crystals being tabular in nature, often exhibiting twinning.

SELENITE ROSE
Sacred Heart

Color(s)	reflective milky white and sandy tan
Chakra(s)	crown, heart
Planet(s)	Moon
Number(s)	13
Element(s)	water
Mohs scale	1.5–2
Astro sign(s)	Cancer

Affirmation My head and my heart are aligned with the Divine. I am a miracle worker. I spread love and well-being to all life. I am balanced, aligned, healthy, and strong. It is easy for me to stand in the center of my power and emanate love.

Spiritual uses Selenite rose helps connect you with your guides, angels, archangels, and Ascended Masters. This is a perfect stone for aligning with the Divine Mother, specifically Mother Mary and Kuan Yin. The symbol of the rose connects you with your sacred heart of love, which is your true nature. This stone further aligns you with the truth that we each carry a seed of love within us. It is up to each of us to cultivate and nurture that seed into a blossoming flower.

Mental uses Selenite rose is a tool that helps you activate the scholar within. It opens the crown chakra to assist you in learning and retaining complex information. This stone will support a budding scholar who needs to integrate complex teachings into his or her knowledge base. This stone is beneficial to clear your thoughts of anything not resonating at the rate of love.

Emotional uses Selenite rose carries the energy of universal love. By reminding you of your true nature, which is love, this stone gives you the ability to expand the love that you are and to attract back to you all that is love and loving. This stone is also useful for balancing your chakras so that you can align all aspects of yourself.

Physical uses Selenite rose is good for aligning your spine and muscles and for bringing your entire body into balance, which helps readjust your emotional body as well. The selenite rose is the perfect stone for parents. It aids parents in being strong when they set boundaries with love. This stone is good for all types of caregivers or anyone who works with other people to help keep them aligned with their hearts while maintaining leadership or a strong position.

Divine guidance Have you had a hard time receiving love or help from others? Are you challenged by cranky people in your life? Cultivate a kinder and more loving attitude, and you'll notice agitating circumstances diminishing. It's time to open your heart to the Divine. You are a blessing here on Earth, and it is time to step into the magnificence of your love. Be an overflowing vessel of divine love.

About the stone:
Selenite rose refers to the mineral gypsum when it crystallizes in rose-like clusters of lenticular crystals mixed with sand. These form in dry, sandy locations and are also called gypsum rose or desert rose.

SEPTARIAN
Dragonheart

COLOR(S)	yellow, brown, grayish-brown, and white
CHAKRA(S)	root, navel, solar plexus
PLANET(S)	Sun
NUMBER(S)	7
ELEMENT(S)	fire
MOHS SCALE	7
ASTRO SIGN(S)	Gemini, Taurus

Affirmation My personal power is completely intact. I am balanced, aligned, and connected with my magnificence. I recognize my self-worth, which has been deeply instilled in my consciousness by the Divine. It is easy for me to get along with all types of people. I am open to new ideas.

Spiritual uses Septarian helps connect you with the contracts you made with your ancestors. With this stone in hand, meditate and/or engage in past- or current-life regression to uncover information that can benefit your present life.

Mental uses The yellow calcite energy in septarian helps you uncover and clear away outdated belief systems attached to old memories and other thoughtforms or mental energy that have accumulated over time in your mind. With this stone in hand, you can begin to reduce their unwanted effects on your behavior and how you react to life's events.

Emotional uses Septarian helps you uncover and release emotions that have been bubbling beneath the surface so that you can proceed toward emotional healing and discontinue unwanted repetitive patterns in your relationships. Use this stone to amplify the benefits of journaling or inner work to heal yourself of emotional wounds. This stone also helps raise your self-esteem.

Physical uses Septarian's powerful combination of brown aragonite and yellow calcite is beneficial for supporting the healing process of broken bones and stressed muscles. With this stone in hand, visualize the knitting of your bones or the relaxation of your muscles, and stay focused on your body functioning in the manner it was designed. This is a good stone for mental health counselors, physical therapists, and orthopedic doctors.

Divine guidance Have you removed yourself from society or stopped interacting with friends? Have you been compartmentalizing your feelings and thoughts? It is time to delve into your consciousness through meditation or contemplation to heal old wounds on all levels, and venture out into the world once again.

About the stone:
Septarian is a variety of concretion composed of several minerals depending on the deposit location. Although the exact process is unclear, it is formed by balls of mud and organic material drying out and cracking, and those cracks later being filled with mineral solutions of calcite or barite. Common minerals in septarian nodules include pyrite, aragonite, limestone, shale, or mudstone, and its appearance shows "cemented" cracks. Its name is from the Latin *septum*, "partition," referring to the cracks.

SERAPHINITE
Holy Connections Inside and Out

COLOR(S)	mossy green with white striations
CHAKRA(S)	crown, heart
PLANET(S)	Uranus, Chiron, Mercury
NUMBER(S)	6
ELEMENT(S)	fire
MOHS SCALE	2–2.5
ASTRO SIGN(S)	Aquarius

Affirmation I feel and know the presence of the Divine within and around me. I attract good friends and acquaintances into my life. My friends and colleagues are people of integrity. I have extraordinary fortune in all aspects of my life, especially in my interpersonal relationships. I am divinely connected to all life.

Spiritual uses Seraphinite is named for the seraphim—winged angelic beings in God's service. This stone facilitates communication with the angelic realm, including Archangel Raphael, by aligning you with the higher planes. It helps you stay connected to the divine spark within yourself as well as with the outer aspects of God. This is a good stone to work with for staying grounded as you aspire toward enlightenment.

Mental uses Seraphinite brings clarity and the energetic integration of complex higher intellectual matters into your knowledge base. Use this stone as your companion as you strive for higher scholarly attributes. This stone helps you to integrate your ability to use telepathy for better communication skills and gaining mental clarity. Use this stone to remove repetitive negative thoughts that were instilled in you as a child or young adult.

Emotional uses Seraphinite evaporates old emotions. It helps to cleanse away feelings that no longer serve you by bringing clarity to the source of the emotional imbalance, thereby releasing its charge or effect on you. Use this stone to cut cords from past relationships that still bind you. Combined with clear intention, this stone can disconnect the charge of emotional buttons, which removes others' ability to agitate you.

Physical uses Seraphinite helps you to release the belief systems or patterns that result in the manifestation of the same diseases or illnesses suffered by your family members. With this stone in hand, choose a different outcome and focus on breaking the mold. This stone reminds you to take the appropriate action to ward off diseases that are considered hereditary.

Divine guidance Do you hear the angels? Are you receiving messages from the Divine? Embrace this gift to live a charmed and enlightened life, help others attain freedom from suffering, and find happiness and peace. Pursue training to develop your intuitive gifts.

About the stone:
Seraphinite is a variety of clinochlore in the chlorite mineral group. It is an aluminum silicate of iron and magnesium in the monoclinic system, and normally found in massive form.

SERPENTINE
Fabulous, Fortunate, and Phenomenal

Color(s)	olive green, yellow or golden, brown, or black
Chakra(s)	heart, solar plexus
Planet(s)	Jupiter, Venus, Earth
Number(s)	24/6
Element(s)	earth
Mohs scale	3–4.5
Astro sign(s)	Taurus

Affirmation I am so fortunate! I connect with the right people at the right time. All of my hard work is paying off in all areas of my life. I am blessed with good health, great prosperity, and fabulous friends and colleagues. Wherever I go and whatever I do, I am blessed.

Spiritual uses Serpentine grounds you as you traverse the depths of your consciousness. With this stone in hand, you will find it easier to meditate, and it will no longer seem like a daunting task. This stone is good for shamanic journeywork, regression therapy, and progression therapy, which help clear your consciousness of the source of negative thoughts. Cultivate kindness and love in yourself.

Mental uses Serpentine helps you keep your mind focused on positive thoughts. This stone reminds you to be aware of negative thoughts so you can immediately release them and replace them with good thoughts. It also supports the beneficial effects of neurolinguistic programming (NLP).

Emotional uses Serpentine is a good tool for therapists, especially practitioners of Emotional Freedom Technique (EFT), a therapeutic psychological tool to heal emotional stress, since this stone helps you get in touch with positive ways to integrate situations and emotions into your life. Use it to help you get to the source of what's eating you. It's also the perfect stone to help heal your heart from relationship challenges, be it the loss of a friendship, lover, or any person with whom you once shared a relationship. It also helps you open your heart and relax into relationships again.

Physical uses Serpentine supports efforts at rebalancing your digestion. While watching your diet and following any medical advice you've received, delve into your consciousness to uncover what you might find difficult to swallow, literally and figuratively. Its green energy can be used with focused intent to open your heart chakra, and increase prosperity, good fortune, and the ability to reap the benefits of all your hard work. This is a good stone for bankers, finance managers, gastroenterologists, cardiologists, and mental health counselors.

Divine guidance Have you noticed that you are attracting negative situations and people in your life? Are you feeling lucky? Are you aware of all of your blessings? Aim for the stars. You can and should expect the best from every positive action you take. You attract money, joy, happiness, and good fortune. With that as your intention, your life will transform.

About the stone:
Serpentine is a hydrated magnesium silicate and crystallizes in the monoclinic system, although always found in massive form. It is found as marble when combined with calcite, dolomite, magnesite, and other impurities.

SODALITE
The Peaceful Intuitive

Color(s)	dark blue with white and black streaks
Chakra(s)	crown, third eye, root
Planet(s)	Jupiter
Number(s)	11
Element(s)	earth
Mohs scale	5.5–6
Astro sign(s)	Sagittarius

Affirmation I am calm. I am relaxed, and all is well. I sail through life on calm, nurturing waters and enjoy good health. I am extremely intuitive. It is easy for me to make decisions. I am at peace with myself and the world around me.

Spiritual uses Sodalite is a grounding tool for use as you channel inspirational, spiritual, and/or metaphysical writings. It helps you keep your focus on your third eye center, which allows you to activate the six "clairs"—clairvoyance, clairaudience, claircognizance, clairsentience, clairolfaction, and clairgustation. This dark blue stone is a perfect tool for meditation, as it helps calm incessant internal chatter. Sodalite is good for connecting with Archangels Michael and Raziel.

Mental uses Sodalite is a good study aid, especially when you are learning something new or unfamiliar. This stone also helps you to maintain your focus on something important when your thoughts are scattered. Its calming effect helps you sort out your thoughts. It is a good stone to help you cancel out angry, vindictive, or negative thoughts.

Emotional uses Sodalite balances rampant emotions. This is a perfect stone for calming and releasing anger and frustration. Use this stone to help quell emotional outbursts brought on by PMS, menopause, or any other hormone-related upsets. This stone helps you acknowledge and accept hormone-related realizations as accurate, but it also helps you find a way to deal with and express them in a way other people can handle.

Physical uses With its calming energy, sodalite reduces inflammation in the body, relieving inflammatory conditions such as headaches and muscle strains. This stone also helps reduce acid in your system for a more healthful acid-alkaline balance. It also aids in lowering blood pressure. This is a good stone for inventors, students, teachers, athletes, physical therapists, and meditation practitioners.

Divine guidance Have you been experiencing physical inflammation? Do you get frequent headaches or sinus conditions? Is a situation in your life inflamed? Steps to reduce emotional, physical, and mental inflammation are in order. Try visualization, meditation, and/or aromatherapy to bring a new calmness to every aspect of your life and body. Peace and tranquility are yours for the asking.

About the stone:
Sodalite is a sodium aluminum silicate with sodium chloride and is generally found in blue colored massive form. It is best known as one of the components of lapis lazuli. Sodalite rarely obtains the rich blue color of lapis, as it usually contains more calcite (white inclusions); lapis, on the other hand, contains pyrite more often than sodalite.

STILBITE
A Quiet Mind

Color(s)	pink, white, yellow, brown, or red
Chakra(s)	heart, throat, third eye, crown
Planet(s)	Mercury
Number(s)	4, 7
Element(s)	water
Mohs scale	3.5–4
Astro sign(s)	Gemini

Affirmation My mind is clear. My emotions are calm. I am at peace. I am grateful for the guidance I receive from my angels. I have a quiet mind. I feel serene and aligned with the Divine. Healing energies flow through me. I am grateful to be of service.

Spiritual uses Stilbite activates your third eye and crown chakras, which allows you to more easily accept and process insight and information from the angelic realm, spirit guides, and ancestors on the Other Side. Also, the pink vibration of this stone opens the heart chakra so you can feel and know the information within your heart. This stone is also a perfect companion to your meditation practice.

Mental uses Stilbite increases your mental capacity. It helps clear your mind so you can think through a situation or challenge. This is a stone for learning new concepts, a foreign language, and/or alternate ways to solve problems. It helps you think outside the box, and it creates new circuits in the brain that help you arrive at solutions or new ideas. This stone also helps support efforts at treating mental challenges such as Alzheimer's disease or dementia.

Emotional uses Stilbite calms your emotions, realigning your perception of your feelings to allow for objectivity. This stone aids in changing the way you look at things, thereby offering creative solutions to embrace feelings. It creates a nurturing environment by amplifying feelings of loving kindness in your energetic space. This stone is helpful for family members and caregivers of those experiencing senility or other challenges affecting normal mental function.

Physical uses Stilbite helps improve brain function. It is useful for those challenged by any disease that affects the brain's ability to function normally. This stone is an excellent companion for practitioners of Healing Touch, Reiki, Integrated Energy Therapy, and the like. It also increases the acceptance of holistic therapies in traditional medical facilities. This is a good stone for neurologists, mental health counselors, strategists, entrepreneurs, and inventors.

Divine guidance Are you taking on a new course of study? Are you trying to figure something out? Have you taken time to meditate? Now is a good opportunity for you to pause, still your mind, and sit in quiet contemplation. Once your mind is cleared, you can proceed with a new course of study and learn what you need to integrate.

About the stone:
Stilbite is a hydrous aluminum silicate containing calcium, sodium, or both, and crystallizing in the monoclinic system. Crystals are tabular and often form in groups resembling sheaves of wheat.

SUGILITE
The Transformative Power of Love

Color(s)	purple
Chakra(s)	crown, third eye
Planet(s)	Uranus, Neptune
Number(s)	22, 8
Element(s)	air
Mohs scale	6–7.5
Astro sign(s)	Aquarius, Pisces

Affirmation I am a miracle worker. Love is vibrating in all aspects of my being. I easily transform and transmute negative energy. I release the past and move forward with love. I attract inner peace and great joy every day in many ways. I see the bigger picture.

Spiritual uses Sugilite is a stone for personal transformation. Archangels Uriel and Zadkiel are associated with this stone. Use it to enhance your meditation practice or assist you in contemplation. The purple and azure energies are associated with the third eye chakra. The black inclusions in this stone ground your spiritual practice so that it can benefit your daily life. It can also increase moments of expanded awareness—those "aha" moments—where everything suddenly makes sense.

Mental uses Sugilite helps you to let go of the past and move forward in a positive way. Use this stone to deflect negative thoughts projected from others and from yourself. The transmutational power of the purple energy transforms negative belief systems, gently guiding you toward more beneficial belief systems. The indigo blue energy calms relentless inner chatter and invites peace and a calm mind.

Emotional uses Sugilite helps you cultivate tools to love and be loved without neediness on your part or the other person's. Use this stone to develop a true understanding of detachment, which can help you develop healthy relationships once you realize reality's impermanent nature. This stone is also a good tool to help you transform disturbing emotions or ignorant beliefs, especially as they relate to relationship with others.

Physical uses Sugilite helps increase physical stamina and endurance. Use it to support treatment for iron deficiency as well as breathing difficulties or other lung-associated health challenges. It is also beneficial for those with anemia, asthma, or allergies. This is a good stone for pulmonary specialists, phlebotomists, dieticians, nutritionists, physical trainers, and marathon runners. It is also a good stone for potters, contractors, and glass blowers.

Divine guidance Are you experiencing repetitive thoughts or incessant inner chatter? Do you grab onto a thought, memory, or life experience and chew it over and over and over again? It's time to let go and release situations from your past—whether they happened five minutes ago or five years ago—and find inner peace and true happiness.

About the stone:
Sugilite is a silicate containing potassium, sodium, iron, manganese, lithium, and aluminum. Sugilite rarely crystallizes but is normally found in massive form; much on the market today is associated with the manganese mines in South Africa.

SUNSTONE
Let the Sun Shine In

COLOR(S)	red, golden orange, or green
CHAKRA(S)	solar plexus
PLANET(S)	Mars, Venus
NUMBER(S)	19/1
ELEMENT(S)	fire
MOHS SCALE	6–6.5
ASTRO SIGN(S)	Aries

Affirmation My light shines brightly. I am self-confident and recognize my value and worth. Other people also recognize my value and worth. I shine the light of compassion, kindness, and love from my heart.

Spiritual uses Sunstone brings you spiritual fortitude and self-confidence so you can develop your spiritual gifts. With this stone in hand, recognize that you have a direct connection with the Divine. This stone reminds you that self-confidence is necessary to improve your own life as well as to be an instrument of peace and love to help all humanity. This stone activates that part of you that remembers your spiritual magnificence. Sunstone is the gemstone of Archangel Ariel.

Mental uses Sunstone's luminosity offers mental clarity and connects you with positive thoughts. Just like the sun, this stone sheds light on obstacles and brings luck and good fortune. It is the stone of manifestation and the mind power in creating reality. This gemstone activates creative thought processes, which help you to bring forth inspiration for inventions and art alike.

Emotional uses Sunstone reminds you of your own personal brilliance and magnificence, thereby raising your spirit and increasing your self-confidence. Its fiery energy evaporates out-of-balance emotions. This is a stone of new beginnings and brings promise and optimism. Use it to help lift you from feelings of depression by bringing you the realization that happiness is always available to you and that it is up to you.

Physical uses Sunstone amplifies the vital life force within you. It promotes passionate action toward a goal with the motivation required to get things done. Operating in the physical world requires money and vitality, so with this stone in hand, follow the light and align yourself with the vibration of the resources you require to move forward with a project or plan.

Divine guidance Have you been feeling down in the dumps? Do you need to add a bit of vibrance to your life? Do you need some brilliance and enthusiasm? This is a time of prosperity and purpose. You are ready to step into your power and be all you were meant to be. You are aligned with magnificence and courage to show yourself in your fullest splendor.

About the stone:
Sunstone is an oligoclase variety of the mineral feldspar, which is potassium aluminum silicate. Sunstone crystallizes in the triclinic system, however is usually found as crystalline masses. The yellow to orange color is due to thin platy crystals of copper, goethite, and/or hematite found in parallel orientation that gives the stones a spangled effect.

TIGER'S EYE, BLUE
Reading Between the Lines

COLOR(S)	deep blue with lighter blue bands
CHAKRA(S)	throat, third eye
PLANET(S)	Uranus
NUMBER(S)	11
ELEMENT(S)	air
MOHS SCALE	7
ASTRO SIGN(S)	Aquarius

Affirmation It's easy for me to see beyond the obvious. I accurately read between the lines and hear what isn't being said. I am grateful for the deeper insights and awareness available to me. I feel safe and know I am divinely protected.

Spiritual uses Blue tiger's eye helps to increase clairvoyant skills. This stone activates all six "clairs" (or sensory gifts)—clairvoyance, clairaudience, claircognizance, clairsentience, clairolfaction, and clairgustation. With its blue energy, this stone aligns you with the cosmic forces that provide inspirational messages to guide you in your life. With this stone in hand, grasp the significance of karma, retribution, and the spiritual consequences and benefits of action or lack of action.

Mental uses Blue tiger's eye helps ground and calms your mental chatter so you have the clarity to move in the right direction at the present moment. This stone is useful when you are feeling confused or when circumstances seem chaotic. Carrying the energy of sight, this stone promotes seeing life from an aerial view, like a hawk, so that you can approach life from a higher perspective.

Emotional uses Blue tiger's eye can be used to help deepen your understanding of difficult situations and people, promoting emotional balance. When you use this stone to gain mental clarity, you will also find that emotional balance is restored as you sort out your feelings and gain perspective.

Physical uses Blue tiger's eye, as well as all the other varieties of tiger's eye, improves vision, especially night vision. This stone is helpful for relieving headaches, migraines, sinusitis, eye problems, sore throats, and earaches. It is useful for fighting infections, reducing inflammation, and lowering fevers. Blue tiger's eye is a good stone for an astrologer, counselor, psychologist, or life coach.

Divine guidance Are you looking at something from only one angle? Do you need to rise above a situation to find truth and see with greater clarity? It is time to take steps to gain a new perspective on life. The time has come to believe in your choices and know that they are good. Trust your ability to see things and read situations clearly.

About the stone:

Also known as hawk's eye, blue tiger's eye is commonly believed to be a quartz (silicon dioxide) chatoyant pseudomorph of a blue variety of asbestos called crocidolite, although newer theories also exist. It can occur naturally, sometimes exhibiting a combination of blue and varying degrees of brown and yellow. In some cases, it is dyed blue.

TIGER'S EYE, GOLD
Eye of the Tiger

COLOR(S)	brown and gold with lighter bands of brown and gold
CHAKRA(S)	solar plexus, navel, root
PLANET(S)	Sun
NUMBER(S)	19/1
ELEMENT(S)	fire
MOHS SCALE	7
ASTRO SIGN(S)	Leo

Affirmation I am safe. I have constant protection surrounding me. I have the courage and self-confidence to create my world. I am grateful for other people's good fortune. It brings me joy to see others experiencing happiness. I extend blessings and goodwill to all.

Spiritual uses Gold tiger's eye enlivens your ability to remember your dreams and use the dreamtime for spiritual advancement. The chatoyancy (the optical reflectance effect) of this stone sparks your imagination, which is the key to understanding your intuition. The gold energy of this stone reminds you to embrace your spiritual potential and allow divinity into your spiritual practice. Use this stone to connect with the spiritual power of the sun as a source for nourishment of your soul. Gold tiger's eye is ideal for connecting with Archangels Jophiel and Sabrael.

Mental uses Tiger's eye aids with mental clarity. The yellow tones brighten and lighten your outlook on all that is positive, and it opens your mind to unlimited possibilities. This stone is a good companion when you are trying to remain grounded and focused on your goals and dreams and how they might be accomplished. It can help you feel self-empowered and unaffected by other people's opinions on how you should act and what you should do. It helps keep your thoughts aligned with your personal truth.

Emotional uses Gold tiger's eye helps you release feelings of jealousy. As you observe the nature or source of your jealousy, employ this stone to focus your attention on raising your own self-confidence. This stone also helps you master emotions during periods of emotional upheaval. It aids you when you need to remember that the sun continues to shine on you and how new beginnings are powerful times for renewal and growth.

Physical uses Gold tiger's eye, like all tiger's eye, helps improve your eyesight. This stone also aids in digestion and absorption of foods for ultimate nutrition. Use tiger's eye to increase vital life force and improve absorption of vitamin D as provided by the sun. This stone is also beneficial for those wishing to improve their career in a leadership position or as a speaker, supervisor, or project leader.

Divine guidance Are you envious of someone else's good fortune? Are others jealous of yours? Know that everyone receives blessings. Anyone can create fortune in their own life with true and pure intentions. Replace any feelings of envy with happiness for another's good fortune, and this energy will be returned to you. Radiate good fortune for all.

> ### About the stone:
> Gold tiger's eye is a quartz (silicon dioxide) chatoyant pseudomorph of a yellow to brown variety. Tiger's eye is thought to be formed by quartz replacement of asbestos called crocidolite, although newer theories exist about the minerals growing simultaneously. The color is caused by the oxidation of crocidolite fibers, creating hydrous iron oxide.

TIGER'S EYE, RED
Passionately Persistent

COLOR(S)	deep red with bands of lighter red
CHAKRA(S)	root
PLANET(S)	Mars, Pluto, Saturn, Vesta
NUMBER(S)	8
ELEMENT(S)	fire, earth
MOHS SCALE	7
ASTRO SIGN(S)	Aries, Scorpio, Capricorn

Affirmation I am safe. I have constant protection surrounding me deflecting anything not for my highest good. I have the courage and self-confidence to create my world. It is easy for me to take action and move forward in life with joy and enthusiasm.

Spiritual uses Red tiger's eye is a useful grounding force in your spiritual practice and motivates you to implement a spiritual discipline if necessary. The red energy is helpful for any type of moving meditation from yoga and tai chi to walking meditation. This stone is a stabilizer to maintain mindfulness and single-pointed focus. The red energy of this stone removes the energy of procrastination and adds verve and vigor to your spiritual practice.

Mental uses Red tiger's eye amplifies your business acumen. Use this stone as a tool to help you read between the lines and to be more open to perceiving the bigger picture. This stone triggers your inner entrepreneur. With its ability to amplify your determination, it helps you think outside the box and implement your ideas into action.

Emotional uses The red energy of this tiger's eye assists you in tapping into your personal power. Use this stone to shore up inner strength and courage when you are feeling emotionally weak and vulnerable. It helps you let go of paranoia or unfounded fears and strengthens your belief in yourself. This stone reminds you that it is safe for you to be powerful.

Physical uses The red energy of this tiger's eye supports the root chakra and strengthens your connection with the earth. This stone helps you maintain focus on your core needs— food, shelter, and water—which are always provided for you with the right intention, translating to money and prosperity. All varieties of tiger's eye improve vision, especially night vision, but red tiger's eye also improves libido by increasing feelings of sexuality and sensuality. This stone helps you strengthen muscles as well as inner strength for stronger vital life force.

Divine guidance Do you need some motivation? Do you find your mind wandering when you are trying to stay focused? If so, you need to find your passion and begin experiencing the rewards that come with it. Do what you love. Prosperity is yours, but you must take action.

About the stone:
Red tiger's eye is a quartz (silicon dioxide) chatoyant pseudomorph of a reddish variety. Tiger's eye is formed by quartz replacement of asbestos called crocidolite. The gold color is caused by iron oxides, and further metamorphic activity may impart the reddish color. However, red tiger's eye is often dyed or heat-treated.

Tiger Iron
Motivation

Color(s)	bands of gold, yellow, brown, red, black, and gray
Chakra(s)	root, navel, solar plexus
Planet(s)	Sun
Number(s)	8
Element(s)	fire
Mohs scale	7
Astro sign(s)	Leo

Affirmation I am grounded, focused, and energized. I have plenty of energy and time to accomplish what I need and want to get done. I am sure of myself and my abilities. My inner strength shines through in everything I do.

Spiritual uses Tiger iron helps you see the truth. This stone is useful when you want more clarity on all levels. It is the perfect grounding stone for applying spiritual principles and incorporating spiritual beliefs into your daily life. Use this stone when you channel or seek spiritual counsel for protection and practically apply the guidance received.

Mental uses Tiger iron promotes courage by feeding your mind with thoughts that encourage high self-esteem. It sparks the imagination, helping you think of or believe in the seemingly impossible. It is also beneficial for maintaining focus and conviction to complete a job or task. With its motivating energy, this is an excellent stone to help you get moving.

Emotional uses Tiger iron encourages your ability to stand up for yourself and set proper boundaries. It calms emotions while activating your life force, amplifies your self-esteem, and integrates that self-confidence into your personality. This fortifying gemstone helps you to feel safe and sound. Use it to help you keep your feelings to yourself when necessary. It is a good stone to carry around when dealing with the corporate world to protect you from getting your feelings hurt.

Physical uses A stone composed of tiger's eye, red jasper, and black hematite, tiger iron has the protective energy of tiger's eye, the deflective shield of hematite, and the energizing vibration of red jasper. With this stone in hand, you are shielded from negativity while being catapulted into action, enabling you to complete tasks, projects, creative ideas, and business ventures with ease.

Divine guidance Have you been distracted lately? Are you easily steered off-course? Are you lacking motivation? You are on fire with great ideas, so go ahead and step into your personal power. Maintain your ground and stand in your truth. Find the motivation and complete that project!

About the stone:
Tiger iron is a rock composed of varying layers of hematite, tiger's eye, and jasper.

TOPAZ, BLUE
What Did You Say?

Color(s)	blue
Chakra(s)	throat, third eye, and solar plexus
Planet(s)	Mercury, Jupiter, Moon
Number(s)	3
Element(s)	air
Mohs scale	8
Astro sign(s)	Virgo, Sagittarius

Affirmation I feel calm and at peace. I have great ideas all the time. My creative juices are flowing. My mind is clear and bright. I communicate well. I always find the right words when speaking or writing, and people listen to me.

Spiritual uses The heavenly blue of this topaz helps you tap into higher realms of awareness to channel Divine wisdom and knowledge. Use it to connect with your guides, angels, and loved ones on the Other Side. This stone promotes a two-way conversation so you not only talk to the angels but you also hear and listen to the messages of the Divine. This is a perfect stone for a mystic.

Mental uses Blue topaz brings inspiration to artists, authors, inventors, or anyone creating something, be it a garden or a meal. It is a stone of creative inspiration, and is useful for overcoming writer's block. Musicians also will find it helpful for tuning in to their muse. This is a stone of mental clarity.

Emotional uses Blue topaz calms the emotions, increasing awareness of your feelings. Its blue energy promotes peaceful vibes when you are feeling angry or frustrated. Since blue is the complementary color for orange, this stone calms inflamed issues related to your naval chakra, helping you express yourself with grace instead of rage. It is a useful tool for journaling your feelings.

Physical uses Blue topaz carries the energy of peacefulness. As such, it is useful for relieving stress-related disorders, including high blood pressure. Add this stone to your bag of remedies by holding it or wearing it when you have a headache. This stone is also a useful tool for helping you find or understand the true source of an illness and discovering the best course of treatment. This is a good stone for speakers, authors, artists, musicians, bankers, and inventors.

Divine guidance Do you aspire to be an artist, musician, or writer? Do you have an idea or a project on your mind? It is time to allow your inner artist to step forward. Allow yourself to express…yourself! This stone is telling you speak up, be heard—and listen well.

About the stone:
Blue topaz is the blue variety of the mineral topaz, a fluosilicate of aluminum containing fluorine and hydroxyl in varying amounts. Topaz crystallizes in the orthorhombic system, with crystals often prismatic and striated in the direction of its length. Crystals are generally only terminated on one end due to basal cleavage. Topaz is often found in alluvial deposits as water-worn pebbles. Blue topaz is sometimes irradiated to impart the color, and the darker blues are rarely seen anymore due to the presence of radioactivity.

TOPAZ, GOLDEN
Shining Star

COLOR(S)	yellow
CHAKRA(S)	solar plexus
PLANET(S)	Jupiter, Sun
NUMBER(S)	1
ELEMENT(S)	fire
MOHS SCALE	8
ASTRO SIGN(S)	Sagittarius, Leo

Affirmation I am a shining star! I focus on all my good attributes and amplify them. I see my path shining brightly before me. I have the courage to step forward with joy and enthusiasm. I help others as I radiate my magnificence.

Spiritual uses Golden topaz enhances your crown chakra and puts a sparkle in your halo. With this stone in hand, the golden flecks of light within your energy field shine every brighter, offering you a step closer to enlightenment. In ancient Egypt and Rome, it was believed that golden topaz received its color from the sun. This stone's golden rays amplify your ability to align with the Divine, Ascended Masters, and Archangels Ariel, Camael, Jophiel, and Metatron. Use this stone to increase your confidence in yourself and your intuition.

Mental uses Golden topaz is a good stone to help you raise your self-esteem, remember your good qualities, and maintain your focus on them. This is a stone of positive energy and good thoughts. It is a helpful adjunct to raise you out of depression and renew your self-confidence. Use it to improve your courage to put good thoughts into action.

Emotional uses Golden topaz increases the courage you need to embrace the magnificent person you truly are. It is also advantageous when you are trying to absorb what's going on in your life and the lives of those around you. This stone helps you lighten up and feel good about yourself. Use it when you have to make a presentation to overcome fear of public speaking. It also comes in handy for challenging conversations.

Physical uses Golden topaz is valuable for digestive issues and challenges. Use this stone to improve brain function as you tap into the spiritual aspect of your mind. It is helpful for those with dementia and Alzheimer's disease. It is also useful for the elderly and anyone nearing transition to the Other Side. This is a good stone for speakers, authors, merchants, teachers, gastroenterologists, and philanthropists.

Divine guidance Do you need to recapture your personal power? Do you need to set boundaries with friends, family, and/or colleagues? Surround yourself with people who recognize your talents, intelligence, creativity, kindness, and thoughtfulness. Their appreciation will amplify your goodness! Shine your light brightly, and be a wonderful contributor to all that is good in your community.

> ### About the stone:
> Golden topaz is the yellow to pinkish-yellowish brown variety of topaz, a fluosilicate of aluminum containing fluorine and hydroxyl in varying amounts. Topaz crystallizes in the orthorhombic system with crystals often prismatic and striated in the direction of its length. Crystals are generally only terminated on one end due to basal cleavage.

Topaz, Silver
The Inner Mystic

Color(s)	silvery blue
Chakra(s)	throat, solar plexus, crown
Planet(s)	Mercury, Mars
Number(s)	33
Element(s)	air
Mohs scale	8
Astro sign(s)	Aries, Gemini

Affirmation I can be and do anything! There is always a silver lining within any challenge. I am able to see the good even when others can't. I am aligned with the Divine. My angels and guides are guiding me every day. I feel the support of the heavenly realm.

Spiritual uses Silver topaz activates the light particles within the auric field of your crown chakra. Use this stone to connect with angels. Imagine this stone's silvery blue energy is sending out a ray of light connecting your heart, throat, and mind with the heavenly realm, spirit guides, and Ascended Masters. Recognize that this energy flows back to you, offering wisdom, knowledge, and sage advice for daily use. This stone awakens your inner mystic.

Mental uses Silver topaz activates the part of you that is able to see the good in all people and all situations. With this stone in hand, amplify your ability to find the positive no matter what so you will always see the proverbial glass as half-full. This is a perfect stone to aid with the visualization of positive outcomes. Use it to imagine potential realities as you script out your life.

Emotional uses Silver topaz is an excellent tool for improving your self-esteem. Recall every positive experience you've ever had, and allow those memories to flood into your consciousness with silver topaz as the main magnet. As the positive memories come rushing in, observe or imagine that anything that is not positive is washed away on the silvery light. The watery energy of emotions is realigned with this stone because of the connective ray to the Divine.

Physical uses Silver topaz is beneficial for the health of your throat, larynx, mouth, tongue, and ears. Use this stone to enhance your ability to express yourself so you are communicating clearly to benefit your career. Financial success is amplified when working with this stone with good intentions. Use it to visualize the outcome in advance.

Divine guidance Are you seeing the glass as half-full or half-empty? Do you take the time to dwell on the positive? Allow the angels to guide you toward all that is good. Take notice of the signs and symbols the angels send to you to help you in your daily life. Be confident, and allow your light to shine.

About the stone:
Silver topaz refers to the silvery-blue variety of the mineral topaz, a fluosilicate of aluminum containing fluorine and hydroxyl in varying amounts. Topaz crystallizes in the orthorhombic system with crystals often prismatic and striated in the direction of its length. Crystals are generally only terminated on one end due to basal cleavage.

TOURMALINE, BLACK
Force Fields Up!

COLOR(S)	black
CHAKRA(S)	root
PLANET(S)	Pluto
NUMBER(S)	11
ELEMENT(S)	water
MOHS SCALE	7–7.5
ASTRO SIGN(S)	Scorpio

Affirmation I am safe and sound. I am out of harm's way. All is well. I surround myself with trustworthy people. I am blessed. I am always divinely protected. I am enveloped in a sphere of goodness and well-being.

Spiritual uses Black tourmaline grounds your spiritual practice into your everyday life. With this stone in hand, delve into the deeper aspects of your consciousness to uncover past lives. This stone also deflects negative energy. Keep it close by for protection while doing readings or any type of spiritual healing. This stone provides the ever-important mindfulness, awareness, and peripheral vision in spiritual practice.

Mental uses Black tourmaline is helpful when you are feeling scattered and constantly being pulled off center. Use it to help you remain focused on the task at hand. Let it clear away repetitive, outdated thoughts so you can continue to achieve your goals and aspirations. This stone helps shield you from the effects of jealousy—yours and others. It also facilitates order in the face of general chaos.

Emotional uses Black tourmaline helps draw out dark, negative emotions holding you back from living a happy life. This stone is useful when you find yourself reacting uncontrollably. This stone helps you uncover deeper hidden reasons for negative actions or reactions toward others. With this stone in hand, find the source of the emotional problem so you can heal the drama and the trauma.

Physical uses Black tourmaline offers protection from electromagnetic frequencies emitted by cell phones, computers, and other electronic devices. This stone is good to help draw out toxins and anything else that isn't good for your physical body. Just as it helps to clear away spiritual, mental, and emotional angst, this stone helps you become conscious of what needs to be cleared in order to have a healthy body.

Divine guidance Do you fear betrayal or feel threatened in some way? Are you perhaps surrounded by negative or untrustworthy people or find yourself in questionable situations? Focus your intention on deflecting the negativity and surround yourself in a loving cloak of protection. Know that your angels and other spirit guides are watching out for you.

> **About the stone:**
> Black tourmaline (also known as schorl) is an iron-rich aluminum borosilicate often containing other impurities. Tourmaline crystallizes in the trigonal system and the crystals are typically long with vertical striations and triangular when viewed at length. Shorter, more tabular crystals may also occur. Tourmaline exhibits piezoelectricity, an electric charge that occurs when pressure is applied to the crystal or it is rubbed.

TOURMALINE, GREEN
Love, Luck, Wealth, and Success

COLOR(S)	green
CHAKRA(S)	heart
PLANET(S)	Venus
NUMBER(S)	3
ELEMENT(S)	earth
MOHS SCALE	7–7.5
ASTRO SIGN(S)	Taurus

Affirmation My actions are heart-centered, and I allow love in my life. I easily manifest my ideas into reality and attract wealth, luck, and success. I honor Mother Earth. My connection to the earth is strong.

Spiritual uses Green tourmaline opens your heart to give and receive. Use this stone to activate compassion, mercy, Divine love, and tolerance. This gemstone reminds you that there is an abundance of help available to us from the spiritual realm and assists you in learning how to perceive the nature spirits and hear their guidance. A wand fashioned from this stone helps connect you to the fairy realm. With green tourmaline in hand, call on the help of Archangels Chamuel, Raphael, and Thuriel.

Mental uses Green tourmaline realigns your consciousness to recognize that receiving is not the same thing as taking. This stone reminds you to allow the good of the universe to flow through you. It helps people who are afraid to give, fearing that giving something away will leave them lacking. With this stone in hand, this belief in lack can be removed. Use this stone to strengthen your belief in the ever-flowing abundance and infinite supply available to us all.

Emotional uses Green tourmaline helps you improve your demeanor and attract new friends or a romantic partner. This stone reminds you that to bring more romance into your life, you must learn how to enjoy your own company. Determine what makes you happy and use this stone to attract relationships that will provide loving companions or a mutually satisfying romantic relationship.

Physical uses Green tourmaline supports heart health through balancing electrical impulses in the muscles and valves. It is also beneficial for those challenged by the symptoms of multiple sclerosis and Parkinson's disease. This stone is also good for business success and loyalty as well as a useful aid for attracting ethical, heart-centered business associates. It is a valuable tool for ecologically focused and fair-trade businesses. This is a good gardener's stone, and as such, is beneficial for herbalists and aromatherapists.

Divine guidance Are you concerned about your finances? Do you believe in unlimited supply in all areas of your life? What kind of friends or colleagues are you attracting? Are they loyal? It's time to recognize that there are myriad opportunities and potentialities available to you in all areas of your life. Decide what types of people you want in your life and know that you have the ability to attract them.

About the stone:

Green tourmaline, also known as verdelite, is an alkali-rich aluminum borosilicate often containing sodium, lithium and potassium. Tourmaline crystallizes in the trigonal system and the crystals are typically long with vertical striations and triangular shape when viewed at length. Shorter, more tabular crystals may also occur. Tourmaline exhibits piezoelectricity, producing an electric charge when the crystal is rubbed or pressurized. Tourmaline also exhibits a strong double refraction and pyroelectricity, producing an electric charge when the crystal is heated to approximately 212 degrees Fahrenheit.

TOURMALINE, PINK
Angelic Resonance

COLOR(S)	pink
CHAKRA(S)	heart
PLANET(S)	Venus
NUMBER(S)	7
ELEMENT(S)	water
MOHS SCALE	7–7.5
ASTRO SIGN(S)	Libra

Affirmation I hear the angels sing. The energy of my own loving vibration nurtures my thoughts and feelings. Unconditional love is mine today and always. Every cell in my being vibrates at the rate of love. I feel good. I am happy. I am grateful.

Spiritual uses The nurturing energy of pink tourmaline brings forth the vibration of the Divine Mother. Use this stone when you need to activate the ability to have mercy and compassion for yourself and others. It activates your sacred heart, aligns your consciousness with the angels, and facilitates communication from the Ascended Masters, especially Lady Nada and Kuan Yin. Pink tourmaline is a perfect stone to invoke the aid of Archangels Chamuel and Tzaphkiel.

Mental uses Pink tourmaline is a nurturing tool that helps you restructure your thoughtforms, or mental energy, into positive statements. It helps you raise your awareness enough to recognize the negative thoughts you carry around and then assists in releasing them. Use this stone with the intention of receiving inspiration. This stone softens the thoughts you have about yourself and helps you treasure yourself with every thought you have.

Emotional uses Pink tourmaline's primary vibration for the emotional body is nurturance. This stone is useful when you need an injection of unconditional love, which starts with first loving yourself unconditionally. It comforts you when you are emotionally vulnerable. Employ this stone to discover what unconditional love means, how it feels, and what to do to actualize it for yourself.

Physical uses Pink tourmaline is a skin regenerator and rejuvenator. Use it with the intention to increase collagen and reduce wrinkles. Use it also to improve heart and lung function. This stone is a good amulet for pediatricians, caregivers, nurses, teachers, mental health counselors, and anyone else who cares for others. It amplifies the vibration of giving and caring, returning it back to the giver multifold, thereby regenerating that person's energy to continue to do his or her good work.

Divine guidance Do you treat yourself well? What kind of self-talk is going on in your mind? How is your connection with guides and angels? Are you a caregiver? Do you remember to take care of yourself? This is a time to pay attention to how well you treat yourself and to be aware of your inner chatter so that you can make necessary changes. It is time to awaken your consciousness fully and focus on love for yourself and all beings.

About the stone:
Pink tourmaline is an alkali-rich aluminum borosilicate often containing sodium, lithium, and potassium. Tourmaline crystallizes in the trigonal system and the crystals are typically long with vertical striations and triangular shape when viewed at length. Shorter, more tabular crystals may also occur. Pink tourmaline refers to a pink variety of the broader family of red or dark pink tourmaline known as rubellite.

TOURMALINE, WATERMELON
An Open Heart

COLOR(S)	pink center with an outer layer of green
CHAKRA(S)	heart
PLANET(S)	Venus, Sun, Juno, Ceres
NUMBER(S)	22/4, 33
ELEMENT(S)	fire
MOHS SCALE	7–7.5
ASTRO SIGN(S)	Libra, Taurus, Cancer, Leo

Affirmation My heart is open to giving and receiving love. I transform the world around me through focusing my energy and intentions on Divine love. Every cell in my body vibrates at the rate of love. Every word I say and thought I think travels on the frequency of love.

Spiritual uses With its pink and green energy, watermelon tourmaline is the ultimate heart chakra stone. This stone epitomizes the Divine as cosmic forces accept you with unconditional love and embrace all aspects of your human nature. Use this stone to attract beneficial spirits and to reveal your true divine nature. This stone also helps you bridge the spiritual energy of the upper three chakras (crown, third eye, and throat) with the lower three (solar plexus, navel, and root) through the center of your chest (heart chakra) to bring heaven and earth together through you.

Mental uses Watermelon tourmaline increases your awareness of your thoughts and whether or not they are good, positive thoughts. As you become aware of these thoughtforms (mental energy), this gem can further assist you in focusing on what you want and letting go of the energy preventing you from attaining your goals.

Emotional uses Watermelon tourmaline represents the heart chakra—the center of the self. It is the place of love, compassion, kindness, tolerance, and goodness. It is the bridge between the lower three chakras (the physical mundane world) and the upper three chakras (the spiritual higher-consciousness world). Use watermelon tourmaline for self-acceptance as well as for attracting romantic love.

Physical uses Watermelon tourmaline is the go-to stone for healing the physical heart and lungs. Use it to help you eat right, get enough exercise, and release unhealthy habits. Use this stone as a smoking cessation aid. It is also the perfect amulet for weight loss. Keep this stone close by if you are in the fields of counseling or caregiving to amplify the potential for a good income.

Divine guidance Are you looking for romance? Do you need more attention and affection? It is time to nurture yourself and treat yourself the way you want others to treat you. This is a good time to rev up your self-acceptance and increase your willingness to allow more love in your life.

> ### About the stone:
> Watermelon tourmaline refers to the pink and green bi-colored variety of tourmaline. When the crystals are sliced crosswise, they exhibit pink in the center surrounded by green. Tourmaline crystallizes in the trigonal system and the crystals are typically long with vertical striations and triangular shape when viewed at length. Shorter, more tabular crystals may also occur.

TURQUOISE
Talks with Spirit

Color(s)	bluish-green and greenish-blue
Chakra(s)	throat
Planet(s)	Jupiter, Mercury
Number(s)	3
Element(s)	air
Mohs scale	5–7
Astro sign(s)	Sagittarius, Gemini

Affirmation I open my consciousness to various forms of expression. I express myself with ease and grace. My creativity is activated. I am a channel of divine inspiration. I receive insights and wisdom from various cultures and philosophies.

Spiritual uses Turquoise helps you connect with cosmic energies. Revered by many Native American peoples, this stone has been used to connect with Father Sky and is often complemented by coral in jewelry and amulets to connect with Mother Earth below, bringing heaven and earth together. This is the go-to stone for channeling, automatic writing, and communication with the angels. Use turquoise to call on Archangel Haniel, the angel of divine communication.

Mental uses Turquoise helps you to know, speak, and live your truth. This is a good stone when you need assistance with the timing of things. Know that the angels are orchestrating your life for your highest good. Turquoise is exceptionally beneficial for storytelling, journalism, and writing of any kind. It is a good stone to gaze at while waiting for inspiration to aid you with any type of project, especially when you are experiencing a mental block.

Emotional uses Turquoise balances the moods swings commonly associated with premenstrual syndrome. This stone helps to remind you that the feelings and realizations you receive during the premenstrual and perimenopausal periods of your life are valid, but you are able to act upon them with grace and ease. This is also a stone of validation when it comes to downloading wisdom and truth. Speak your truth with love and beauty.

Physical uses Turquoise calms inflammations and agitation. Its calming energy helps you to release tension, reduce anger, and relieve headaches. This stone is an excellent reminder to drink enough water. It also helps with healing maladies of the ears, nose, throat, larynx, and neck. This is the stone for ENT (ear, nose, throat) doctors, speech therapists, vocal coaches, singers, auctioneers, and radio and TV hosts.

Divine guidance What do you wish to express? How do you wish to express it? Is there something you need to say to someone? Expression comes in many forms. Meditate on what you would like to communicate, and then have the courage to do so. Consider exploring one or more types of Native American spiritual teachings.

About the stone:
Turquoise is a hydrous copper aluminum phosphate with iron present in varying degrees. Turquoise crystallizes in the triclinic system, although it is normally found in massive form as nodules or in veins, and sometimes displays botryoidal growth. The material varies in porosity.

UNAKITE
A Balancing Act

Color(s)	pink and green
Chakra(s)	heart, solar plexus, navel
Planet(s)	Moon, Venus
Number(s)	6
Element(s)	water, earth
Mohs scale	6–7
Astro sign(s)	Cancer, Pisces, Taurus

Affirmation My emotions are balanced. I am able to observe my reactions to others in an objective and loving way. Love allows me to awaken my consciousness. I understand the underlying cause of challenging situations, and I move through them with ease and grace.

Spiritual uses With its pink and green energy, unakite reminds you to set your intention on love, compassion, and kindness. Use this stone to remind you to be tolerant and gentle with all beings. This is a good stone to use as a supportive aid if you are studying the Tree of Life, Kabbalah, or kundalini (life force).

Mental uses Unakite is the stone of balance. Use it to help you balance your mind with your heart and emotions. This stone helps you make decisions using your head *and* your heart. It also aids in calming internal debate and incessant chatter that goes on in your mind, and it offers peace and comfort in the face of anxiety.

Emotional uses Unakite is a good relationship stone, since it helps to foster a healthy and happy relationship through balanced emotions. With this stone in hand, you are less susceptible to being influenced by distorted emotions or personal bias. It helps you be more objective and let go of pre-conceived notions of how something should be handled, making it more likely for you to achieve your goals. Unakite is perfect for aligning with Arch-angels Chamuel and Muriel to invite assistance in balancing emotions.

Physical uses With its heart-centered pink and green energy, unak-ite assists you in staying focused on healing any problems with your physi-cal heart. It gently opens up your consciousness to understand the source of heart disease. It aids in business success for anyone in the world of beauty, aromatherapy, and fashion design. It also is beneficial for marriage counselors and divorce attorneys.

Divine guidance Are you experiencing emotional upset? Are you able to "swallow" everything that is happening in your life? Balance your-self through self-nurturing activities. Pay attention to what you eat. Em-brace your emotions. Imagine that the food you eat provides all the nutri-ents necessary for good health. When you nurture yourself, you develop a more caring attitude not only toward yourself, but toward others as well.

About the stone:
Unakite is a granite rock containing quartz, pink feldspar, and green epidote. The stone was first found in the Unakite Range in North Carolina, hence the name.

VANADINITE
Supernova Shining Star

COLOR(S)	rusty orange
CHAKRA(S)	root, navel
PLANET(S)	Sun
NUMBER(S)	0
ELEMENT(S)	earth
MOHS SCALE	2.5–4
ASTRO SIGN(S)	Leo, Scorpio

Affirmation I understand the factors controlling my life. I know that I am the one in control. I have the power to shine like a star! I easily attract all I need and want with joy and enthusiasm. The more I give, the more I get.

Spiritual uses Vanadinite vibrates with the energy of the cosmos. The sparkling orange energy in this gemstone offers the opportunity to channel inspired works—from musical compositions to technological gadgets. This stone can help you to remember why you are here on the planet at this time. With this stone in hand, meditate on remembering your sacred contract and life purpose. Then use it to help you take action and do it!

Mental uses Vanadinite changes the mental composition of your thoughts. It breaks down old repetitive ways of thinking and reconstitutes them with a new flair. Though you may be weary of the old thoughtforms, this stone helps you to restructure those thoughts, giving them new life with a positive twist.

Emotional uses Vanadinite is used for the disintegration of emotional states that have been firmly established in the navel and root chakras. Instead of total disintegration, it destabilizes the negativity associated with challenging memories or experiences. This stone therefore helps you reintegrate the lessons captured from the experience, making you a much more powerful person because of it.

Physical uses Vanadinite helps you with any health challenges that can be interpreted as a form of breaking down and changing of chemical equations. It helps you find the nutritional, herbal, and medicinal tools to return you to a state of robust health. This stone also helps with the absorption of iron. It is a good stone for chemists, nutritionists, herbalists, and aromatherapists.

Divine guidance What on earth do you need to do? Is it time to break down the old emotional walls and rebuild positive avenues for joy and happiness? Do you need a shot of enthusiasm? It is time to step into your power and be the person you were meant to be. Find that courage, step up to the plate to live your life's purpose.

About the stone:
Vanadinite is a lead chlorovanadate. It crystallizes in the hexagonal system forming small prismatic crystals that are sometimes partially hollow; occasionally it produces terraced hopper crystals.

Appendices

Appendix A:
Astrological Signs

Aries (March 21–April 19)—amazonite, amber, ametrine, ammonite, carborundum, carnelian, cathedral quartz, garnet, golden calcite, optical calcite, orbicular jasper, orthoceras fossil, petalite, red calcite, red jasper, red tiger's eye, ruby, silver topaz, sunstone, tiger iron

Taurus (April 20–May 20)—bismuth, chlorite phantom quartz, dioptase, dolomite, emerald, goldstone, green calcite, green moss agate, green tourmaline, hematite, kunzite, moldavite, Picasso stone, pink calcite, rhodochrosite, rose quartz, septarian, serpentine, tree agate, watermelon tourmaline, unakite

Gemini (May 21–June 20)—amazonite, amber, amethyst druzy, ametrine, Botswana agate, chevron amethyst, copper, dogtooth calcite, emerald, fluorite, golden calcite, hiddenite, pietersite, septarian, silver topaz, stilbite, tabular quartz, tourmalinated quartz, trilobites, turquoise, yellow jasper

Cancer (June 21–July 22)—bloodstone, celestite, cobaltoan calcite, emerald, hiddenite, girasol quartz, howlite, Isis quartz crystal, magnesite, moonstone, muscovite, optical calcite, orange calcite, orbicular jasper, selenite, selenite rose, watermelon tourmaline, unakite

Leo (July 23–August 22)—amber, carnelian, chalcopyrite, citrine, dogtooth calcite, golden topaz, gold tiger's eye, heliodor, peacock copper, peridot, petalite, pyrite, record-keeper crystals, ruby, rutilated quartz, sapphire, tiger iron, watermelon tourmaline, vanadinite

Virgo (August 23–September 22)—amazonite, apatite, blue-dyed agate, blue lace agate, blue topaz, Botswana agate, carnelian, charoite, dioptase, fluorite, iolite, kyanite, peridot, pietersite, prehnite, sapphire, silver topaz, trilobites

Libra (September 23–October 22)—apophyllite, black obsidian, blue lace agate, chalcedony, chrysocolla, Dalmatian jasper, danburite, dolomite, epidote, goldstone, jade, kunzite, morganite, opal, relationship quartz crystals, rhodocochrosite, rhodonite, rose quartz, ruby in zoisite, watermelon tourmaline

Scorpio (October 23–November 21)—Apache tears, black obsidian, cobra jasper, copper, covellite, dogtooth calcite, elestial quartz, golden sheen obsidian, honey calcite, Isis quartz, jet, leopardskin jasper, phantom quartz, red tiger's eye, smoky quartz, snowflake obsidian, time link quartz, tourmalinated quartz, vanadinite

Sagittarius (November 22–December 21)—azurite, azurite/malachite, blue topaz, dumortierite, golden topaz, lapis lazuli, magnetite octahedron, morganite, pietersite, purple-dyed agate, sodalite, turquoise

Capricorn (December 22–January 20)—andalusite, black onyx, brown agate, green aventurine, red calcite, chalcopyrite, dioptase, epidote, hematite, Herkimer diamonds, Kambamba jasper, mookaite jasper, red jasper, zebra jasper, lodestone, malachite, peridot, prasiolite, prehnite, quartz laser wands, red tiger's eye, rhodonite, sardonyx

Aquarius (January 21–February 19)—amber, amethyst, amethyst druzy, ametrine, angelite, aquamarine, axinite, blue calcite, blue-dyed agate, blue tiger's eye, chalcedony, charoite, chevron amethyst, dolomite, elestial quartz, galena, kyanite, larimar, magenta-dyed agate, magnetite, scolecite, seraphinite, sugilite, time link quartz

Pisces (February 20–March 20)—angelite, aquamarine, aragonite, axinite, blue lace agate, blue calcite, brucite, celestite, channeling quartz, chevron amethyst, chrysoprase, cobaltoan calcite, golden sheen obsidian, green-dyed agate, green aventurine, green calcite, hiddenite, kyanite, labradorite, larimar, leopardskin jasper, lepidolite, magenta-dyed agate, moldavite, opal, orbicular jasper, petrified wood, phantom quartz, prehnite, rainbow obsidian, scolecite, sugilite, turritella shell agate, unakite

Appendix B:
Planets and Asteroids

Planets

The Sun—amber, carnelian, chalcopyrite, citrine, dogtooth calcite, golden calcite, golden topaz, gold tiger's eye, heliodor, peacock copper, pyrite, quartz laser wands, record-keeper quartz, rutilated quartz, window quartz, ruby, septarian, sunstone, tiger iron, watermelon tourmaline, vanadinite

Mercury—amazonite, amber, ametrine, apatite, azurite, azurite-malachite, bismuth, blue topaz, Botswana agate, chevron amethyst, dioptase, dogtooth calcite, epidote, fluorite, galena, golden calcite, iolite, petalite, pietersite, sapphire, scolecite, seraphinite, silver topaz, stilbite, tabular quartz, tourmalinated quartz, trilobite, turquoise, yellow jasper

Venus—apophyllite, bismuth, black obsidian, blue chalcedony, channeling quartz, green calcite, copper, Dalmatian jasper, danburite, dioptase, dolomite, emerald, goldstone, green moss agate, green tourmaline, jade, kunzite, magenta-dyed agate, moldavite, morganite, opal, pink calcite, petalite, Picasso stone, pink tourmaline, relationship quartz, rhodochrosite, rhodonite, rose quartz, ruby in fuchsite, ruby in zoisite, rutilated quartz, serpentine, sunstone, tree agate, unakite, watermelon tourmaline

The Moon—bloodstone, blue topaz, cobaltoan calcite, chrysanthemum stone, girasol quartz, hiddenite, howlite, magnesite, moonstone, optical calcite, orange calcite, orbicular jasper, selenite, selenite rose, snowflake obsidian, unakite

Earth—amethyst druzy, andalusite, blue-dyed agate, cathedral quartz, chrysocolla, chlorite phantom quartz, green aventurine, green moss agate, hematite, kyanite, moldavite, prehnite, ruby in fuchsite, serpentine, tree agate

Mars—ammonite, carnelian, covellite, garnet, hematite, orbicular jasper, orthoceras fossil, red calcite, red jasper, red tiger's eye, ruby, ruby in zoisite, silver topaz, sunstone

Jupiter—amber, angelite, azurite, azurite-malachite, channeling quartz, dumortierite, emerald, jade, lapis lazuli, magnetite octahedron, morganite, ortherceras, pietersite, purple-dyed agate, sardonyx, serpentine, blue topaz, turquoise

Saturn—andalusite, brown agate, bismuth, black onyx, chalcopyrite, dioptase, Herkimer diamond, Kambamba jasper, lodestone, malachite, mookaite jasper, opal, prasiolite, quartz laser wands, red jasper, red tiger's eye, rhodonite, sardonyx, zebra jasper

Uranus—amethyst, ametrine, angelite, aquamarine, axinite, blue calcite, blue lace agate, blue tiger's eye, blue-dyed agate, charoite, chevron amethyst, dolomite, galena, Isis quartz, kyanite, magnetite octahedron, scolecite, seraphnite, sugilite

Neptune—angelite, aquamarine, aragonite, blue lace agate, blue calcite, brucite, celestite, charoite, chevron amethyst, chrysoprase, golden sheen obsidian, green calcite, green-dyed agate, green aventurine, hiddenite, labradorite, larimar, leopardskin agate, lepidolite, moldavite, orbicular jasper, opal, petrified wood, phantom quartz, rainbow obsidian, scolecite, sugilite, turritella agate, trilobite

Pluto—Apache tears, axinite, black obsidian, black tourmaline, charoite, cobra jasper, covellite, dogtooth calcite, golden sheen obsidian, honey calcite, Isis quartz, jet, leopardskin jasper, peridot, phantom quartz, red tiger's eye, smoky quartz, time-link quartz, tourmalinated quartz

Note: The order of the planets given here is based on the planets' average distances from the sun.

Asteroids

Chiron—Apache tears, blue calcite, elestial quartz, gold sheen obsidian, hiddenite, leopardskin jasper, time link quartz, seraphinite

Vesta—Isis quartz, onyx, pink tourmaline, red tiger's eye, selenite rose, stilbite

Juno—danburite, gold tiger's eye, hiddenite, kunzite, magenta-dyed agate, relationship quartz, tourmalinated quartz, unakite, watermelon tourmaline

Ceres—bloodstone, brown agate, cobra jasper, cobaltoan calcite, green moss agate, howlite, magnesite, opal, orange calcite, tree agate, watermelon tourmaline

Pallas—amber, ametrine, black obsidian, Botswana agate, bismuth, carnelian, citrine, dumortierite, hematite, iolite, leopardskin jasper, malachite, orbicular jasper, petalite

Appendix C: Chakras

Crown (7th Chakra)—amethyst, amethyst druzy, ametrine, apophyllite, azurite, azurite-malachite, bismuth, celestite, chalcedony, chalcopyrite, channeling quartz, charoite, chevron amethyst, chrysanthemum stone, clear quartz, dogtooth calcite, chrysocolla, citrine, Dalmatian jasper, dioptase, dolomite, fluorite, girasol quartz, golden topaz, heliodor, Herkimer diamond, howlite, kyanite, labradorite, lapis lazuli, laser wands, lepidolite, magnesite, moldavite, mookaite jasper, moonstone, orbicular jasper, optical calcite, orthoceras, petalite, phantom quartz, purple-dyed agate, rutilated quartz, sapphire, scolecite, selenite, selenite rose, seraphanite, shell fossil, silver topaz, snowflake obsidian, sodalite, stilbite, sugilite, tektite, time link quartz, tree agate, trilobite, white onyx, window quartz, yellow jasper, zebra jasper

Third Eye (6th Chakra)—amethyst, amethyst druzy, ametrine, apophyllite, azurite, azurite-malachite, bismuth, blue chalcedony, blue-dyed agate, blue tiger's eye, blue topaz, brucite, celestite, chevron amethyst, chalcopyrite, charoite, chrysocolla, clear quartz, copper, covellite, dioptase, dumortierite, fluorite, goldstone, Herkimer diamonds, indochinite tektite, iolite, kyanite, labradorite, lapis lazuli, laser wands, lepidolite, moldavite, mookaite jasper, moonstone, optical calcite, orthoceras, phantom quartz, pietersite, purple-dyed agate, rutilated quartz, sapphire, scolecite, sodalite, stilbite, sugilite, tektites, window quartz, yellow jasper

Throat (5th Chakra)—amazonite, andulasite, angelite, apatite, aquamarine, azurite-malachite, bismuth, blue calcite, blue chalcedony, blue lace agate, blue-dyed agate, blue tiger's eye, blue topaz, celestite, clear quartz, dioptase, dumortierite, fluorite, kyanite, larimar, magenta-dyed agate, scolecite, silver topaz, stilbite, turquoise

Heart (4th Chakra)—ametrine, azurite-malachite, Botswana agate, chlorite phantom quartz, chrysoprase, cobaltoan calcite, clear quartz, copper, danburite, dioptase, dolomite, emerald, epidote, fluorite, goldstone, green aventurine, green calcite, green-dyed agate, green moss agate, green tourmaline, hiddenite, jade, Kambamba jasper, kunzite, labradorite, larimar, magenta-dyed agate, malachite, moldavite, mookaite jasper, morganite, optical calcite, orbicular jasper, peridot, petalite, pink calcite, pink tourmaline, prasiolite, prehnite, red jasper, relationship quartz, rhodochrosite, rhodonite, rose quartz, ruby in fuchsite, ruby in zoisite, sardonyx, selenite rose, seraphinite, serpentine, stilbite, tabular quartz, tree agate, unakite, watermelon tourmaline, window quartz

Solar Plexus (3rd Chakra)—amber, ametrine, apatite, blue topaz, chalcopyrite, charoite, chrysoprase, citrine, clear quartz, cobra jasper, copper, danburite, dogtooth calcite, epidote, fluorite, gold tiger's eye, golden calcite, golden obsidian, golden topaz, goldstone, green calcite, heliodor, hiddenite, leopardskin jasper, lepidolite, magnetite, malachite, mookaite jasper, moonstone, morganite, optical calcite, orange calcite, peridot, phantom quartz, Picasso stone, pietersite, prehnite, purple-dyed agate, pyrite, relationship quartz, rhodochrosite, rutilated quartz, septarian, serpentine, silver topaz, sunstone, tiger iron, unakite, yellow jasper

Navel (2nd Chakra)—amazonite, amber, andalusite, apache tears, aragonite, azurite-malachite, bloodstone, Botswana agate, brucite, carnelian, clear quartz, cobra jasper, copper, golden sheen obsidian, gold tiger's eye, leopardskin jasper, mookaite jasper, moonstone, orange calcite, goldstone, orthoceras, Picasso stone, pietersite, pyrite, red calcite, red jasper, tiger iron, rutilated quartz, septarian, unakite, vanadinite

Root (1st Chakra)—andalusite, Apache tears, axinite, black obsidian, black onyx, black tourmaline, bloodstone, Botswana agate, brown agate, chalcopyrite, chrysanthemum stone, clear quartz, cobra jasper, covellite, Dalmatian jasper, galena, garnet, gold tiger's eye, golden sheen obsidian, goldstone, green moss agate, hematite, honey calcite, indochinite tektite, jet, leopardskin jasper, lodestone, magnetite, mookaite jasper, orthoceras, petrified wood, Picasso stone, pietersite, prasiolite, pyrite, rainbow obsidian, red calcite, red jasper, red tiger's eye, rhodonite, ruby, ruby in fuchsite, rutilated quartz, sodalite, sardonyx, septarian, shell fossil, smoky quartz, snowflake obsidian, tiger iron, tourmalinated quartz, tree agate, vanadinite, zebra jasper

Appendix D:
Careers and Professions

Actor—channeling quartz, peacock copper

Acupuncturist—azurite, chrysanthemum stone

Animal communicator—cobra jasper, larimar, tabular quartz

Arborists—green moss agate, green tourmaline, tree agate

Archeologist—amber, chalcedony, channeling quartz, chrysanthemum stone, Kambamba jasper, septarian, stilbite, turritella shell agate, trilobite fossil

Architect—brown agate, honey calcite, pyrite

Aromatherapist—brown agate, chlorite phantom quartz, green moss agate, green tourmaline, tree agate, unakite, vanadinite

Artist—angelite, aragonite, blue calcite, blue topaz, Botswana agate, carnelian, celestite, dolomite, Indochinite tektite, moldavite, peacock copper, record-keeper quartz

Astrologer—angelite, blue calcite, blue tiger's eye, celestite, indochinite tektite, moldavite

Athlete—aragonite, chalcopyrite, copper, elestial quartz, howlite, leopardskin jasper, orange calcite, red tiger's eye, sardonyx, selenite, septarian, serpentine, sodalite, trilobite

Author—amazonite, angelite, blue calcite, blue topaz, carnelian, chalcopyrite, channeling quartz, copper, golden topaz, iolite, tabular quartz

Banker—amazonite, blue topaz, citrine, emerald, green aventurine, jade, pyrite, serpentine

Boater—amazonite, aquamarine, brucite, larimar, orbicular jasper

Body worker—leopardskin jasper, orange calcite, sardonyx, selenite

Book publisher—celestite, channeling quartz, golden calcite

Broker—amazonite, green aventurine

Builder—honey calcite, pyrite, sardonyx, sugilite

Cardiologist—green aventurine, green tourmaline, magenta-dyed agate, moldavite, pink calcite, pink tourmaline, rose quartz, unakite, watermelon tourmaline, zoisite with ruby

Caregiver—hematite, Isis quartz, pink tourmaline, selenite rose, stilbite

Chemist—vanadinite

Chiropractor—andalusite, Apache tears, aragonite, axinite, black tourmaline, chalcopyrite, copper, dolomite, elestial quartz, garnet, howlite, labradorite, leopardskin jasper, orange calcite, prehnite, sardonyx, selenite, septarian, trilobite

Clairvoyant—angelite, amethyst, azurite, black onyx, blue tiger's eye, celestite, charoite, dumortierite, galena, golden sheen obsidian, heliodor, Herkimer diamond, hiddenite, Isis quartz, jet, labradorite, lepidolite, magnesite, moonstone, optical calcite, pietersite, sodalite

Conservationist—amethyst druzy, apatite, black tourmaline, brown agate, green moss agate, honey calcite, howlite, pink tourmaline

Contractor—honey calcite, pyrite, sardonyx, sugilite

Counselor—angelite, apatite, blue tiger's eye, magenta-dyed agate, muscovite, pink tourmaline, tabular quartz, time link quartz, septarian, serpentine, stilbite, unakite

Dental profession—andalusite, apatite, aragonite, axinite, azurite-malachite, blue lace agate, chrysocolla, dogtooth calcite, dolomite, howlite, leopardskin jasper, prehnite

Dermatologist—Botswana agate, morganite, opal, pink calcite, pink tourmaline, rose quartz

Dietician—apatite, dioptase, golden calcite, golden sheen obsidian, serpentine, sugilite, unakite, yellow jasper

Doula—carnelian, clear quartz, cobra jasper, garnet, orange calcite, moonstone, red jasper, selenite

Drug-rehabilitation therapist/specialist—ametrine, amethyst, black obsidian, iolite, jet, lapis lazuli, peridot, phantom quartz, rose quartz, watermelon tourmaline

Ear, nose, and throat specialist—blue lace agate, Botswana agate, turquoise

Ecologist—amethyst druzy, apatite, black tourmaline, brown agate, green moss agate, honey calcite, howlite, pink tourmaline

Editor—amazonite, angelite, aquamarine, blue calcite, blue topaz, carnelian, chalcopyrite, iolite, prehnite, record-keeper quartz, zebra jasper

Electrician—azurite-malachite, black tourmaline, copper, covellite, dioptase, fuchsite, malachite, scolecite

Electronics professional—black tourmaline, fluorite, galena, iolite, elestial quartz, smoky quartz, scolecite

Entertainer—channeling quartz, peacock copper

Entrepreneur—emerald, hiddenite, onyx, red tiger's eye, stilbite

Environmentalist—amethyst druzy, apatite, black tourmaline, brown agate, green moss agate, honey calcite, howlite, pink tourmaline

Esthetician—kunzite, morganite, opal, rhodochrosite, rose quartz

Explorer—indochinite tektite

Farmer—andalusite, apatite, blue topaz, brown agate, cobra jasper, green moss agate, green tourmaline, honey calcite, petrified wood, tree agate

Feng shui practitioner—golden calcite

Fertility specialist—carnelian, clear quartz, cobra jasper, garnet, orange calcite, moonstone, red japser, selenite

Finance manager—amazonite, blue topaz, citrine, emerald, green aventurine, jade, pyrite, serpentine

Fisherman—aquamarine, ammonites, aragonite, brucite, blue chalcedony, orbicular jasper

Florist—angelite, aragonite, Botswana agate, brown agate, chlorite phantom quartz, green moss agate, tree agate

Food supplier—golden calcite

Gardener—andalusite, apatite, blue topaz, brown agate, cobra jasper, green moss agate, green tourmaline, honey calcite, petrified wood, tree agate

Gastroenterologist—citrine, green calcite, gold tiger's eye, larimar, magnesite, peridot, serpentine, yellow jasper

Ghost hunter—phantom quartz

Glass blower—goldstone, indochinite tektite, moldavite tektite, obsidian

Gymnast—aragonite, selenite

Gynecologist—azurite-malachite, chrysocolla, turquoise

Hair stylist—angelite, blue lace agate, celestite, carnelian, dolomite, seraphinite, tabular quartz

Healthcare practitioner—charoite, pink calcite, prehnite, rhodochrosite, rose quartz, ruby in fuchsite, snowflake obsidian, window quartz

Heart surgeon—green aventurine, green tourmaline, moldavite, pink tourmaline, ruby in zoisite, selenite rose, serpentine, stilbite, unakite, watermelon tourmaline

Herbalist—brown agate, green moss agate, green tourmaline, tree agate, vanadinite

High board diver—aquamarine, larimar

Hospice caregiver—angelite, celestite, elestial quartz, indochinite tektite, Isis quartz, moldavite, orange calcite, pink calcite

Intuitive reader—angelite, amethyst, azurite, black onyx, blue tiger's eye, celestite, charoite, dumortierite, galena, golden sheen obsidian, heliodor, Herkimer diamond, hiddenite, Isis quartz, jet, labradorite, lepidolite, magnesite, moonstone, optical calcite, pietersite, sodalite

Inventor—bloodstone, blue topaz, Botswana agate, copper, indochinite tektite, moldavite, sodalite, stilbite, sunstone, window quartz

Journalist—amazonite, angelite, aquamarine, blue calcite, blue topaz, carnelian, chalcopyrite, iolite, prehnite, record-keeper quartz, zebra jasper

Judge—amazonite, octahedron-shaped stones

Landscape architect—brown agate, honey calcite

Law enforcement—amazonite, black tourmaline, galena, hematite

Lawyer—amazonite, angelite, celestite, blue lace agate, blue calcite

Leader—gold tiger's eye, indochinite tektite, sapphire, selenite rose

Librarian—blue tiger's eye, record-keeper quartz

Manicurist—aragonite, morganite

Marathon participant—dolomite, garnet, ruby, sugilite

Marriage counselor—danburite, hiddenite, unakite

Massage therapist—leopardskin jasper, sardonyx, selenite, wand-shaped stones

Maternity nurse—bloodstone, carnelian, hematite, rose quartz, snowflake obsidian

Mediator—amazonite, black tourmaline, blue lace agate, blue calcite, hematite

Meditation facilitator/practitioner—celestite, channeling quartz, sodalite

Mental health counselor—serpentine

Merchant—citrine, chalcopyrite, green aventurine, green tourmaline, emerald, jade, pyrite

Metaphysical gift wholesaler—celestite, channeling quartz

Metaphysician—celestite, channeling quartz

Musician—angelite, blue calcite, blue topaz, carnelian, copper, record-keeper quartz, vanadinite

Mystic—blue topaz, cathedral quartz, celestite, golden topaz, jet, Kambamba jasper, pink calcite, ruby, silver topaz

Neurologist—lepidolite, moldavite, muscovite, optical calcite, stilbite

New Age retailer—amethyst, celestite, channeling quartz

Numerologist—angelite, blue calcite, blue tiger's eye, celestite, channeling quartz

Nurse—charoite, pink calcite, prehnite, rhodochrosite, rose quartz, ruby in fuchsite, snowflake obsidian, window quartz

Nutritionist—apophyllite, aragonite, charoite, chlorite phantom quartz, golden calcite, gold tiger's eye, green aventurine, Kambamba jasper, muscovite, sugilite, vanadinite

Optometrist/Ophthalmologist—optical calcite, blue tiger's eye, gold tiger's eye

Parent—black tourmaline, blue lace agate, hematite, relationship quartz, selenite rose

Phlebotomist—bloodstone, garnet, hematite, sugilite

Physical therapist—aragonite, chalcopyrite, copper, elestial quartz, howlite, leopardskin jasper, orange calcite, red tiger's eye, sardonyx, selenite, septarian, serpentine, sodalite, trilobite fossil

Physical trainer—aragonite, chalcopyrite, copper, elestial quartz, howlite, leopardskin jasper, orange calcite, red tiger's eye, sardonyx, selenite, septarian, serpentine, sodalite, trilobite fossil

Pilates instructor—aragonite, chalcopyrite, copper, elestial quartz, howlite, leopardskin jasper, orange calcite, red tiger's eye, sardonyx, selenite, septarian, serpentine, sodalite, trilobite fossil

Pioneer—indochinite tektite

Podiatrist—aragonite, brown agate, green moss agate, red calcite, tree agate

Psychologist—angelite, apatite, blue tiger's eye, magenta-dyed agate, muscovite, pink tourmaline, septarian, serpentine, stilbite, tabular quartz, time link quartz, unakite

Regression therapist—amber, black tourmaline, celestite, covellite, malachite, orbicular jasper, phantom quartz

Reiki practitioner—apophyllite, celestite, orange calcite, peridot, stilbite

Researcher—channeling quartz, moldavite, window quartz

Seamstress—prehnite

Sex therapist—lapis lazuli, red calcite, pietersite, ruby in zoisite, red tiger's eye

Speaker—amazonite, angelite, blue lace agate, celestite, citrine, indochinite tektite

Speech therapist—amazonite, angelite, blue lace agate, turquoise

Spiritual counselor—amethyst, angelite, charoite, clear quartz, sugilite

Supervisor—gold tiger's eye, indochinite tektite, sapphire, selenite rose

Swimmer—aquamarine, larimar

Teacher—amazonite, amethyst druzy, ametrine, chevron amethyst, golden topaz, iolite, morganite, pink tourmaline, relationship quartz, tabular quartz, selenite, sodalite

Travel profession—aquamarine, bloodstone, channeling quartz, chrysocolla, green aventurine, lodestone, orbicular jasper, serpentine, sodalite, watermelon tourmaline

Vascular doctor—azurite-malachite, magnetite, morganite

Veterinarian—andalusite, cobra jasper, Dalmatian jasper, dogtooth calcite, zebra jasper

Visionary leader—blue lace agate, celestite, indochinite tektite, moldavite

Weight management counselor—apatite, citrine, malachite, peridot, yellow jasper

Writer—amazonite, angelite, aquamarine, blue calcite, blue topaz, carnelian, chalcopyrite, iolite, prehnite, record-keeper quartz, zebra jasper

Yoga instructor—celestite, channeling quartz, chrysocolla, fluorite, garnet, leopardskin jasper, petrified wood, record-keeper quartz, red tiger's eye, ruby, sardonyx, zebra jasper

Appendix E: Archangels

Archangel Ariel (general health and vitality)—carnelian, citrine, garnet, golden topaz, red jasper, ruby, sunstone

Archangel Auriel (realignment of the Divine Feminine and subconscious fears)—cobaltoan calcite, girasol quartz, moonstone, petrified wood, pink calcite, rhodochrosite, selenite

Archangel Camael (realignment of the Divine Masculine, anger, aggression, and emotions)—azurite-malachite, carnelian, chrysoprase, chrysocolla, garnet, golden calcite, golden topaz, lapis lazuli, ruby

Archangel Chamuel (relationship healing)—danburite, emerald, green calcite, green tourmaline, kunzite, malachite, rose quartz, pink calcite, pink tourmaline, rhodochrosite, unakite

Archangel Gabriel (inspiration and guidance, dream interpretation, and inner knowing)—amethyst, celestite, danburite, Herkimer diamond, kunzite, scolecite, selenite

Archangel Haniel (Divine communication, determination, and alignment with soul's purpose)—amazonite, angelite, blue lace agate, blue calcite, celestite, clear quartz, kunzite, rose quartz, turquoise

Archangel Jophiel (inner wisdom and beauty)—amber, aragonite, citrine, chalcedony, cobaltoan calcite, gold tiger's eye, golden calcite, golden topaz

Archangel Melchizedek (aiding the spiritual journey on Earth and connection with the mystic within)—ammonite, black obsidian, blue topaz, cathedral quartz, jet, malachite, red calcite, ruby, rutilated quartz, silver topaz

Archangel Metatron (activation of the ascension process to higher states of consciousness, enlightenment, Akashic records, and the soul's evolution)—amethyst, apophyllite, bismuth, cathedral quartz, danburite, Herkimer diamond, golden calcite, golden topaz, kunzite, kyanite, lapis lazuli, morganite, selenite

Archangel Michael (protection, faith, and removal of fears, phobias, and obsessions)—clear quartz, kyanite, lapis lazuli, sodalite

Archangiel Muriel (rebalancing of emotions)—aquamarine, aragonite, larimar, unakite

Archangel Raphael (healing for yourself and others)—emerald, green calcite, green moss agate, green tourmaline, malachite, moldavite, seraphinite

Archangel Raziel (embracing the gifts of clairvoyance, prophecy, revelation, and the great mysteries)—amethyst, Herkimer diamond, sodalite

Archangel Sabrael (release of jealousy, viruses, and negative forces)—black obsidian, chrysoprase, gold tiger's eye, hematite, jet, peridot

Archangel Sandalphon (distance healing, Earth healing, and planetary group healing)—apophyllite, clear quartz, elestial quartz, indochinite tektite, kyanite, moldavite, peacock copper, selenite

Archangel Seraphiel (reawaken your angelic self-inviting peace and release of personal and family karma)—apophyllite, angelite, amber, celestite, danburite, kyanite, petrified wood, selenite.

Archangel Thuriel (animal healing and human connection with nature)—blue lace agate, green moss agate, green tourmaline, larimar

Archangel Tzaphkiel/Zaphkiel (the feminine aspect of God, understanding and mindfulness)—amethyst, kyanite, magenta-dyed agate, moonstone, pink tourmaline, rhodochrosite, selenite

Archangel Uriel (illumination and peace)—charoite, cobaltoan calcite, garnet, magenta-dyed agate, peacock copper, ruby, selenite, sugilite

Archangel Zadkiel (transformation, transmutation, and the Violet Flame)—amethyst, charoite, green calcite, moldavite, peridot, petrified wood, sugilite

Guardian Angel (one's main guardian)—amazonite, angelite, blue lace agate, blue calcite, celestite, clear quartz, kunzite, morganite, rose quartz

Appendix F:
Crystal Grids and Alignments

A crystal grid is a method of placing crystals in geometric formations on or around a person, place, or thing to achieve a formed intention within the space or person. Crystal grids can be combined with crystal alignments with larger groups of people at sacred sites. A crystal alignment is when crystals are placed on and around the body to clear, balance, and align the chakras. It usually includes a guided-imagery meditation in which the participant is instructed to envision the results he or she is seeking.

This section contains a list of stones that would work well to help realign or bring harmony to a person, place, or thing. I am providing you with some recommendations on where to place the gems via diagrams. These diagrams are intended to guide you and provide inspiration to activate your own intuition. Trust your inner guidance when choosing gemstone and geometric configurations.

Keep in mind that the list of gemstones provided is a menu of suggested choices. You don't need to use all the stones I suggest, but you can if you wish. Often two or three different types of stones are plenty, and even one type is enough.

To get started, do the following:

1. Identify your goal.

2. Visualize the outcome as if it has already become a reality.

3. Contemplate who else is involved and what part of your home or your life it affects.

4. Decide where you want to make the grid.

5. Look at the various suggested stones from the lists below.

6. Use your intuition and follow your gut to determine the perfect stone for your personal situation.

7. Construct the grid. Place the stones and establish a clear intention of the end result.

Remember that the most important ingredient is to take the time to form a clear intention of love, peace, well-being, harmony, joy, abundance, health, and happiness.

Bathroom

Aura cleansing—amethyst, chrysoprase, howlite, kyanite, rose quartz, selenite

Good digestion—apatite, chrysoprase, citrine, malachite, peridot

Safety—amethyst, black obsidian, black tourmaline, hematite, rose quartz, selenite

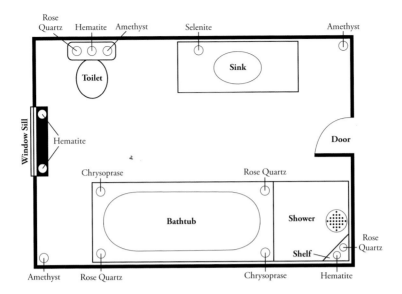

This diagram gives you an idea of one of the many possibilities for arranging the stones in your bathroom. This drawing demonstrates the Aura Cleansing Grid and the Safety Grid. Note that pieces of amethyst are placed in opposite corners of the room. Visualize an energetic thread connecting them. Similarly, the rose quartz is placed in opposite corners, so perform the same visualization. The hematite is on the windowsill to deflect negativity and create a shield. The selenite on the counter near the sink is intended to amplify the whole grid.

Bedroom

Dreaming—amethyst, ammonite, Herkimer diamonds

Peace—angelite, blue lace agate, clear quartz

Protection—amethyst, black obsidian, hematite, rose quartz, selenite

Sensuality—garnet, hematite, relationship quartz points, rose quartz, ruby

Sound sleep—amethyst, hematite, rose quartz

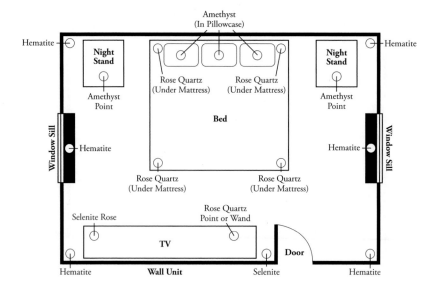

This rose quartz and hematite grid is my personal favorite for the bedroom or anywhere you need nurturing vibes combined with protection. It is formed with rose quartz and hematite. The rose quartz is placed throughout the room on furniture and nightstands as well as between the mattress and box spring. The hematite is placed in the four corners of the room. The visualization to go with this grid is to imagine the bedroom encased in a sphere of rose quartz with a protective outer shell of hematite. This same visualization can be used in any circumstance—for a child or adult, for an animal, or for a place or space. Visualize an energetic thread connecting the hematite creating a shield of protection and deflecting negativity. Similarly, the rose quartz is placed in portions of the bed and around the room, creating an orb of love and goodness. Add an amethyst point on nightstands to ward off nightmares and encourage pleasant dreams.

Children's Playroom or Place for Study

Creativity—carnelian, chrysacolla, orange calcite, turquoise

Focus—amethyst pyramids, fluorite octahedrons, fluorite octahedrons, hematite, tiger's eye, pyrite cube

Many stones help our childrens' development,
encouraging creativity, happiness, and peace.

Happiness—citrine, orange calcite, pink calcite, unakite

Harmony—amethyst, blue lace agate, rose quartz, sodalite

Peace—blue lace agate, clear quartz, lapis lazuli, sodalite, turquoise

Dining Room

Harmony—amethyst, blue calcite, golden calcite, green calcite, pink calcite

Healthy eating—chrysoprase, clear quartz, howlite, rose quartz, selenite

Socializing—amazonite, amethyst, citrine, clear quartz clusters, tabular quartz, turquoise

Exercise Room

(Includes yoga studios, gyms, and Pilates studios)

Focus, safety, and endurance—clear quartz, citrine, hematite, leopardskin jasper, red jasper, selenite

General, for Any Location

Healing—amethyst, green aventurine, rose quartz

Love—clear quartz, green aventurine, rose quartz

Protection—amethyst, black tourmaline, hematite, rose quartz, selenite

There are many possibilities for placing gemstones, crystals, and minerals around each room of your home, and all are quite beautiful.

Kitchen

Cooking skills—carnelian, chrysocolla, citrine, jade, rose quartz, fluorite

Digestion—amber, citrine, golden calcite, malachite, orange calcite, peridot

Health—green aventurine, garnet, peridot, rose quartz, amethyst

Positive thinking—citrine, golden calcite, jade, rhodochrosite

Living Room

Family harmony—amazonite, angelite, blue lace agate, lapis lazuli, pink calcite, rose quartz, sodalite

Joy—citrine, clear quartz, golden calcite, pyrite clusters, rose quartz

Relaxation—amethyst, angelite, chrysoprase, pink calcite

Many specimens of minerals, gems, and crystals
can be as subtle as small decorative accents … or as bold as centerpieces.

Nature and Outdoors

Pool Area

Water safety—aquamarine, blue lace agate, chrysoprase, selenite

BBQ Grill Area

Healthy food—apatite, clear quartz, green calcite, hematite, rose quartz, smoky quartz

Garden

Nature spirit connection—andalusite, clear quartz, green moss agate, green tourmaline, tree agate

Flowers

Devic force alignment—clear quartz, green moss agate, kunzite, pink tourmaline, rose quartz

Nature Spirits

Communication—brown agate, green moss agate, lodestone

Office

Communication—amazonite, blue lace agate, angelite, turquoise, clear quartz

Concentration—fluorite octahedrons, hematite, pyrite cubes

Creativity—carnelian, turquoise, clear quartz

Prosperity—pyrite cluster, emerald, green aventurine, citrine

People

Anger removal—amethyst, angelite, azurite, celestite, charoite, chrysacolla, lapis lazuli, lepidolite, malachite, rose quartz, sodalite, sugilite, turquoise

Communication—amazonite, angelite, aquamarine, blue topaz, celestite, chrysacolla, turquoise

Fertility—orange calcite, red goldstone, red jasper, chrysacolla

Grief—Apache tears, kunzite, pink calcite, rhodonite, rose quartz, rubellite (pink tourmaline), watermelon tourmaline

Negativity—amethyst, black tourmaline, golden sheen obsidian, hematite, jet, lapis lazuli, onyx, rainbow obsidian, smoky quartz, snowflake obsidian, tourmalinated quartz

Romance—carnelian, clear quartz, kunzite, rose quartz, ruby

Self-worth—chrysoprase, citrine, golden calcite, orange calcite, peach moonstone, yellow topaz

Physical, mental, or emotional abuse—amethyst, black tourmaline, chrysacolla, citrine, golden calcite, golden sheen obsidian, hematite, lepidolite, malachite, rainbow obsidian, rose quartz, smoky quartz, sodalite, tourmalinated quartz

Planet

Global healing and alignment—andalusite, chrysacolla, danburite, kunzite, kyanite, selenite, tabular quartz

Glossary

Adularescence: An optical phenomenon, similar to labradorescence and aventurescence, produced most notably by moonstones.

Akashic Records: A metaphysical record of the history of the cosmos, which includes everything that has happened in the past, all that is happening in the present moment, and all potential future realities.

Angels: Luminous beings—neither masculine nor feminine—that act as divine messengers. There are many types of angels, including Archangels, guardian angels, seraphim, cherubim, and more. They act and react based on thoughtforms (mental energy) and their charges' specific requests. Because humans have free will, angels need to be asked to assist us or intervene on our behalf.

Animal medicine: The healing aspects that a particular animal provides in order to bring something to your awareness. By understanding the messages and mannerisms of various animals whose energy enters your life either physically or mentally, you can make necessary adjustments in how you perceive yourself and reality. This concept is associated with Native American spirituality and the spirituality of many indigenous tribes around the world.

Animal totems (power animals): The essence of animal energy that aids you in your everyday life. Similar to spirit guides, animal totems energetically travel with you to enhance your efforts in your spiritual pursuits and practices such as shamanic journeywork to find answers for self-improvement. This concept is associated with Native American spiritualities and the spiritualities of many indigenous peoples around the world.

Anhydrous: A crystalline compound containing no water.

Aromatherapy: A form of alternative medicine that uses volatile plant oils, including essential oils and other aromatic compounds, for psychological and physical well-being. It is always best to use 100-percent pure therapeutic-quality or medical-grade aromatherapy products.

Ascended Master: A spiritually enlightened being who has incarnated as a human being in a past life or many past lives, such as St. Germain, Sanat Kumara, Kuthumi, Kuan Yin, Isis, or Walt Disney, to name a few. Through the process of spiritual transformation, these beings are believed to have ascended and are therefore directly connected to universal wisdom and knowledge.

Automatic writing: A form of writing in which the writer allows channeled messages to flow through him or her. After stating intention, prayer, and protection, the recipient allows spirit to provide information and messages from the Other Side, angels, and Ascended Masters. It is advisable for the recipient to discern what level of entity is permitted to write through them in this manner.

Botryoidal: Having a shape reminiscent of a cluster of grapes.

Cabochon: A cabochon, from the Middle French *caboche* (head), is a gemstone that has been shaped and polished as opposed to faceted, usually a convex top with a flat bottom.

Carbonaceous: A rock or sediment consisting of or containing carbon or carbon compounds.

Chakra: A Sanskrit word for "wheel" or "vortex." The seven main chakras, or energy centers, that make up your body begin at the base of the spine with the root chakra and end at the head with the crown chakra—and all of them are energetically connected. When one or more of your chakras becomes blocked or out of alignment, it affects your mental state or your emotional balance. It can also affect you spiritually. Eventually, the blockage presents itself on the physical level with imbalance or some health condition that seems to show up out of nowhere. Read my book *Chakra Awakening* for a deep understanding of the chakras.

Chatoyant: Showing a band of bright reflected light caused by aligned inclusions in the stone.

Clairaudience: The ability to receive messages or guidance through intuitive hearing or sound that has not been produced by physical sound waves. The voice within is the connection to the higher self and to one's guides and angels.

Claircognizance: The ability to know something intuitively.

Clairgustation: The intuitive ability to recognize a taste in the mouth that provides insight into a matter at hand. Medical intuitives often use this sensory gift to identify their clients' physical challenges.

Clairolfaction: The ability to intuitively pick up a smell that doesn't physically exist as scent particles, providing guidance or a clue into a situation at hand.

Clairsentience: The ability to clearly sense or feel, and therefore know.

Clairvoyance: The ability to receive intuitive messages through visions in the mind's eye, including dreams and daydreams, through the vibration or energy of spiritual sight. This vibration resides primarily at the third eye.

Consciousness: A term used to explain awareness in relationship to oneself and the the surrounding world. It is a compilation of one's belief systems and thoughts that are part of the natural thinking process. The foundations of consciousness are established early in life, yet can be realigned and changed with intent. Other terms associated with consciousness are *mindfulness, wakefulness, sense of self, perceptions of reality,* and *philosophical outlook.*

Crystal alignment: The use of crystals placed on and around the body to clear, balance, and align the chakras. It usually includes a guided-imagery meditation in which the participant is instructed to envision the results he or she is seeking.

Crystal grid: The use of gemstone in geometric formations placed on or around a person, place, or thing to achieve the formed intention. Crystal grids can be combined with crystal alignments with larger groups of people at sacred sites.

Dendritic: Having a branched form, branchlike inclusions, or resembling a tree.

Devic forces: *See* Elemental spirits.

Divine Feminine: The universal mother, or Great Mother, represented by any and all of the following: the Goddess, Gaia, Isis, Mary Magdalene, Mother Mary, Lady Nada, Kuan Yin, and the Asteroid Goddesses as they are represented from an astrological viewpoint (Pallas Athena, Juno, Vesta, and Ceres), among many more. The Divine Feminine represents the state of receptivity and being-ness.

Divine Masculine: The universal father, represented by any and all of the following: God, Mikael, Christ, Chiron, and many others. All represent the energy of doing, taking action, moving forward. This is the energy of the protector and the provider. The universal father loves us, provides shelter and safety, and watches over us in a state of action.

Druzy: Also known as drusy or druse; a rock encrusted with aggregate small crystals.

Elemental spirits: A force in nature or energy, with or without intelligence, related to the four elements—earth, air, fire, and water. Names given to these forces include gnomes and dwarves to represent earth; sylphs to represent air; salamanders to represent fire; and undines, nymphs, and mercreatures to represent water.

Essential oils: The oils and other constituents of distilled organic compounds, such as plant hormones, vitamins, and phytochemicals, which can be used in a carrier oil to be applied to the skin for rebalancing the physical, mental, and emotional bodies.

Feminine Christ: The energy associated with the female gender of Christ Consciousness or the Divine Feminine. Often used interchangeably with Kuan Yin, Isis, and even Mary Magdalene, who is believed by some to have been the wife of Jesus the Christ.

Gemstone guardians: Elemental spirits connected with the gemstone kingdom, such as fairies, gnomes, and other devic forces. The guardians are associated with the structure and energy of rocks.

Hexagonal: Of or denoting a crystal system or three-dimensional geometric arrangement having four axes, three of which are equal in length and lie at an angle of 120° from each other, and the fourth of which is perpendicular to the other three.

Igneous: Relates to a rock that solidified from lava or magma.

Inclusion: A liquid, solid, gaseous, or other type of foreign body enclosed within a mineral or rock.

Labyrinth: A maze with a single path to the center and back. This type of maze symbolizes our ability to learn things about ourselves that bring us within and then back out again with answers and a new personal truth. Walking a labyrinth can be a spiritual, meditative, and contemplative process.

Medicine wheel: A teaching tool in the shape of a wheel that contains thirty-six positions, each one providing a story and connection with the many cycles of life we spiral through daily, monthly, yearly, and throughout a lifetime. The teachings of the medicine wheel provide a map to understanding all life.

Meditation: A practice of quieting the mind. It's called a practice because it takes practice with every moment of the experience to stay focused on nothing. There are various forms of meditation using guided imagery to enable the practitioner to focus on calming thoughts to attain higher states of awareness. A goal of meditation is often geared toward attaining compassion and understanding.

Metamorphic: A rock that has undergone transformation by heat, pressure, or other natural means.

Metaphysical: Beyond the physical. This concept encompasses what the physical and scientific world cannot define yet clearly exists. Many of the principles and discussions within this book are metaphysical.

Microcrystalline: A material formed of microscopic crystals. Microcrystalline minerals will not exhibit a crystal shape but will appear in massive form.

Mohs scale (of mineral hardness): A scale that measures the scratch resistance of minerals, gemstones, and rocks, created by the German geologist and mineralogist Friedrich Mohs in 1812.

Monkey mind: A Buddhist term used to express the idea that the mind is restless, chattering, unsettled, confused, and difficult to control.

Monoclinic: Of or denoting a crystal system or three-dimensional geometric arrangement having three unequal axes of which one is at right angles to the other two.

Nagual: A shape shifter or trickster who can magically turn into an animal, commonly a jaguar. Nagualism is associated with pre-Columbian shamanism. In this belief system, all humans have an animal counterpart.

Nature spirits: Devic forces associated with the trees, plants, rocks, streams, mountains, ocean, rivers, deserts, and all of nature. Words used to represent these forces include gnomes, elves, salamanders, fairies, and undines. While they are unseen, for the most part, they are quite real and have many followers around the planet.

Negative ions: Odorless, tasteless, and invisible molecules that create positive vibrations. Negative ions are believed to produce biochemical reactions that increase levels of the mood chemical serotonin, helping to alleviate depression, relieve stress, and boost daytime energy. There is an abundance of negative ions in forests and mountains, at beaches and waterfalls, and after a thunderstorm or rainstorm.

Nodule: A small, rounded lump of a mineral or mixture of minerals that is distinct and usually harder than the surrounding rock or sediment. Nodules often form by replacement of a small part of the rocks in which they form.

No mind: The complete absence of thought.

Oligoclase: A feldspar mineral common in siliceous igneous rocks, consisting of a sodium-rich plagioclase (with more calcium than albite).

Oracle: A person, place, or thing through which advice or prophecy is given.

Orthorhombic: Of or denoting a crystal system or three-dimensional geometric arrangement having three unequal axes at right angles.

Orthoclase: A white to pale yellow, red, or green mineral of the feldspar group, found in igneous, sedimentary, and metamorphic rocks.

Pagan: Someone who has a spiritual or religious practice or belief that honors or worships deities found in pre-Christian, classical, aboriginal, or tribal mythologies. Pagan practices include shamanism and/or magical rituals. Their spiritual attention is primarily on the Divine Feminine and on earth-based spirituality.

Plagioclase: A form of feldspar consisting of aluminosilicates of sodium and/or calcium, common in igneous rocks, typically white.

Pleocroism: The phenomenon of different colors appearing when certain crystals are viewed from different directions.

Polymorph: An organism or inorganic object that takes various forms.

Prismatic: Of or denoting a crystal habit or three-dimensional geometric arrangement resembling a prism; having four or more sides of similar width and length, elongated in one direction.

Pseudomorph: A mineral completely replaces another and retains the same outward shape of the replaced mineral.

Rainbow body: A physical mastery state of Dzogchen, which is the natural state of the mind as well as a body of teachings and meditation practices aimed at achieving that state. It is the central teaching of the Nyingma school practices by Tibetan Buddhist sects.

Rainbow bridge: The bridge that carries departed ones to the Other Side upon passing from this physical life.

Rebirthing (aka Rebirthing Breathwork): A tool for healing, personal growth, and spiritual awakening. Through the use of conscious breath, it helps you uncover emotions and belief systems stored in your consciousness. Though officially created by Leonard Orr in 1974, this circular breathing rhythm practices has been used in yogic practices for centuries.

Rhombohedral: Of or denoting a lattice system or three-dimensional geometric arrangement having three equal axes and oblique angles. It is a subset of the trigonal crystal system, but not all trigonal crystals are rhombohedral.

Schiller: A lustrous colored reflection from certain planes in a mineral grain.

Sedimentary rocks: Types of rock that are formed by the deposit of material at the earth's surface and within bodies of water.

Self-actualization: The realization of one's ultimate true potential. Maslow's Hierarchy of Needs theory brought this concept to full prominence.

Self-observation: A tool to awaken one's conscious awareness, which when activated can help one more effectively use the power of his or her thoughts to create reality. Self-observation is the intentional act of observing one's own behaviors, reactions, and actions as an interested, objective observer—that is, without judgment.

Shamanic journeywork: A journey to the center of one's self achieved in various ways. Many shamanic journey practitioners use drumming at the rate of the heartbeat to induce a trance-like state. In this state, the practitioner usually connects with either the subconscious (the lower world) or the super-conscious (the upper world) to find answers, understanding, and healing. Some shamanic journeywork incorporates the use of power animals or animal totems as an ally or guide during the journey.

Shamanism: A path to understanding various rituals and ceremonies, typically involving the four elements or four directions, to transform oneself in body, mind, and spirit.

Spirit guides: Disincarnate beings who exist in another dimensional reality. These guides become allies when we consciously choose to invite them into our spiritual circle of consciousness. It is important to choose your spirit guides wisely, just as you choose your friends wisely.

Stalagmitic: A mineral deposit built up on the floor of a cave by dripping water, often from a stalactite above.

Stalactitic: A mineral deposit formed from the dripping of mineral-rich water.

Tabular: A crystal that forms in the shape of a tablet. In quartz crystals, two of the six sides are much wider than the other four.

Telepathy: Communication without the use of the spoken word; a form of mental energy used for mind-to-mind and heart-to-heart communication.

Termination: The point on the end of a crystal. A double termination refers to a crystal having points on both ends, which is more rare.

Tetragonal: Of or denoting a crystal system or three-dimensional geometric arrangement having three axes at right angles, two of them equal in length.

Triclinic: Of or denoting a crystal system or three-dimensional geometric arrangement having three unequal axes all intersecting at oblique angles.

Trigonal: Of or denoting a crystal system or three-dimensional geometric arrangement having three equal axes separated by equal angles that are not right angles.

Thoughtforms: Mental energy.

Word patrol: The practice of employing awareness when speaking or thinking so that one's words and thoughts create a desired reality rather than an unwanted situation. For example, when employing word patrol, one would say "I'm hungry" rather than "I'm starving" to avoid creating a reality in which the body goes into starvation mode.

Suggested Reading

Ancient Teachings for Beginners by Douglas DeLong. Llewellyn Publications, 2000.

Animal-Speak by Ted Andrews. Llewellyn Publications, 1996.

Asteroid Goddesses: The Mythology, Psychology, and Astrology of the Re-Emerging Feminine by Demetra George and Douglas Bloch. Nicolas-Hays, 2003.

Astrology: A Cosmic Science by Isabel Hickey. CRCS Publications, 2011.

Chakra Awakening: Transform Your Reality Using Crystals, Color, Aromatherapy, and the Power of Positive Thought by Margaret Ann Lembo. Llewellyn Publications, 2011.

Heal Your Body by Louise Hay. Hay House, 1987.

Many Lives, Many Masters by Brian Weiss. Touchstone, 1988.

Messengers of Love, Light and Grace by Terry Lynn Taylor. HJ Kramer/ New World Library, 2005.

Numerology and the Divine Triangle by Dusty Bunker and Faith Javane. Whitford Press, 1979.

Opening to Channel by Sonaya Roman and Duane Packer. HJ Kramer, 1993.

Personal Power through Awareness by Sonaya Roman. HJ Kramer, 1986.

Sacred Path Cards: The Discovery of Self Through Native Teachings by Jamie Sams. HarperOne, 1990.

Spiritual Development for Beginners by Professors Jan and Richard Potter. Llewellyn Publications, 2006.

References and Bibliography

Achad, Frater. *Melchizedek Truth Principles*. Marina del Rey, CA: DeVorss & Co, 1963.

———. *Ancient Mystical White Brotherhood*. Lakemont, GA: CSA Press, 1971.

Adams, John. *The Crystal Sourcebook: From Science to Metaphysics*. Edited by John Milewski and Virginia Harford. 1st ed. Santa Fe, NM: Mystic Crystal Publications, 1987. [*Author's Note:* This book includes information about Marcel Vogel's experiments with crystals.]

Andrews, Ted. *Animal-Speak: The Spiritual and Magical Powers of Creatures Great and Small*. Woodbury, MN: Llewellyn Publications, 1993.

———. *Animal-Wise: The Spirit Language and Signs of Nature*. Jackson, TN: Dragonhawk, 1999.

Argüelles, Jóse. *Surfers of the Zuvaya: Tales of Interdimensional Travel.* Santa Fe: Bear & Company. 1989.

Caddy, Eileen. *The Spirit of Findhorn.* Scotland: Findhorn Press, 1994.

Das, Lama Surya. *Awakening the Buddhist Heart: Integrating Love, Meaning, and Connection into Every Part of Your Life.* New York: Broadway Books, 2000.

Davidson, John. *The Secret of the Creative Vacuum: Man and the Energy Dance.* Essex, England: C.W. Daniel Company, 1989.

Gardner-Gordon, Joy. *Color and Crystals: A Journey through the Chakras.* Feasterville Trevose, PA: Crossing Press, 1988.

George, Demetra. *Asteroid Goddesses: The Mythology, Psychology, and Astrology of the Re-Emerging Feminine.* York Beach, ME: Nicolas-Hays, 2003.

Foundation for *A Course in Miracles. A Course in Miracles.* Mill Valley, CA: Foundation for Inner Peace, 1976.

Hay, Louise. *Heal Your Body.* Carlsbad, CA: Hay House, 1984.

Hickey, Isabel M. *Astrology: A Cosmic Science.* Watertown, MA: Isabel Hickey. 1970

Javane, Faith, and Dusty Bunker. *Numerology and the Divine Triangle.* Atglen, PA: Schiffer, 1979.

Kinstler, Clysta. *The Moon Under Her Feet: The Story of Mai Madgalene in the Service of the Great Mother.* New York: HarperCollins, 1983.

Mead, Jerry D. "Wine on the Rocks," *International Wine Review.* February/March 1989. [*Author's Note:* This article includes information about Marcel Vogel's experiments with crystals.]

Melody. *Love is in the Earth: A Kaleidoscope of Crystals; The Reference Book Describing the Metaphysical Properties of the Mineral Kingdom.* Wheat Ridge, CO: Earth-Love, 1991.

Milanovich, Norma, and Shirley McCune. *The Light Shall Set You Free.* Scottsdale, AZ: Athena, 1996.

Miller, Hamish, and Paul Broadhurst. *The Sun and the Serpent.* Hillsdale, NY: Pendragon Press, 1989.

Neville, E.W. *Planets in Synastry.* Atglen, PA: Whitford Press. 1990

Ouspensky, P. D. *In Search of the Miraculous: Fragments of an Unknown Teaching.* New York: Harcourt Brace Jovanovich, 1949.

Raphaell, Katrina. *Crystal Enlightenment: The Transforming Properties of Crystals and Healing Stones.* Vol. 1. Santa Fe: Aurora Press, 1985.

———. *Crystal Healing: The Therapeutic Application of Crystals and Stones.* Vol. 2. Santa Fe: Aurora Press, 1987.

———. *Crystalline Transmission: A Synthesis of Light.* Vol. 3. Santa Fe: Aurora Press, 1990.

Raven, Hazel. *The Secrets of Angel Healing: Therapies for Mind, Body and Spirit.* London: Godsfield Press, 2006.

Rinchen, Geshe Sonam. Translated by Ruth Sonam. *The Thirty-Seven Practices of Bodhisattvas.* Ithaca, NY: Snow Lion Publications, 1997.

Rudhyar, Dane. *The Astrological Houses: The Spectrum of Individual Experience.* Garden City, NY: Doubleday & Company, 1972.

Sakoian, Frances, and Louis S. Acker. *The Astrology of Human Relationships: Techniques for Guiding or Evaluating Your Personal, Social & Business Relationships.* New York: Harper & Row, 1973.

Sams, Jamie. *The 13 Original Clan Mothers: Your Sacred Path to Discovering the Gifts, Talents & Abilities of the Feminine Through the Ancient Teachings of the Sisterhood.* New York: HarperCollins, 1993.

Shinn, Florence Scovel. *The Writings of Florence Scovel Shinn.* Camarillo, CA: DeVorss, 1996.

Snider, Jerry and Richard Daab. "The Advocacy of Marcel Vogel," *Magical Blend,* 1989.

Solara. *The Star-Borne: A Remembrance for the Awakened Ones.* Charlottesville, VA: Star-Borne Unlimited, 1991.

Spero, Maria. *Chichen Itza: A Guide to the Ruins.* Self-published by Maria Spero, 1990.

———. *Exploring the Yucatan Peninsula.* Self-published by Maria Spero, 1995.

———. *Uxmal.* Self-published by Maria Spero, 1995.

Stein, Diane. *The Women's Book of Healing.* Woodbury, MN: Llewellyn Publications, 1987.

Stone, Joshua David, Ph.D. *The Ascended Masters Light the Way: Beacons of Ascension.* Flagstaff, AZ: Light Technology Publishing, 1995.

Sun Bear, Wind Wabun, and Crysalis Mulligan. *Dancing with the Wheel: The Medicine Wheel Workbook.* New York: Prentice Hall Press, 1991.

Taylor, Terry Lynn. *Messengers of Light: The Angels' Guide to Spiritual Growth.* Tiburon, CA: HJ Kramer, 1989.

Thurman, Robert "Tenzin," and Annie Bien. *Kalachakra for World Peace.* Washington, DC: Capital Area Tibetan Association, 2011.

Tompkins, Peter. *The Secret Life of Plants.* New York: Harper, 1989.

Valentine, Tom. "Marcel Vogel: The Man Who Would See Magnetism," *Magnets in Your Future,* June 1986, Volume 1, no. 6.

Virtue, Doreen, and Lynnette Brown. *Angel Numbers: The Angels Explain the Meaning of 111, 444, and Other Numbers in Your Life.* Carlsbad, CA: Hay House, 2005.

Waters, Frank. *Book of the Hopi.* New York: Penguin, 1977.

White Eagle. *Spiritual Unfoldment 2*. Camarillo, CA: DeVorss, 2008.

Yogananda, Parmahansa. *Autobiography of a Yogi*. Nevada City, CA: Crystal Clarity, 2005.

Ywahoo, Dhyani. *Voices of Our Ancetors: Cherokee Teachings from the Wisdom Fire*. Boston, MA: Shambhala Publications, Inc. 1987.

Index

CHRYSOPRASE